THE PERSONAL BELIEFS OF JIMMY CARTER

Includes the complete text of
Living Faith and *Sources of Strength*

THREE RIVERS PRESS • NEW YORK

ALSO BY JIMMY CARTER

Sources of Strength

Turning Point: A Candidate, a State and a Nation Come of Age

Talking Peace: A Vision for the Next Generation

An Outdoor Journal

Everything to Gain: Making the Most of the Rest of Your Life
(with Rosalynn Carter)

The Blood of Abraham: Insights into the Middle East

Keeping Faith: Memoirs of a President

A Government as Good as Its People

Why Not the Best?

POETRY:
Always a Reckoning

FOR CHILDREN:
The Little Baby Snoogle-Fleejer
(with Amy Carter)

LIVING FAITH

Jimmy Carter

www.randomhouse.com

THREE RIVERS PRESS is a registered trademark and the Three Rivers Press colophon is a trademark of Random House, Inc.

Living Faith was originally published in hardcover in slightly different form by Times Books, a division of Random House, Inc., in 1996. This version was originally published in softcover by Times Books, a division of Random House, Inc., in 1998.

Sources of Strength was originally published in hardcover by Times Books, a division of Random House, Inc., in 1977. This version was originally published in softcover by Three Rivers Press, a division of Random House, Inc., in 1997.

Printed in United States of America

Library of Congress Cataloging-in-Publication Data is available on request.

ISBN 1-4000-5038-3

10 9 8 7 6 5 4 3 2 1

First Edition

To my wife, Rosalynn

She'd smile, and birds would feel that they no longer
had to sing, or it may be I failed
to hear their song.

Within a crowd, I'd hope her glance might be
for me, but knew that she was shy, and wished
to be alone.

I'd pay to sit behind her, blind to what
was on the screen, and watch the image flicker
on her hair.

I'd glow when her diminished voice would clear
my muddled thoughts, like lightning flashing in
a gloomy sky.

The nothing in my soul with her aloof
was changed to foolish fullness when she came
to be with me.

With shyness gone and hair caressed with gray,
her smile still makes the birds forget to sing
and me to hear their song.

Contents

Preface

Living Faith is my eleventh book, and its hardcover publication resulted in more responses and comments than from anything else I've written. Readers seemed to find something in the text that appealed to them, perhaps a shared faith that always seems to be the same, even in a modern, fast-changing, technological world.

Interestingly enough, many of the letters were from members of my own extended family, most of whom I had never met. Although I regularly receive about 3,000 letters a month and cannot respond to many of them personally, in this case I decided to answer all those that indicated a blood relationship with me. I maintain a computer program that includes this information, and the number of cousins grew rapidly—to more than 3,000 names. We finally decided to have a family reunion, but to limit the number by including only direct descendants of my great-great-grandfather Wiley Carter. Since he was born in 1798, this provided an opportunity to celebrate the two hundredth anniversary of his birth.

On May 2, 1998, more than 800 members of our family assembled, more than doubling the total population of my hometown! Although most of them were from the South-east, we also had strong delegations from New England and the West Coast. We had a surprisingly harmonious and enjoyable weekend sharing information, reminiscences, and promises to stay in touch, at least with our closest relatives. A newly discovered cousin, a Mormon who lives in Salt Lake City, volunteered to do additional research about our family tree in the Church of the Latter-Day Saints' extensive genealogical records.

One of the highlights of the reunion was a Bible study with several hundred kinfolk at Marantha, my home church. We discussed what had precipitated our coming together, and we decided that it might be this special time in history that caused us to pause and consider some basic principles of our lives, as well as to look back at our roots.

Many people may be reading these pages during 1999 and 2000, as we welcome the new millennium. There will undoubtedly be numerous media stories, both secular and religious, about the significance of this turning point. I've already noticed arguments, even books written, about which year is the end of the twentieth century, and experts are laboring and spending hundreds of millions of dollars to assure that our computers don't think the following day is January 1, 1900!

There will also be end-of-the-world predictions, and other religious prophecies based on selectively extracted verses from the Holy Bible, especially the Book of Revelation. (The phrase "thousand years" occurs six times just during the first seven verses of Revelation 20.) This period of a millennium is not taken lightly by many sincere evangelical Christians, and there are sharp divisions generated by different interpretations of the meaning. In fact, some "dispensational premillennialists" criticized part of the text in *Living Faith*, which they considered to be incompatible with their beliefs.

I don't claim to understand the nuances of these interpretations of the Bible. It seems to me that Jesus cautions us not to make predictions about the future timing of scriptural events. When his disciples asked him about his second coming and the end of the world, he cautioned them, "But of that day and hour knoweth no man, no, not the angels of heaven, but my Father only" (Matthew 24:36). Later, Peter writes, "One day is with the Lord as a thousand years, and a thousand years as one day" (2 Peter 3:8).

On a number of occasions, Jesus commands us to live as though our ending was imminent. In this book, I have attempted to describe in a layman's terms, as simply as possible, how my life has been affected by the words and acts of Jesus Christ, about the mistakes I've made and the lessons I've learned. Perhaps the beginning of the twenty-first century will be an additional incentive for each of us to look back at our family roots, our previous actions, and also forward to an unpredictable future. It is clear to me that the basic elements of life never change—our living faith that shapes our relationship with God and with one another.

LIVING FAITH

Introduction

This is a book about the values and experiences that have shaped my life, and how the religious beliefs I inherited have been transformed into a living faith. I have waited a long time to write these words, because religion is a private matter—and my own faith has been the subject of much public speculation. Yet I think that my close relationship with God is something I share with many Americans of different traditions.

I hope this book will be illuminating for those who have wondered whether a "born-again Christian" president was a contradiction in terms, or why a candidate for the highest office in the land who was far ahead in the polls gave a particular interview to *Playboy* magazine and almost lost the election.

I've had a varied life and a dramatic one, with times of wonderful accomplishment alongside devastating setbacks. Some of my career changes were of my own choosing, and others have been forced on me by what I considered at the time to be failures. I have moved from a naval career to farming, to business, then to a political life, and, since the end of my presidency, to a challenging and delightful life as a college professor, a volunteer activist, and a grandfather. I have been blessed with a loving and enduring marriage and have attained many of the goals I set for myself as a young man. But I have also witnessed the deaths of my father and siblings when they were far too young, confronted public defeat more times than I wanted, and faced bankruptcy as well as the self-doubt, private losses, and disappointments that are part of the human lot.

Throughout these three score and ten years, my faith as a Christian has provided the necessary stability in my life. Come to think of it, stability is not exactly the right word, because to have faith in something is an inducement not to dormancy but to action. To me, *faith* is not just a noun but also a verb.

Faith is the foundation of this book, and it is a rich, complex, even elusive concept, used in varied ways in the Scriptures. In Christian tradition, the concept of faith has two interrelated meanings, both implying fidelity: confidence in a being (God), and action based on firm belief.

The clearest New Testament definition is "Faith is the

assurance of things hoped for, the conviction of things not seen" (Hebrews 11:1). The text continues, "By faith we understand that the universe was formed at God's command, so that what is seen was not made out of what was visible" (Heb. 11:3). The Bible goes on to say that we are justified, sanctified, and reconciled with God by faith, not by works or by obeying the law; the just shall live by faith; God gave each of us a measure of faith; we walk by faith, not sight; we are children of God by faith; we are saved by grace through faith; faith is the gift of God, and it is more precious than gold; to face life, we should put on the shield of faith, the breastplate of faith and love; we are taught in faith and truth.

In this book, I explore some of the ways my Christian faith has guided and sustained me, as well as the ways it has challenged and driven me to seek a closer relationship with God and my fellow human beings.

These chapters began as an outgrowth of the Bible classes I have been teaching ever since I became an adult. When I was a young midshipman at the U.S. Naval Academy, I taught the children of the officers and enlisted men stationed at Annapolis. Later, while serving on submarines, I conducted religious services on special days, such as Easter. A dozen or more of the crew would sit on folding bunks between the torpedoes, and I would stand alongside the launching tubes to read the text, ask and answer some questions if I could, and say a prayer.

After I left the navy and returned home to Plains,

Georgia, I taught young boys and girls in Sunday school regularly for about fifteen years, as my father had always done when I was a child. Even as president, while I was attending Washington's First Baptist Church, the regular teacher and I would set aside a few Sundays each year for me to teach the adult class.

Today, in Plains, I lead an adult class at Maranatha Baptist Church, a congregation of about forty-five families, most of whom have lived and worshiped together for several generations. ("Maranatha," meaning "Come, Lord," is the first Christian prayer of which we have any record [1 Corinthians 16:22].) Since most of our adult members are teaching their own classes, keeping the nursery, or managing other Sunday school affairs, almost all my students are visitors. They are families who drive over from nearby towns, entire Bible classes from more distant communities who come in buses to worship with us, or vacationers who stop by on journeys to or from Florida. Quite often, one or two will whisper to me that they have never been in a church before, or not since they were baptized as babies.

Along with the visitors who join us from nearby towns or distant communities are two special groups. One is from a nearby community known as Koinonia Partners (*koinonia* is a Greek word meaning "brotherhood"). This farm was organized in the early 1940s by Dr. Clarence Jordan, who designed it to break down the strict racial barriers that existed in the South during those days. A few dedicated and courageous white Christians invited poor black families to live, work, and worship with them on an equal basis. For years they survived economic boycotts by almost all the local merchants and attacks by the Ku Klux Klan and other white segregationist groups, who burned their property and fired bullets through their homes at night. For more than fifty years, they have lived on the proceeds of their farming and with the help of supporters throughout the country.

The other regular members and frequent visitors in my class come from the international headquarters of Habitat for Humanity, which originated at Koinonia about twenty years ago. Habitat is described more fully later in this book; it is a worldwide program of building homes for "God's people in need." Both the temporary volunteers and permanent workers at Koinonia and Habitat attempt to demonstrate their own religious faith by serving the poor and needy in an often sacrificial way.

Most of the time it is a pleasure for me to study the suggested Scripture, consider at least overnight how best to present the lesson, read some commentaries, prepare an outline, and then meet with my class on Sunday mornings. I treat theological arguments gingerly but am bolder when it comes to connecting my religious beliefs with life and current events in the world, even when the issues are controversial.

I learned long ago that the best way to finesse a difficult Bible passage is to involve the class in a give-and-take discussion. Questions back and forth keep us all awake and help us understand the subject. We have lively debates but few injured feelings. Some of the exchanges continue after the services are over, even in letters that come to me during the following weeks.

I have discovered during these years of teaching that it is far better not to preach and just share the lesson on an equal basis with those who have come to join me. The more memorable experiences are when we meld into a common group, all striving to decipher the meaning of the Bible verses and to apply the message to our own lives. My hope is similarly to maintain an equal or shared relationship with the readers of this book, so that we can search together for religious truths, how they relate to us, and perhaps how they can affect our lives.

These classes often include representatives from a dozen Protestant denominations, including Mennonites and Amish, as well as Jews and Catholics. One recent Sunday, I had visitors from twenty-eight foreign countries. We all have a feeling of being part of a community of people trying together to make sense of our lives and of our world. Because of this diversity, I've had to go more deeply into other people's questions—some of which I have never raised in my own life.

And so I began writing this book by trying to use the most meaningful of these classes as a base for thinking about a "living faith." However, as the months went by and I wondered aloud with my family and friends, I realized that the story was more complicated than biblical texts and their relationship to my life. I saw that the debate about faith in American life has, if anything, intensified since I was president.

As a new millennium approaches, we Americans face many issues within which religion, politics, and private matters tend to mix explosively. They create sharp divisions among us, in our private and public lives and even in individual religious denominations. It seems increasingly difficult to separate church and state issues, and even the purely religious issues have to be addressed by politicians.

I have confronted the separation of church and state from both directions. I think often of the strong reaction of our visiting revival preacher when I decided to run for my first political office back in 1962. He asked me, "How can you, as a Christian, a deacon, and a Sunday school teacher, become involved in politics?" I gave him a smart-aleck response: "I will have 75,000 people in my senate district. How would you like to have a congregation that big?"

More recently, since our White House years, my move has been away from politics and toward religion, but for me the two are still related. There is no doubt that my having been a national political leader is what attracts most visitors to my Sunday school class, and it is clear to me that these worshipers are increasingly eager to help shape our nation's political agenda.

When I look back on my life, I can see how startling the changes have been. Eric Hoffer, the self-educated long-shoreman and philosopher, described the 1930s as a time of hope and more recent years as a time of desire. As a child, I knew the '30s to be a time of hope, when the economic situation was so bad that everyone believed it could only improve. Nowadays, things are so plentiful, at least as shown in movies and on television, that we want not only what we already have but also what everyone else has.

I was brought up in a fairly isolated rural community called Archery, about three miles west of Plains, and in a family that was close and cohesive. Home was our haven, in times of pain or pleasure. There was no doubt that my father made the final decisions, but all of us knew that Mama's influence and opinions were always major factors in how our family was managed. There were certain aspects of life, particularly in the running of the household and the raising of my sisters, that were almost exclusively my mother's purview. Together, our parents were dominant, and we children respected and obeyed them. In fact, I never deliberately disobeyed them.

Now most Americans move around frequently and are exposed to many influences, and our environments and customs are multifaceted. But for me as a child, there were just a few sources of knowledge about myself or any other people. Our contacts with the world beyond our community were limited. Without electricity in our house, time on the battery radio was restricted, even on the rare nights when we stayed up after dark. We did listen as a family to *Little Orphan Annie*, *Fibber McGee and Molly*, and *Amos 'n' Andy*, and my parents would sometimes let me stay up until 8:00 P.M. to hear Glenn Miller's band playing the current musical hits. But that was all the outside world I knew.

In addition to my family and our farm neighbors, almost all African-American, I knew other people just through

school and the church. Our prom parties, which parents
would carefully orchestrate to let boys and girls get
acquainted, were sponsored by the church.

Sunday mornings were for Sunday school and preaching at Plains Baptist Church, where Daddy was a teacher
and a deacon. After church we always had the best meal
of the week, usually fried chicken, mashed potatoes, hot
biscuits, and all kinds of vegetables, followed by pies made
from sweet potatoes or fruits of the season. Afterward, our
activities were severely limited. There were no stores open,
movies in the nearby county seat were out of the question, and shooting a gun or playing cards was prohibited.
Fishing in the nearby creek or small pond was a close call,
but it came to be permitted if done discreetly. It would not
have been appropriate to walk down a public road with a
fishing pole.

My mama and daddy played cards—but certainly not on
Sunday. Rosalynn points out that others, including her
own family, wouldn't play cards at all.

At the age of twelve, when I was deemed old enough to
drive a car by myself, my sisters and I went back to the
church on Sunday evenings for meetings of the Baptist
Young People's Union, or BYPU. (Our brother Billy was
thirteen years younger than I.) This was very important,
because the BYPU sponsored most of the teenage social
events.

I need not go on, since the picture is fairly clear. It was
a simple, family-centered, deeply religious, working existence, with easy interracial play with my black neighbors.

I imagine that, except for automobiles and a hand-cranked telephone, our lives were similar to those of our great-grandparents.

There was a special closeness among neighbors. Sickness or death were community affairs. Even in later years, when my father was on his deathbed, the yard was full of people who came to offer cakes, pies, and fried chicken so that we wouldn't have to do anything but care for him. Daddy had cancer, and everyone knew that his illness was terminal. He grew weaker every day because he couldn't eat or digest any food, but folks would go out, even if it wasn't quail season, kill a couple, and bring the carefully cooked birds to my daddy with some pecan pie or something they knew he really liked. There was a sharing not just of food but of presence.

Now, of course, family life even in the small Plains community is quite different. Some activities once strictly concealed in our proper society are probably no more prevalent but are now out in the open. Divorce has become acceptable, even for active church members. Without trying to analyze it too deeply, I see that one of the most significant changes is the relationship between young people and their parents. The ties are substantially broken during the teen years, no matter how much parents want to retain strong influence over their growing children. The outside world is a much more powerful influence, with the availability of rapid transportation, television, and particularly a broader circle of friends (and adversaries), whose influence often exceeds that of our own families.

But many families still have a core of principles that do not change. Where do we turn now when there is a moral question? What things in the 1990s are the same as they were in the 1930s? We need a permanent foundation on which our lives can be fashioned. Without a central core of beliefs or standards by which to live, we may never experience the challenge and excitement of seeking a greater life. We will have ceased to grow, like Jesus, "strong in spirit, filled with wisdom; and the grace of God upon him" (Luke 2:40).

People in the New Testament church came to Paul and asked him what things they could depend on if they changed their way of living and adopted the Christian faith that he espoused. He replied, "We look not at what can be seen but at what cannot be seen; for what can be seen is temporary, but what cannot be seen is eternal" (2 Corinthians 4:18). The things we cannot see are paramount, and do not change—those about which Jesus taught. Can we see truth, justice, forgiveness, or love? I try to remember this verse during some of the more trying times of my own life, and I use it frequently in my classes and in counseling people who are distressed about crises in their lives.

It is not difficult to identify the changes in our lives, some welcome and others quite painful. But we don't want the verities of our lives to change. We need to have something unshakable, like a mother's love, something that can't be destroyed by war, the loss of a loved one, lack of success in business, a serious illness, or failure to realize our ambitions. We need some foundation on which we can build a predictable and dependable existence.

This cannot be found in either our nation's laws or religious denominations. I would like to say as an American who has been president of the United States that the accepted values of my country are constant—but they aren't. There's a great deal of change, all the time, in the interpretation of laws and in the passage of new ones. Some laws violate what seem to be accepted principles and create serious division within our society. Also, almost every religious denomination is fragmenting over controversial secular issues.

But despite the confusion and controversy among religious organizations, there are basic principles that, for me, have never changed. For a Christian, the life and teachings of Jesus offer a sound moral foundation that includes all the most basic elements that should guide us. Since these highest standards are eternal, we have an obligation to comprehend what they are and what they mean for us. Our faith can provide enough courage to apply these biblical lessons to our daily lives. If specific guidelines or examples are not always available, at least our basic principles can help narrow the options.

For me, sharing any problem through prayer provides a powerful element of calm and objectivity. Then, when I might fear or regret the consequences of a choice I have made, an awareness of the presence of the Spirit of God can give me courage. John says that Christ knows us all (John 2:24), and Paul reminds us that nothing can separate us from the love of God (Romans 8:39).

Somewhat to my own surprise, this has become a book whose core is love—the love that is possible among those who are closely related, among strangers allied by a common dream or faith, and even between people who begin by despising each other but find a way to see the image of God in each other's humanity.

When I return to my beginnings, I see a number of times when what I believed I wanted most was challenged by a more difficult path. When I had the courage to choose that path, even in the midst of despair and uncertainty, I was given a glimpse of deeper truths that continue to sustain me.

CHAPTER ONE

The Search for Faith

Religious faith has always been at the core of my existence. It has been a changing and evolving experience, beginning when I was a child of three, memorizing Bible verses in Sunday school. When I was nine years old, I was promoted to the Sunday school class taught by my father, so I had the double influence of the church environment and my own father as my teacher. My faith at first was simple and unequivocal; there was no doubt in my mind about the truth of what I learned in church.

Yet even as a child, I was dismayed to find myself becoming skeptical about some aspects of my inherited faith. We learned in church that Jesus had risen from the dead three days after his crucifixion, and that all believers would someday enjoy a similar resurrection. As I grew older, I began to wonder whether this could be so. I became quite concerned about it, worried not so much about the prospect of my own death as about the possibility that I might be separated from my mother and father. These two people were the core of my existence, and I couldn't bear the idea that I wouldn't be with them forever.

By the time I was twelve or thirteen years old, my anxiety about this became so intense that at the end of every prayer, until after I was an adult, before "Amen" I added the words "And, God, please help me believe in the resurrection." What made it worse was that I thought I was the only person with such concerns. I felt guilty that I doubted what the preacher said and what my father taught me in Sunday school.

This was not the kind of thing we would have talked about at home. Although my father was at ease teaching the lessons in church, I think he would have been embarrassed to bring up Christian subjects with me while we were at work in the fields or sitting together at the dinner table. In a way, I saw a different father in Sunday school. I admired Daddy greatly as a man who excelled in many things: he was an unbeatable tennis player, an outstanding baseball pitcher, and a fine hunter and fisherman; he knew how to raise bird dogs so they could find and point quail, and he was a successful farmer and businessman. I took his faith and his Sunday school teaching for granted, and I kept my doubts to myself. It would have been inconceivable to express doubts to him about anything in the Bible.

So even at an early age, I was developing a kind of dual approach to biblical teachings. My sense of faith was pre-eminent: I *knew* that there was a God who was our creator and that I was being observed and judged in all I did; I *knew* that Jesus Christ had accepted the punishment for my sins and that through faith in him I could be saved. But I had a nagging degree of skepticism about the relationship between my faith and the scientific point of view I was already developing through my schoolwork and my reading.

Of course, church was much more to me than a source of knowledge about God. It was the center of social life for our family and for the whole community. For example, we had no Boy Scout troop in Plains then, so my father would take his Sunday school class into the woods to camp out all night or go fishing, teaching the town boys something about the outdoors.

Beginning when I was ten or twelve, church was also the place where we became acquainted with our female class-mates in a social setting. The church would sponsor closely chaperoned "prom parties" for the young people on Friday nights. Each of us would bring a pound of food—a pound of fried chicken, pork barbecue, bread, potato salad, or cake. Then we'd stroll, talk, and dance. The chaperones made sure there were no wallflowers at these parties, and we had to check back in with them frequently enough to minimize opportunities for "improper" conduct. Prom cards were used to keep track of partners for dances, and no one could dance more than three times, or spend more than fifteen consecutive minutes, with the same partner.

These parties were fun, and as I grew older I came to realize that they were also the way our parents arranged for us to explore the field for possible future spouses.

Every summer, our Baptist church held a revival week, designed to heighten the religious commitment of the church members and to convince nonmembers to join. (The Methodist church held its own revival at a different time of year, and the more devout Christians in town would attend both.) The visiting preachers who conducted the ten revival services offered a two-part message. They preached what we called "hellfire and damnation" sermons to convince us that anyone who didn't accept Christ as a personal savior was going to hell. Interspersed was a description of the glorious alternative of redemption and heaven offered by Jesus. Their eloquence and the power of their message were often overwhelming.

Practically everyone in Plains would come to some of these services. There was a morning sermon at ten o'clock, attended by the women while their children were in school and their husbands worked in the stores and fields, and a nighttime service, which entire families could attend. The climax of each sermon was when nonmembers were asked to come forward and declare their intention of accepting Christ as savior. This was the most important step in life, marking the moment at which a person became a member of the Christian community. It was much more important for us Baptists than the rite of baptism, which came soon afterward and symbolized a burial of our old selves with immersion, rebirth into a new life with Christ, and membership in our church.

We didn't believe in what we called "child conversions," although I understand that in some Baptist churches children as young as eight might make the step of accepting Christ and becoming church members. We were encouraged to wait until we were older, and I decided to accept Christ during a revival service when I was eleven. I was then baptized with other new converts on the Sunday following revival week.

What does it mean when I say that I "decided to accept Christ"? Jesus was the Messiah, the long-awaited savior, who came both to reveal God to us and to heal the division between God and humankind. As Jesus told his disciples, "If you have seen me, you have seen God" (John 14:9). Furthermore, the Gospels recount how Jesus, having lived a perfect and blameless life, accepted a death of horrible suffering on the cross on our behalf, as an atonement for the sins we have committed. Accepting Christ as my savior means believing all these things and entering into a relationship with God through him, so that my past and future sins no longer alienate me from my Creator.

Putting our total faith in these concepts is what is meant by being "born again." It's when there is an intimate melding of my life with that of Jesus: I become a brother with him, and God is our mutual parent. This frees me from the strings that previously limited my relationship with my creator.

Being born again is a new life, not of perfection but of striving, stretching, and searching—a life of intimacy with God through the Holy Spirit. There must first be an emptying, and then a refilling. To the extent that we want to know, understand, and experience God, we can find all this in Jesus. It is a highly personal and subjective experience, possible only if we are searching for greater truths about ourselves and God.

This experience is challenging, even painful at times, but ultimately deeply rewarding. It provides answers to the most disturbing questions about our existence, the purpose of life, and how to deal with sorrow, failure, loneliness, guilt, and fear. In it, we come to know that our gifts from God are not earned by our own acts but are given to us through his grace. As Paul says, "Therefore, since we have been justified through faith, we have peace with God through our Lord Jesus Christ, through whom we have gained access by faith into this grace in which we now stand" (Romans 5:1–2).

The love of Christ lets us feel the fullness of God. Ephesians 3:16–19 describes this experience well:

> I pray that, according to the riches of his glory, he may grant that you may be strengthened in your inner being with power through his Spirit, and that Christ may dwell in your hearts through faith, as you are being rooted and grounded in love. I pray that you may have the power to comprehend, with all the saints, what is the breadth and length and height and depth, and to know the love of Christ that surpasses knowledge, so that you may be filled with all the fullness of God.

Being born again didn't happen to me when I was eleven. For me, it has been an evolutionary thing. Rather than a flash of light or a sudden vision of God speaking, it involved a series of steps that have brought me steadily closer to Christ. My conversion at eleven was just one of these steps.

Through it all, my worry over the doubts I felt about some Christian teachings continued, and my skepticism was somewhat heightened when I went away to college. I took part in the usual all-night discussions with my freshman and sophomore classmates about big philosophical topics: Why was I created? What is the purpose of life? Who or what is God? We questioned everything, and we thought we were quite profound.

Then I went to the U.S. Naval Academy, and I became an engineer and later studied advanced science. This was also the first time that I got to know significant numbers of people who were not Protestant Christians. (There were a handful of Jews in our nearby county seat of Americus— respected community members—but their religion was never discussed.) At the Naval Academy, there were many students who attended Protestant religious services, a substantial number who attended Roman Catholic services, and a relatively small number who attended Jewish services. (We also had a few who claimed to be Moslems, Hindus, or atheists, but the rest of us all figured that this was so they wouldn't have to go to the mandatory chapel services.) So for the first time, I had the opportunity to learn something about other faiths.

Worshiping God remained an important part of my life. During my three years at the academy, I attended chapel regularly, and I got to know the chaplain pretty well. I also taught Sunday school; my students were the nine-to-twelve-year-old daughters of the enlisted men and officers who were assigned permanently to the naval base at Annapolis. Out of 3,500 midshipmen, only a handful were equally active in chapel activities, so this was a significant religious commitment on my part.

When I graduated from Annapolis, Rosalynn and I were married, and she moved from the Methodist church in which she'd grown up to join me as a Baptist. However, the following seven years I spent in the navy were a relatively dormant phase in my religious life. With me assigned to various ships at naval bases in Virginia, Hawaii, California, and Connecticut, it wasn't convenient for Rosalynn and me to be part of a single nurturing church community.

Nonetheless, I sought out opportunities to worship when and where I could. For instance, when I got off duty on Sunday mornings after several days at sea, I would almost invariably find a Christian church service to attend on the naval base, despite the fact that I was eager to get home to my young bride. It didn't matter to me what kind of service I went to—I attended either Protestant or Roman Catholic services, and took communion at the Catholic masses; I just went to whichever service was earliest, so I could get home sooner.

Seven years after Annapolis, I was enjoying a burgeoning navy career when I was called home to my father's deathbed. This proved to be a turning point in my spiritual life.

During the weeks before and after my father's death, my

family's immersion in the Christian community of Plains was an overwhelming experience for me. I felt that we had a family with not five people in it but several hundred. This was something I had almost forgotten since I'd left home as a teenager. My appreciation for the warmth and power of this Christian fellowship was a major factor in my decision to leave the navy and return to live in Plains.

As soon as we'd moved home, I volunteered to teach Sunday school at the Plains Baptist Church again, taking over my father's own class (the juniors, aged nine to twelve). After a year, Rosalynn joined me as a teacher of the junior girls, while I taught the boys. Soon I became head of the junior department, and also a deacon, one of the important lay ministries in the Baptist church.

My religious questions persisted, however, made more intense, in a way, by my father's death. This was the first real tragedy in my life. (I had lost my grandparents earlier, but they had lived in another community and I was not very close to them.) I found my father's death hard to understand. How could a good man, not nearly as old as many others in Plains, be deprived by God of his productive life? It seemed to me a harsh act, one I could only attribute to what I thought of as the God of the Old Testament, a stern, judgmental figure, very different from the loving, forgiving Jesus I knew from the Gospels.

This is when I began to explore in some depth the writings of theologians. I had never taken a course in religion or theology, but now I bought a large number of books by authors like Dietrich Bonhoeffer, Karl Barth, Martin Buber, Paul Tillich, Hans Küng, and particularly Reinhold Niebuhr, and I began to read and examine their ideas.

I explored more deeply what religion is, considering how my scientific outlook and knowledge, my continuing doubts about the biblical accounts of miracles, and my uneasiness about the relationship between God the Creator and God in Christ could be accommodated to the traditional faith I'd inherited. A torturous time of searching followed. I struggled to understand and differentiate the varying definitions of religion and the nature of God that I found in the works of theologians and philosophers, looking for a point of view with which I could feel comfortable.

I was fascinated by the outlooks of these thinkers, but my own relationship to faith remained an open question. An important part of the answer came to me from the writings of Paul Tillich. One of his themes is that doubt is an acceptable, even necessary aspect of faith—that faith implies a continuing search, not necessarily a final answer.

I found myself turning repeatedly to the story in the Gospel of Mark when a father comes to Jesus in search of a cure for his son, who is suffering seizures. The father asks Jesus to heal his son, saying, "If you can do anything, have pity on us and help us." Jesus replies, "If you can believe! All things are possible to him who believes." And the father responds, "I believe; help my unbelief!" Jesus rebukes the spirit and drives it away from the son, healing him completely (Mark 9:17–27).

The assurance Jesus offers in this story—that we will not be turned away on account of our doubts or skepticism

but that he will "help our unbelief"—has meant a great deal
to me, especially in times of pain or trouble. At such times,
I've felt strongly the need of something more permanent
and profound than a successful career, being president, or
even my relationship with Rosalynn. Jesus' acceptance has
given me this.

Maybe some Christians never lack faith—they are the
lucky ones. However, I don't know of anybody who has
never had doubts about any aspect of the Christian faith.

We would like to have an absolutely certain base on
which to build our lives—unquestioned faith in everything
that the Bible tells us about God, about Jesus, about a
quality life, about life after death, about God's love for us.
Perhaps we are afraid that opening the door to a little questioning might shake the foundation of our faith or anger
God. But I came to realize that it is a mistake not to face
our doubts courageously. We should be willing to ask questions, always searching for a closer relationship with God,
a more profound faith in Christ. It is foolish to think that
our own doubts can change the truth.

When I contemplated abandoning my naval career, I
prayed fervently that God would guide me to the right
decision. Later, when I lost the 1966 governor's election
and was tempted to abandon my faith altogether, my search
for God's will sustained me through my anger and disillusionment. I have seen many people with broken lives, some
on the verge of alcoholism or even suicide, turn and con-
struct new and vibrant lives based on religious faith. The
combined testimonies of countless people with similar

experiences have helped to perpetuate religious faith as an integral part of the lives of billions of believers.

Yet the acquiring of faith is not an easy or frivolous thing. How can we prove that God created the universe, that the prophets communicated with God, that Jesus was the Messiah, or that the resurrection occurred? How can we prove that our lives are meaningful, that truth exists, or that we love or are loved? When I become absorbed in these questions, it helps me to fall back on my faith as a Christian.

The Danish existentialist Søren Kierkegaard said, "Faith means the betting of one's life upon the God in Jesus Christ, . . . the giving or commitment of one's whole life." My faith—my life commitment—has been instilled in me since childhood. Despite periods of doubt, it has been confirmed and strengthened by the tangible spiritual benefits I have received from the "assurance of things hoped for, the conviction of things not seen" (Hebrews 11:1). It is only through faith that I can maintain a relationship with the omnipotent Creator and my personal savior. Without this, I would feel destitute.

My reading of theology, which helped to open these new ideas about faith for me, was an illuminating experience in which I began to feel at ease with my religion for the first time since I was a little child.

I also began to see that my Christian faith and my scientific outlook could be compatible, not conflicting. One of the Bible passages that has helped me understand this is found in Paul's letter to the Romans. Speaking about the pagan peoples of the day, Paul wrote, "That which is known about God is evident within them, for God made it evident to them. For since the creation of the world His invisible attributes, His eternal power and divine nature, have been clearly seen, being understood through what has been made, so that they are without excuse" (Romans 1:19–20). Paul's point was that the glories of the world around us prove God's existence.

Like Paul, I see the glory of God around me, in the unfathomable mysteries of the universe and the diversity and intricacies of creation. We stand in wonder at how a tree grows from an acorn, how a flower blooms, or how DNA can shape the appearance and character of a living creature. It is almost humanly incomprehensible that in our Milky Way galaxy there are billions of stars equivalent to our sun, and then billions of other galaxies equivalent to our own. At the other end of the scale, I marvel that the inseparable atom I learned about in high school is really a collection of remarkable components, matter and anti-matter, rotating in different directions yet held together by forces of immense power, and some particles able to pass through the entire earth without being deflected.

Even more miraculous is the human form, in which the trillions of neuron connections in a single human brain exceed the total number of celestial bodies in the known heavens! Scientific knowledge only enhances my sense of God's glory filling the universe. Over the centuries, scientists have discovered more and more about these truths—truths that have always existed. None of these discoveries contradicts my belief in an ultimate and superior being; they simply confirm the reverence and awe generated by what becomes known and what remains unexplained.

As a believer, I have no problem with discoveries in astronomy, geology, and paleontology: that the universe is enormous and expanding, the earth is ancient, and human beings have evolved from primitive ancestors. It is not difficult for me to accept the "big bang" theory of the origin of the universe, at least until it is refuted by further exploration of the heavens and a new explanation is evolved to explain what God has done. Nor does it shake my religious faith to realize that the early authors of the Scriptures thought that the earth was flat, that stars were little things like Christmas tree ornaments that could fall on us, that the entire process of creation occurred during six earthly days, and that the first woman came from the rib of the first man, both Adam and Eve created in modern human form. The gap between their understanding and ours just indicates that knowledge was revealed later to Galileo, Newton, Darwin, Einstein, and Hubble—and to most of us.

One of my favorite authors is Stephen Jay Gould, an evolutionary biologist who writes monthly articles for *Natural History* magazine, which are later published in book form. His most intriguing book for me was *Wonderful Life*, in which he described the remarkable creatures that evolved almost overnight (in geological terms) during the Cambrian period, about 530 million years ago. He claimed that if a few genes or some environmental factors had been different, the "tape of life" as we know it would have played out in a completely different way. Everything has been a matter of chance or accident, including the evolution of human beings.

Feeling a bit presumptuous, I wrote to Gould disagreeing with this premise and asserting that there were factors other than pure happenstance that influenced the course of evolution. He later contradicted my argument—with good humor—in another of his books, *Bully for Brontosaurus*. Such discussions will continue on many fronts, as more scientific discoveries are made. The fact is that between true scientific facts and faith in a supreme being, the Creator of all, there can be no disparity—except among people who argue about things that cannot be or have not yet been proven.

Later, I wrote a poem on the subject:

A CONTEMPLATION OF WHAT HAS BEEN CREATED, AND WHY

I tried to fathom nature's laws
from twirling models and schoolroom sketches
of molecules and parts of atoms,
and nearly believed—but then came quarks,
bosons, leptons, antiparticles,
opposite-turning mirror images,
some that perforate the earth,
never swerving from their certain paths.
I've listened to conflicting views
about the grand and lesser worlds:
a big bang where it all began;

of curved, ever-expanding space;
perhaps tremendous whirling yo-yos
that will someday reach the end
of cosmic gravity and then
fly back to where they can restart
or cataclysmically blow apart—
and then, and then the next event.
And will it be an accident?

Unlike Professor Gould, I am sure that none of this is an accident. If Paul expected the ancient Romans to believe in God because of their relatively limited observations of the world around them, shouldn't our faith be stronger, since we know so much more?

In its own way, technology offers a lesson in the nature of faith. Aren't there plenty of things in modern life that we believe but can't understand? The computer, radio, television, space travel—all once seemed miraculous, but most of us now accept them as routine. We can set up an antenna and bring in 150 different television programs. The waves are all around us, plus countless radio signals, waiting for us to extract them from the ether for our pleasure or information. There is no way for us to detect in advance that the signals are here, or for most of us to explain how these electromagnetic waves can be changed into music or colored, moving pictures almost instantaneously. These are amazing things that few of us comprehend, but we believe them.

In the same way, I cannot fully understand many religious concepts, even some aspects of the life of Christ—the extremes of love and judgment, power and weakness, the demand for perfection and total forgiveness, the omnipotence of God and his human Son weeping and tempted. The totality of it is overwhelming, but I accept it with confidence—through faith.

In addition to the intellectual realization of a supreme being, we have a purely subjective need to meet a personal yearning. We have an innate desire to relate to the all-knowing, the all-powerful, and the ever-present—to some entity that transcends ourselves. I am grateful and happy when I feel the presence of God within me, as a tangible influence on my thoughts and on the ultimate standards of my life. It is reassuring to me to know that God will always be with me and cares for me. I think of the words of Isaiah: "When you pass through the waters, I will be with you; and through the rivers, they shall not overwhelm you; when you walk through fire you shall not be burned, and the flame shall not consume you. For I am the Lord your God. . . . You are precious in my sight, and honored, and I love you" (Isaiah 43:2–4).

Our Sunday school class often becomes involved in a discussion about how to achieve this closeness to God. Except in moments of crisis, when we reach desperately for some sustaining force, the relationship requires some effort on our part, some reaching out. I remind my class of the man in terrible trouble who prayed, "God, if you'll just get me out of this mess, I promise never to bother you with

my prayers again." We need God's presence at all times—
not just when life is at its most difficult.

This desire for a personal relationship with God cannot
be abolished, even under pressure. A basic reason for the
disintegration of the once-powerful Soviet Union is that
the government required its citizens to put all their faith
in the central authority. The communist apparatus—
including the army, the party, and the government—was
declared to be sufficient to meet all human needs. As Karl
Marx said, religion was considered merely "the opium of
the people." Eventually, this entire system collapsed, a
hollow shell. Eighty years after the Soviet government officially declared atheism dominant and prohibited religion,
the seeds of faith still exist, and there is now an explosion
of religious fervor in Russia.

There are other elements in our lives that make us turn
to Christ, to seek God's will, to excel in our own standards
of morality or belief. We want to prove that our lives are
meaningful. At the same time, faith has to be predicated on
a *desire* to believe. The Leonard Cohen song about Christ's
walking on the water says that Jesus knew that "only
drowning men could see him." Faced with death, in a
storm, the disciples wanted to believe.

I've been disconcerted to find my own religious beliefs
incompatible with those of many prominent Baptists. In
1976, during my first campaign for the presidency, I was
taken aback when the evangelist Jerry Falwell condemned
me because I "claimed" to be a Christian. At the time, I dis-

counted the importance of this criticism, especially since few people then knew who Jerry Falwell was, but before the end of my term in office, he and his organization, the Moral Majority, became quite famous. This was the first national emergence of the so-called Christian Right, later joined by Pat Robertson, the Christian Coalition, and others.

In 1979, this conservative wing of Christianity was strong enough to take over leadership of the Southern Baptist Convention (SBC), which had always been my church "home." I was a longtime, stalwart supporter of the SBC, which represented Baptist congregations totaling 14 million members. I'd served on the fifteen-man board of the Convention's Brotherhood Commission, which sets policy for all the men's affairs and programs, and had even conducted the wedding ceremony for the commission's executive director while I was governor of Georgia (the only wedding I've ever performed). So I was dismayed when the fundamentalists took control of the convention's organization and began purging the more moderate leaders and defining narrowly the criteria for seminary professors and curricula.

In the United States today, there seems to be a growing split between two ways of practicing the Christian faith. On the one hand, there are those who believe that Christianity gives its adherents material benefits. Such churches promise their members comfort, security, financial wealth, and prestige, and they often display an evangelistic zeal that is quite impressive. Many of these churches are very active in public affairs and have become powerful political forces. On the other hand, there are those who consider ministering to the poor, the despised, and the homeless as important elements of Christianity. The first group often looks upon the second as less than truly Christian, sometimes using the phrase "secular humanist" to describe them.

I have been faced with this charge. A high official of the Southern Baptist Convention came into the Oval Office to visit me when I was president. As he and his wife were leaving, he said, "We are praying, Mr. President, that you will abandon secular humanism as your religion." This was a shock to me. I didn't know what he meant, and I am still not sure. He may have said this because I was against a constitutional amendment to authorize mandatory prayer in public schools and had been working on some things opposed by the "religious right," such as the Panama Canal treaties, a Department of Education, and the SALT II treaty with the Soviets.

These differences among Christian groups sap a tremendous portion of our ability, time, money, and influence. Much of our energy is spent in internecine warfare, in arguments and debates that not only are divisive but incapacitate us for our work in the name of Christ.

Our faith should be a guide for us in deciding between the permanent and the transient, the important and the insignificant, the gratifying and the troubling, the joyful and the depressing. We must study the principles on which our faith is founded, but we can't become obsessed with the belief that we have a special ordination from God to interpret the Scriptures and to consider anyone who disagrees with us wrong and inferior. The tendency of fundamentalists, in Christianity and other religions, to condemn those who differ from them is perhaps the most disturbing aspect of their current ascendancy.

Of course, the fellowship of faith is even larger than the Christian world. The first great Christian theologian, Paul, repeatedly emphasized the fundamental importance of faith as a unifying force between Christians and Jews. A burning question in the early church was whether God's covenant with Abraham was exclusively for the Jews. Some feared that if they became Christians they would forgo God's blessing. Paul made it clear that it was the patriarch's faith and not his ethnicity that was significant. He relied on the Scripture: "For the promise that he should be the heir of the world was not to Abraham or to his seed, through the law, but through the righteousness of faith" (Romans 4:13). The covenant with God is shared by Jews and Christians, with faith in one God as the unifying element.

Although the word *faith* is used only twice in the King James Version of the Old Testament (245 times in the New Testament), the writer of Hebrews relates faith directly and by name to a large number of biblical heroes of earlier times whose actions were determined by it. Through faith, Noah built his ark and became the heir of righteousness. Abraham and his wife, Sarah, although "as good as dead," had descendants as numerous as the stars because of their faith. Joseph, near death, had faith enough to call for the exodus of the Israelites from Egypt. Moses gave up the "pleasures of sin" to lead the Jews to freedom, depending on his faith to sustain him through forty years in the wilderness. And through faith, Gideon, Samson, David, Samuel, and the prophets conquered kingdoms, administered justice, shut the mouths of lions, quenched flames, escaped the edges of swords, and had weaknesses turned to strengths. The power of faith is a unifying bond between Christian and Jew and between the heroes of ancient Israel and those of New Testament times.

When people become alienated from one another, it is important to search for a healing force. A husband and wife may have a child who can hold them together. Members of an athletic team who don't really like one another will cooperate in the heat of a game. Our faith in God should play such a unifying role among believers. This may seem obvious, but all too often we forget or ignore it.

Christians of various denominations and shades of practice should emphasize shared concepts that are so great and so important that, compared with them, other differences fade into relative insignificance. Our faith should transcend all merely human issues, such as whether we are immersed or sprinkled in baptism, have few or many ordinances, have servant pastors or a hierarchical church with bishops and maybe a pope. We can rise above all this when we come together as common believers, but doing so requires both an elevation in spirit and a degree of personal humility.

The closest fellowship Rosalynn and I have with those outside our family is through the Maranatha Baptist Church. But *church* does not mean just "Maranatha" or "Baptist" or "Protestant"; it is the totality of those united in the love of Christ. The ultimate vision of the church should be as a worldwide community in which all believers are joined. As I have come to know, reaching out to others in the name of God can be one of the most deeply rewarding experiences any person can enjoy.

CHAPTER TWO

A Rooted Life

For more than fifty years now, the key factor in my good life has been my relationship with Rosalynn. Even during our first date, going to a movie, I knew that she was the girl I wanted to be my wife. Eight months later, she rejected my marriage proposal, having promised her father that she would finish her college work first. I persisted, and, after going with a number of other boys, she acquiesced. In the years since then, we have had many joys as well as difficult times, but a foundation of mutual affection and shared religious faith has helped us survive the challenges to our marriage. There is no doubt that we both have grown in the process.

For our first seven years, we were a navy family, moving

every year or so from one ship or naval base to another. We lived in Virginia, Connecticut, Hawaii, California, back in Connecticut, and then in upstate New York. Our personal life was narrow and focused on each other, since we had little interest in other couples or in life at the officers' clubs during the all-too-rare times when I was at home. Rosalynn was timid around other people then, and eager to accommodate my wishes. Since I was at sea much of the time, she had the household responsibilities—paying the rent, buying groceries, and caring for the children when they came.

For some reason, I was not always able or willing to talk with Rosalynn about problems or worries related to my ship duty, and she was uncomfortable when I was silent or uncommunicative, concerned that I was displeased with her or was falling out of love. Sometimes she cried, and I became angry and even more withdrawn when I could not see any reason for her tears. Despite our love, it was not always easy for us to adjust to each other.

I'm not sure what caused this discomfort in our relationship. Maybe I inherited a male-dominant role from what I thought as a child was the relationship between my parents. (It was only later that I understood my mother's strong will and how she expressed her views to my father in private and often prevailed.) Another factor was that I lived for at least twenty-five days each month in a completely male environment, onboard ship. The relationships were friendly competition with my peers, compliance with orders from my superiors, and expectation that those junior to me would honor my commands. It was incon-

ceivable to exhibit signs of weakness or even emotions that
were not totally under control. Also, it is likely that I considered Rosalynn's household and family responsibilities
relatively insignificant compared with mine.

Our most intense crisis came when my father died. I was
an ambitious young submarine officer, heading the pre-
commissioning crew of the USS *Sea Wolf,* one of the first
two nuclear-powered submarines being designed and built
under the supervision of the legendary Adm. Hyman Rickover. This was the choice assignment in the navy, and I was
clearly destined for a successful career, with promotions
likely to be coming as early as navy regulations would
allow.

I secured a two-week leave from Admiral Rickover to
visit my father and spent this time by Daddy's bedside and
making some calls on old friends around Plains. I was
amazed to discover the extensive nature of my father's contributions to the lives of our neighbors. Dozens of black
and white friends came to our door, greeted me almost as a
prodigal son who had come home, and described what my
father meant to them. These visitors were grieved for him
and our family because he could not live more than another
few weeks, but they were also wondering what they would
do without him.

The extent of my father's charitable giving surprised me
and all of my family. His benevolence had been largely
secret and was only revealed by these people coming to
visit us during the weeks before and after his death. The
principal of the school told us that when any children were
approaching graduation and didn't have proper clothes for

the ceremony, Daddy would always buy them. We discovered that for almost twenty years he had sent a monthly check for twenty-five dollars to a family in town because the husband and father had died. That was a lot of money in those days.

Much of my father's generosity had occurred during the Depression years, when we and our neighbors had little or no money. In 1935, for example, the farmers had to depend on three sources of income: cotton, peanuts, and hogs. Cotton was selling for five cents a pound, and peanuts and hogs for one cent a pound—far below the costs of production. For a farmer to work an acre of peanuts meant buying or saving seed, breaking the land, cultivating it at least seven times, plowing up and shaking dirt from the peanuts, putting them on stacks, letting them dry, threshing them, and hauling them to market. All of this yielded a *gross* income of seven dollars an acre. So throughout our community and much of the rural South, there was virtually no money. In a world like this, my father's charitable acts were all the more remarkable.

He was also deeply involved in every aspect of our town's social and political life. He served on the school and hospital boards, he was a church deacon and taught the junior Sunday school class, and he held a seat in the state legislature. Several times each year, he would haul a truckload of farmers down to the agricultural college at Tifton, about a hundred miles from Plains, so they could learn in one-day training courses how to build better fences or fishponds or how to grow better peanuts or make more cotton.

The diversity of my father's life impressed me deeply—

how he utilized what talent he had in an extraordinarily broad way. I was working hard in the navy, devoting all my talent and ability to learning how to build and operate atomic submarines, and I was proud of what I had accomplished. But I now began to feel that this was a narrowly focused life. The basic question I asked as I reflected on my father's passing was: Whose life is more important in the eyes of God—mine or his?

On the way back to my navy duties in Schenectady, New York, knowing that my father had only a few days to live, I could not erase these memories from my mind, or the question of how the significance of his life compared with my own, even if my highest career ambitions would be realized. I had been committed to the navy since I was a little child, never giving any serious thought to an alternative career. Now I felt I was faced with a completely unexpected question: Should I resign from the U.S. Navy and return to spend the rest of my life in the little town of Plains?

Without telling Rosalynn that I was even considering such a decision, I began to weigh all the major factors. Very important was a feeling of disloyalty to Admiral Rickover and the embryonic nuclear submarine program. The navy had made a tremendous investment in my training and special graduate instruction in nuclear technology. Although I had performed all my assigned duties to the best of my ability, I still felt, at that time, that I was the debtor in the relationship.

Another consideration was that Rosalynn and I had no money, except for some war bonds that we had bought each month out of our relatively small navy salary. I never considered what my father's estate might be or for whom he might have provided in a will. The natural presumption was that everything would go to my mother, and the maximum that any of us children might receive would be a one-fifth interest. Also, after eleven years in the navy, including my time at Annapolis, I knew very little about farming or any other commercial enterprise.

In the navy, we lived our own lives, relatively isolated as a family except for the loose friendships we formed with other navy couples. I think this may have been one of the attractions of the navy life for Rosalynn, who saw her role as the focal point around which our three boys and I revolved. She had not reached her nineteenth birthday when we were married and began our lives as a navy couple. Later, when we spent a few days at home on leave, she claimed that she was still treated as a child by our families. So as a navy wife, she relished her independence, quite different from what she imagined she would have if we moved back into a tiny community where our two mothers were likely to be dominant.

On the other hand, I missed having a religious dimension in my life. Although Rosalynn and I occasionally went to the most convenient Protestant or Catholic church services, usually on naval bases, I didn't feel that I was maintaining any significant commitment to my Christian faith. By contrast, I had been profoundly affected by the sense of a large, close-knit Christian family during my last visit to Plains. There was a genuine outpouring of sympathy, love, and sharing during Daddy's terminal illness that reminded me of my early days in the community. Also, looking at the diversity of my father's activities, I became convinced that my own life would be broadened and not restricted if I went back home.

The overriding issue in this torturous decision was how I wanted to spend the rest of my life. Should I be focused on a promising and honorable career as a professional naval officer, serving my country while working on the cutting edge of science and technology? Or did I want to embark on an almost totally unpredictable future, in a small town among people I had not known for more than twelve years?

I continued to face this momentous decision alone. Prayer came naturally to me, and I repeatedly asked God to give me wisdom in assessing all the factors involved.

Over the period of a few days, the balance of advantages became increasingly weighted in my mind in favor of going back home, and by the time I shared the proposal with Rosalynn my decision was made. Rosalynn rebelled in every possible way, but I was adamant. Her resentment was bitter and persistent. However, the intensity and duration of her objections did not deter me from submitting my resignation. A few weeks later, after my father's death and after my resignation from the navy had been accepted, we drove from Schenectady to Plains. Except for our three noisy boys in the backseat, we made the long trip in almost complete silence.

My decision to leave the navy and return home was a crucial event in the life of my family and in my personal and spiritual growth. In time, it led to a deepening of my understanding of and commitment to my religious faith, as well as to the kind of career, both public and private, that I've chosen to follow ever since. But to understand fully this decision and the effects it has had on my life, you need to know something more about the moral framework I originally inherited from my family and my community. This set of principles, rooted in my Christian faith, has both shaped me and been shaped by my personal experiences, and it remains to this day a central element of my identity.

It is difficult for any of us to assess our own habits and actions objectively. Without a set of guidelines, it is not possible to acknowledge and correct the mistaken beliefs and habits that tend to become a way of life.

In my life, there has been a series of codes of conduct by which my activities could be both shaped and judged. They began with my home life and the standards established by my parents, and moved outward in widening circles to encompass my service in the navy, my years as a businessman and citizen in Plains, my political career, and my work after leaving public office. I've found few serious incompatibilities among the ethical codes I encountered along the way; each step tended to expand and strengthen the preceding ones. Some might consider politics an exception, but this is not the case. Contrary to popular opinion, for me and most others in political life, moral principles are actually very high. I'm sure that I did some things that would have displeased my parents or my superior officers if they had been aware of them, but their potential approval or disapproval always provided a framework within which I tried to live.

We all must choose the "guiding lights" that we want to follow. It's easy to set our sights lower. In the navy, I could do my duty and tell the truth but had no real reason or opportunity to be involved in voluntary community activities that would improve the lives of others. If businesspeople follow just the normally accepted practices of the commercial and professional world, they have little incentive to be concerned about the well-being of those with whom they have no dealings. Truth, justice, and loyalty are virtues common to these spheres and to politics, but rarely are included the additional principles of kindness, humility, compassion, forgiveness, mercy, or sacrificial love.

For all of us, particularly people of faith, there is a higher expectation, as expressed for me by Jesus: "All things whatsoever you would that men should do to you, do you even so to them; for this is the law and the prophets" (Matthew 7:12). A similar standard is set in most religious traditions. As described in the Gospels, Jesus demonstrated in his life how this rule should be put into practice. For Christians, it is not just one of the general rules of our religion but *the* rule concerning our personal behavior.

There are many *unenforceable* standards in our private lives, with only self-imposed incentives to comply with them. If we are interested in lives that excel, we will wish to do more than just obey the law. How do we act when there is no accountability for what we do? What restrains us from being rude to others, ignoring the plight of needy people, giving false information when it's to our advantage, abusing a defenseless person, promulgating damaging gossip, holding a grudge, or failing to be reconciled after an argument? These are things for which we will not be punished, and therefore the fear of retribution is missing as a motivation.

Where can we find an element of transcendence in establishing our own ideals and habits? We are all constrained to balance what we actually are with the image we want to display. We learn to bridge this gap by self-delusion ("I really believe this must be true") or by rationalization ("I didn't mean to say that, and besides, it didn't do any harm"). But if we aspire to grow as human beings, we should struggle to close the gap by making our inner selves truer reflections of our own highest values, which, for me, grow from my Christian faith. In fact, most of the beautiful acts of Jesus as recounted in the Gospels do not relate to compliance with existing laws; they were extraordinary because he reached beyond what was required or expected.

What is the standard by which we make a difficult choice when morality or fairness is concerned? Although Christians consider the Bible the best guide to our life's priorities, it is certainly not easy to apply biblical teachings to every act in our modern lives. So all of us develop other rules through habit and experience. When I was a child, the expectations of my father and mother shaped the framework of my "proper" life, and they were also the judges of my performance.

My father was my idol, and provided the example for me

in work habits, the treatment of others in business dealings, community service, accomplishments in competitive
sports, and the recreational activities of a man. Everyone in
our community respected him in all these facets of life. No
one worked harder or had more innovative ideas.

Although I did well in athletic competition in school, I
never equaled my father—at least until I left home for college and the navy—on the tennis court, off the diving
board, on the pitcher's mound, catching fish, or shooting a
gun. (Today I think I could hold my own with him as
a marksman and could even outdo him with a fly rod.)

Daddy accepted the racial segregation of the South as a
way of life. However, he was known to treat both his
employees and his customers, regardless of race, equally
and with meticulous honesty. If an associate had a bad crop
or family trouble, Daddy was both helpful and extremely
generous. But he had little patience with anyone who fell
short of his own standards, and he was unforgiving when
someone lied to him or tried to cheat on a settlement.

After I returned home from the navy, I tried to assume
most of the voluntary projects that my father had under-
taken, and I soon discovered how burdensome they were.
In addition to the duties I've already mentioned, he had
been active in the Plains Lions Club and was a leader in the
protection and promotion of the rural electrification
system. In effect, many of my goals in civilian life were his
accomplishments, including the beginning of my political
career as a member of the Georgia legislature.

*   *   *

My father had also taught me what it means to live under strict discipline. Sometimes I was deeply resentful when he punished me, but I knew where I stood, what was expected of me, and the consequences of disobeying the rules.

Once when I was fishing with a friend on the creek nearest our home, we caught the biggest snapping turtle we'd ever seen. We wanted to show it to my parents, so we suspended it from a sapling and started home through the swamp and woods in the middle of the afternoon. We walked through a slow drizzle until after sundown, when we finally saw some tracks, which we were distressed to discover were our own! Realizing that we were lost, we dropped the turtle and concentrated on walking in a straight line. Then the skies cleared and we saw Venus, an evening star at the time, and walked westward by its guidance, in as straight a line as possible through the trees, vines, and swampy ground. I was thankful for my father's training about the more prominent heavenly bodies.

I had mixed emotions. The thing I wanted most was to see my daddy, but that was also what I feared most, realizing that we had violated all the woodsmen's techniques he had taught me. I also knew he would have mounted a search party when we did not return home.

We finally saw lights, which turned out to be in a farmer's cabin about ten miles from our house. Luckily, he had a mule and wagon, and volunteered to carry us home. Too exhausted to walk any farther, we accepted his offer. After traveling for a couple of miles, we met Daddy in his pickup.

We rode six miles over the dirt roads without speaking, my father obviously displeased. He turned to me when we arrived at home and said, "I thought you knew more about the woods than to get lost." Then he reached out to me, and I rushed to embrace him. I knew I deserved to be chastised, but just being in my father's arms was one of my most joyful and memorable experiences. For a few hours, without either of us knowing where the other was, there had been a vacuum in our lives.

My mother set a different kind of standard for me. She served as a registered nurse, and we saw her ministry among the poor families in our community. She worked almost full-time during the Depression years, either twelve-hour days for four dollars or twenty-hour days for six dollars. Between her regular care for private patients, she served as a volunteer medical practitioner—virtually a family doctor—for the extremely poor families who lived in our rural community of Archery. With a group of women helpers, she made additional income each autumn by harvesting pecans from the trees on our farm.

Mama refused to recognize the strict racial segregation of our South Georgia community and throughout her life was considered by some of our neighbors somewhat strange concerning this issue. Even as a child, I could detect a difference between my mother and other people in how she addressed the integration question. In our community this was not a public issue in the 1930s and 1940s, and the unspoken racial customs and subtleties were rigidly observed. But Mama often disobeyed these rules. She would never assume an attitude of superiority toward the black women who worked alongside her in harvesting, shelling, and preparing pecans for market. As a nurse, if anything, she gave our poorest and most needy farm neighbors—usually black—her highest priority.

In those days black people when visiting white people did not go to their front door. The most distinguished resident of Archery was William Johnson, who served five midwestern states as a bishop in the African Methodist Episcopal Church. Such a man was not about to come to a back door. Instead, he would have his driver park his Cadillac or Packard in the front yard and blow the horn. The strange niceties of the day were observed when my father would go out to talk to him.

However, a problem developed after the bishop's son Alvan went to Harvard to study. When he returned home on vacation, he would come to our front door and be received by my mother, who was eager to hear of his experiences in an Ivy League school. If he was home, Daddy would simply leave the front room and ignore the fact that Alvan had made this unprecedented entry. I never knew of any words between my parents on the subject, but they may have discussed it in private—without changing their ways.

My parents and my father's brother and his wife always took their vacations during baseball season, and would travel to a different major league city each year to attend as many ball games as possible. It just happened that they were present in 1947 when Jackie Robinson broke the major league color barrier by playing his first game with the Brooklyn Dodgers. At that moment, Mama became an avowed admirer of Branch Rickey, the general manager who had boldly signed Robinson, and she remained an avid supporter of the Dodgers throughout her life. She stayed up late at night to listen to their West Coast games after they moved to Los Angeles. After Mama's death, we found a gift from the team in her closet, carefully preserved—an entire Dodger uniform, including cleats.

When asked by a news reporter about the origin of her "liberal" attitude on the race issue, Mama explained that it came from her father. When she was a teenager, around 1915, she worked in the Richland post office, where Grandpa was the postmaster. He refused to make any racial distinctions on his job, and, amazingly for those days, he even invited black officials and other visitors to eat lunch with him in one of the rooms of the post office.

My father died in 1953, before the civil rights movement really affected the South, but I have no doubt that Mama's attitude made the acceptance of racial integration much easier for us children, and for others in the community. After her death, some of her friends told me that at their weekly poker games, and at more public social affairs, they were always careful not to tell any jokes or make any remarks that had a racial connotation—out of respect for Mama.

When my parents' influence was divergent or after I was an adult, I absorbed guidance and experience from other sources. Where race was concerned, that source was service in the navy.

It was only after I entered the navy in my late teens that

I came to understand that black and white people should be treated with complete equality. At first, I did not share this new belief with my family. Coming home for brief periods of leave every year or two, I wanted the reunion with my parents to be pleasant and harmonious, and I quickly discovered that the benefits of racial integration on a submarine were not a subject I could discuss freely without a confrontation with my father.

My first personal experience with total racial integration was at the U.S. Naval Academy, when a young student became the first African-American to join the brigade. His name was Wesley Brown, and he was two classes behind me. Although Midshipman Brown was not in my battalion, he and I both ran cross-country. My primary memory of him is that he was always judged by his performance—and he always crossed the finish line ahead of me. A few members of my senior class attempted to find ways to give him demerits so that he would be discharged, but the senior officers at Annapolis investigated every allegation, and Brown's good performance prevailed.

Later, President Harry S Truman ordered an end to racial discrimination in all the armed services, a directive that was honored, so far as I ever knew, without dissension in the navy ranks. On submarines, with the officers and crew required to live much more closely and intimately than on most surface ships, we related easily without any racial incidents.

Once our ship, the USS *K-1*, went into Nassau in the Bahamas for a few days of rest between long periods of undersea training. The governor-general sent a message inviting us to attend a ball the next evening. Our crew members were all excited when his aide reported that a number of young ladies would also be invited.

I was on duty the next afternoon, when the aide returned to tell us that, of course, the invitation applied only to the white crewmen. When I delivered this message to the captain, he assembled everyone in the mess hall and informed the crew. We voted unanimously to reject the terms of the invitation and received permission to compose a message in response to the Bahamian officials. After deleting the expletives, the captain had it delivered.

Although the values I absorbed from my father and mother were different, each of my parents shaped me in a way I've never outgrown. I always remember a comment by Judge Elbert Tuttle, one of the great jurists of our country. A Republican appointed by President Dwight Eisenhower, he made some of the most definitive and courageous rulings on civil rights during the troubled seg-regation days in Georgia. When he retired, he was inter-viewed by Walter Cronkite, who said, "Judge Tuttle, I understand you've never drunk whiskey." And the judge said, "That's right, I've never in my life tasted an alcoholic drink." Cronkite asked, "Why not?" and the judge gave a simple reply: "Because my mama told me not to."

Similarly, because of my father's strong influence, I have never smoked. Daddy smoked two or more packs of ciga-rettes a day, beginning as a young army officer during World War I, when Americans first adopted the habit on a large scale. With our government's approval, the tobacco companies had contributed free cigarettes to soldiers. On several occasions he tried, unsuccessfully, to quit. In those days, tobacco advertising was even promoting cigarettes as means to better health, endorsed by doctors, so Daddy had no way of knowing that they would ultimately cause his early death. But he resented the grip of a habit he could not break.

When I was about twelve years old, Daddy called me into the bathroom, closed the door, and said he had a very serious subject to discuss with me. This was an unprecedented and sobering experience, and I was very nervous. Then he said he didn't want me to smoke until I was twenty-one years old, and I agreed, with great relief. I kept my promise until my twenty-first birthday, when I was a midshipman. I bought a pack of cigarettes and took one puff, didn't like it, gave the others away, and never smoked another cigarette. I didn't know until years later what the tobacco companies have always known, that people are not likely to become addicted to tobacco unless they begin smoking at an early age.

This past winter a young friend and I were visiting a tobacco farmer in South Georgia. When the farmer congratulated my friend for ignoring the "propaganda" and lighting up a cigarette, the young man described in an anguished voice his knowledge of the consequences of his smoking, saying, "My wife and I realize that our little child can never be a long-distance runner, and she may have more serious health problems. She's already breathed too much of our smoke."

This has been a tragic element in my life, since both my parents and all my siblings have smoked and died of cancer. One of the great worries that Rosalynn and I share is that some of our children still smoke cigarettes. Despite their best efforts, including scientific and medical counseling, they have not broken free from this affliction.

Although my father was clearly the head of our family, as I noted earlier, I've come to realize how much strength he derived from my mother.

As a young farm boy, I remember my father, though confident in his own ability, being deeply concerned about the future of his crop. He would go out in the yard at night, and we would peek through the front door to see him walking up and down, looking at the sky. Everything he owned, everything he could borrow, was invested in the growing corn, cotton, and peanuts in our fields. If it didn't rain enough, we wouldn't make a very good crop yield, but even worse would be too much rain. Then the Bermuda grass and nut grass couldn't be controlled with hand hoes and mule-drawn plows, and the crop would be totally lost.

Daddy was filled with worry, but as a strong and proud man he didn't share it much with the family. He never said, "I'm really concerned about the rain," but when he came back in the house, my mother would often say, "Earl, everything's going to be all right." Her quiet words meant a lot to him.

My mother's example also showed me that we are never too old to learn. I lecture at a number of colleges and often meet students and others their age who think they know it all and who really have closed their hearts and minds to expansion. But every morning when my eighty-five-year-old mother got out of bed, she was probing for answers, eager to learn more about the people in the Plains community, the Brooklyn Dodgers and baseball strategy, American politics, what was going on in India, or how to make a better pecan crop.

In this constant probing for new information, she differed from my father. When I would come home from life on a navy submarine, my very busy father would ask me just a few questions. He always called me Hot. He'd say, "Hot, are you getting along all right?" I'd say, "Yes, sir." "You need anything?" I'd say, "No, sir." "You like the navy still?" "Yes, sir." And that would be about it.

By contrast, Daddy's brother Alton had my mother's curiosity. I'd go down to Plains Mercantile Co. and talk to my uncle, and he would stand behind his chest-high desk and ask me questions for two hours, perhaps interrupted by a customer or two. By the time we finished talking, he would know all about my submarine, how many people were on it, what kind of food we ate, where we got freshwater at sea, how often I bathed, the money I made every month, the difference between Soviet and American subs—things like that.

Since my father was the dominant force in our family, it was not until several years after his death that Mama began to expand her life beyond our small community. She first joined her older sister and served as housemother for a fraternity at Auburn University. Then she helped organize and operate a nursing home for the elderly in Blakely, Georgia.

One day while at home in Plains, she saw a television advertisement calling for Peace Corps volunteers, stating, "Age is no barrier." She put in an application, requesting only that she be assigned to "a place where people are dark-skinned and desperately in need." As a registered nurse, she was sent to Vikhroli, a small village near Bombay, India, to work in a nationwide program of family planning.

Mama had great difficulty using the Marathi language in her discussions with mostly illiterate people about family planning, including birth control techniques. Finally, she decided to memorize a few words at a time and record each phrase when it was comprehensible. Then she put these together and delivered her recorded message while she hid behind a screen and wiggled some puppets she had made. Although somewhat successful, this was not the best use of her nursing abilities, and the local doctor recruited her to work part-time in his clinic. With permission from the wealthy owners of the village, she was soon working with him full-time.

Mama felt so deeply about these Indian people that she gave them all the food that we would ship to her from home. She was paid a very few dollars each month by the Peace Corps, and she spent all of it on medicine for the clinic.

She lost thirty-five pounds while she was in Vikhroli and returned home in a wheelchair. It would seem that my mother gave up more than she got, that she made a real sacrifice in going to India. But I can tell you that it enriched and transformed her life. After Mama came back at the age of seventy, she made more than 500 speeches. She became famous because of her humor and total frankness, and she always used her own experiences to convince audiences that all of us can have new and greater lives, no matter how old we are, if we're willing to take a chance on something exciting and unpredictable. That, too, is part of the moral framework my parents gave me.

CHAPTER THREE

Finding Peace at Home

A s I've said, during the early years of our marriage, I was very reluctant to let Rosalynn know when I had an unresolved problem or was in trouble. I'm not proud to admit that, as far as education and knowledge of public affairs was concerned, I considered myself superior to her, and I supposed she shared this opinion. I didn't want her to know that I was vulnerable to doubt and failure, and both in the navy and when we started our business I did not share everything with her.

Even as late as 1962, when I ran for the Georgia state senate, I agonized over the decision by myself and told Rosalynn I was going to file the qualifying papers only when she asked why I was putting on Sunday pants on a workday. As time went on, however, I came to recognize her wisdom and sound judgment, and what a great relief it was to have both of us seeking answers or solutions. Now it is almost inconceivable to me that she was not intimately involved in every significant decision of my life, as she has been for the past thirty years.

In the fall of 1953, when I left the navy after my father's death, we came home to Plains with three boys, the oldest in the first grade. Rosalynn had her hands full. We lived in a tiny apartment in a public housing project. I struggled alone with our farm supply business, and the first year we had one of the worst droughts in history. None of the farmers could pay their bills. After investing all our savings and what I could borrow in an inventory of seed, fertilizer, and other supplies, we finished 1954 with a total income of less than $300 and a heavy debt. I had to buy more inventory, but my application for a $10,000 loan from the local bank was rejected, unless my mother or uncle would guarantee my note. I refused to ask them, and eventually I secured a small line of credit from the company whose fertilizer I was selling. The next year, 1955, was better, and we had a profit of almost $3,000.

As was the case for most people in Plains, our church became the center of our lives. Almost immediately, Rosalynn and I began teaching Sunday school, the junior girls and boys respectively, between nine and twelve years old. In addition, I was director of the Royal Ambassadors, a Baptist equivalent of the Boy Scouts, and I instructed the boys both in outdoor experiences and about Christian missions. The name of the group came from 2 Corinthians 5:20: "Now then we are ambassadors for Christ, as though God was making his appeal through us." I also formed a Boy Scout troop and was scoutmaster, and Rosalynn was den mother for the Cub Scouts.

The disharmony between me and Rosalynn over our return to Plains and abandonment of navy life slowly dissipated as we became involved in community affairs. But then another problem developed. My farm warehouse customers threatened us with a boycott because we were seen as too liberal on the issue of racial desegregation. Although I didn't know which of my immediate neighbors or farm customers were members of the Ku Klux Klan, almost all the white men in Plains belonged to the White Citizens' Council. This was a loose organization publicly sponsored by most of Georgia's political leaders, including the incumbent U.S. senators, the governor, and other officials of the state and local governments. They collected annual dues of five dollars, issued membership cards, and had one or two public meetings each year. No one except the top leaders ever knew what happened to the dues money.

The Council members always professed to be nonracist and peaceful in their purposes, but they were strongly against racial integration. It was understood that a line was being drawn among white citizens concerning the civil rights movement. The two Council leaders in Plains were the railroad depot agent and the town marshal, both of whom knew everyone and had time to sign up members, keep records of local dues collected, and deliver pamphlets and notices. When they first called on me in my warehouse office, I told them I was not inclined to join the Council. That night I discussed the issue with Rosalynn, and we agreed that we could not yield to the community pressure, even if the decision might severely reduce our already marginal income from the warehouse. When the marshal came back to see me, I informed him that I did not intend to be a member. He told me I was making a serious mistake and claimed that every other white man in town had signed up.

I did not hear anything more until, one day in the early summer of 1955, about twenty of my best customers came to see me. They were respected men whom I knew well, longtime friends of my father. The spokesman for the group, whose name was Paul, said they realized that I had been in the navy for a long time, away from the South, and had worked on ships where the crews were integrated. They were sure I was not completely familiar with some of the changes that had taken place in my absence.

He then quietly outlined the segregationist principles with which I was, of course, thoroughly familiar, including the supposed biblical foundation for the separation of races, potential damage to the quality of our schools if black and white students were together, and eventual destruction of the white race through the intermarriages that would inevitably occur. He reminded me about the prominent politicians who were leaders of the group and added that the Council members were equally concerned about the welfare of our black neighbors, among whom, he claimed, only a few radicals, mostly outsiders, wanted to make any change. He said that the Council was against any form of violence and that they were in no way connected with the Klan or other militant organizations.

He pointedly reminded me that all of them had traded with my father, had fond affection for our family, and knew that I was struggling with my new business after the previous disastrous year. They had decided among them to pay the annual dues for me, but they needed my signature on the membership form. There was no need for me to play an active role in the organization.

I believed then and believe now that most of the men had what they thought were my best interests at heart and were trying to protect me from criticism. It was a very difficult moment, and I knew that I was facing the prospect of losing a substantial portion of my trade in the surrounding community, but I decided to resolve the issue once and for all.

In a somewhat shaky voice, I told the group how much I appreciated their trying to be helpful and their loyalty in continuing to be my customers. I understood their arguments and concerns, some of which also troubled me. However, I had decided not to join the White Citizens' Council and could not change my mind. It was not the payment of dues that was a problem; even with their money I could not contribute to an organization in which I did not believe.

Paul voiced his regret at my response, and the group left without any expressions of anger. For several weeks, very few customers came to trade with me. Fortunately, this was at the beginning of a dormant period in our annual business cycle, shortly after the crops were "laid by" and about

two months before harvesttime. During this time, I
thought a lot about leaving Plains and getting a job with
some large company involved in the young but expanding
nuclear power industry. In fact, I had standing offers from
General Dynamics and General Electric, the two companies with which I had been working on the building of the
nuclear submarine *Sea Wolf*. I did not discuss this question
again with Rosalynn, though, because I really did not
intend to leave home.

One by one, I visited the men who had come to see me
and found them to be much less concerned individually
than they had seemed in the group that day. In fact, some
of them resented the pressure that had been put on them to
join the Council.

This was a serious crisis, but it brought Rosalynn and
me even closer together. She began to help me at the warehouse, keeping the books, sending out monthly bills, and,
after a year or two, settling up with a few of our customers for their entire year's trade. Our hard work and the
slowly improving racial attitudes in Georgia let us survive
financially.

The following year, I was chosen by the grand jury to
serve on the Sumter County School Board, in the position
formerly held by my father. This was a prestigious appointment, since the state constitution gives school boards
almost complete authority over the education system,
including all personnel decisions, the assignment of students, purchase of school buses and other equipment and
supplies, construction and maintenance of buildings, and

the right to levy adequate property taxes to finance the operation.

In Georgia, little official interference was permitted in these decisions, even from the governor's office. Following the Supreme Court's 1954 decision in *Brown v. Board of Education*, which struck down school segregation laws in all states, these local school boards were the focal points for decisions about racial integration. We five (white) men and our counterparts throughout the state had to face this issue, and, although it took more than a decade, each of the 200 local boards of education in Georgia eventually authorized school integration without violence. We avoided the public confrontations between governors and U.S. officials that occurred in Mississippi, Arkansas, and Alabama.

Unfortunately, the overall issue was not resolved easily. For the following fifteen years (and even until today), strong segregation sentiments remained. The influence of the White Citizens' Councils slowly faded in all the Southern states except Mississippi, but in our county the John Birch Society gained a stronghold. In our county seat, Americus, a majority of bankers, doctors, and lawyers were active members. The daily *Times-Recorder* always ran the John Birch column prominently on its editorial page. A number of private schools were organized by white parents who refused to permit their children to be educated with black students.

Strong social and economic pressures were exerted to prevent further integration. The churches, free from government authority, were most immune to change.

There was a widely published photograph of black people kneeling in prayer in front of an Americus church, confronted by a stern line of Methodist stewards with arms crossed, guarding the front door of God's house of worship.

As late as 1965, after I had been a Georgia state senator for three years, another boycott was organized against our family business. After our eldest son graduated from high school, the entire family took a three-week summer vacation to Mexico. We traveled without a specific itinerary, often staying in smaller cities, practicing our Spanish, and seeing the sights. When we returned home, I noticed that very few people came to my office as they usually did to buy feed, settle small accounts, or just visit for a while.

After a few days, one of our relatives told me that he had been visited by some prominent John Birchers who informed him where we had supposedly spent the last several weeks. I soon discovered that they had gone to the county courthouse, examined the public agricultural records, obtained a list of everyone who had ever sold peanuts to us, and then visited them all to urge that they no longer deal with our warehouse. Their story was that we had visited a communist training camp in northern Alabama for a month, learning how to expedite racial integration in the South. These were some of the most successful leaders in our county, including the president of a large insurance agency and the man who had served in the state legislature for eight years, filling the seat my father had held.

I immediately confronted these two men, who had concocted the story. Both of them claimed they had irrefutable evidence that their information was correct. It was only after I returned with hotel receipts and other records from places in Mexico that they grudgingly admitted I had not been trained by communists. Then, as had been the case ten years earlier, I had to visit my customers one at a time in order to defuse the crisis.

Most of our friends who were racial moderates, including the president of our college, the owner of the only local radio station, and the county attorney, were forced to leave the community. We survived the boycott and other pressures because of several advantages. Although it was not often mentioned, there was a clear social advantage in belonging to one of the old, pioneer families. Buried in family cemeteries near Plains are Rosalynn's and my ancestors who were born in the eighteenth century. Their many descendants were devoted members of the Baptist, Methodist, and Lutheran churches, and my father and his brother had been quite active in community affairs. My uncle was mayor of Plains for twenty-eight years. Perhaps equally important in our determination to stay was that our family ties were too strong to break. Ancestral lands and five generations of neighboring kinfolks were much more difficult to relinquish than a law practice, a radio station, or even the top position at the local college.

In a way, our approach to the race issue was also excused because of my mother's acknowledged "eccentricity" and because we were known to have spent a number of years in the navy. Furthermore, by the time of the boycott, Rosalynn and I were personally rooted in Plains. I was deeply immersed in our new career, and I had no doubt that I had made the right decision on leaving the U.S. Navy. Our church life provided a foundation for almost everything we did. I had been elected a deacon and was teaching the Sunday school class that my father had taught. Increasingly, our leaving home was inconceivable.

I was really enjoying the opportunities for me to use all of my abilities in our growing warehouse business, in producing on our farm some of the finest seed peanuts in Georgia, in helping to preserve the public school system in the early throes of racial integration, and in serving as Boy Scout master, on the local library board, and on the hospital authority. I was making a rapid climb up the hierarchy of Lions International to district governor, responsible for fifty-four Southwest Georgia clubs. I helped to pull seven counties into a regional group to share our opportunities for development, and I was one of the organizers and the first president of the Georgia Planning Commission. It makes me tired now to look back on it all, but then it was giving me a full and gratifying life.

Plains was and is a wonderful place to live. As in all Southern communities, its white people were faced with a quandary during the civil rights days, but they struggled through the ordeal and ultimately made the right decision. The "professional" segregationist leaders who influenced both the legal system and most of the religious congregations eventually faded into the background. With each passing year during the 1950s and 1960s, more and more citizens in our town came to understand that "separate but equal" was compatible with neither the U.S. Constitution nor the teachings of Jesus Christ.

However, divisions on the race issue remained throughout this time, and it was natural for Rosalynn and me to seek companions who shared our basic views. Through silent agreement, we broke off relations with a few farm couples with whom we had earlier spent a lot of time. Two of them were relatives of ours, and there was an obvious coolness when we attended the same family reunions. As late as 1977, while I was living in Washington, our congregation split, roughly along Baptist political lines, with about twenty-five of the more "moderate" members leaving to form a new church. It has now grown to about fifty families, and our more conservative "mother" church is also thriving.

In some things, we just have to be patient. The Bible says, "For you have need of patience, that, after you have done the will of God, you might receive the promise" (Hebrews 10:36). As Paul told the Romans, "Be devoted to one another in brotherly love. Honor one another above yourselves. Be joyful in hope, patient in affliction, faithful in prayer" (Romans 12:10, 12). Now, after two more decades, most of the divisions have healed. We shake hands and talk to everyone at the reunions, and the Plains churches share fifth Sunday night services and visit each other during our respective revival weeks and on other special occasions.

* * *

During these years, Rosalynn and I formed close friendships with a few other couples, mostly farmers, and began
a fairly intense social life, almost exclusively on Saturday
nights. For most of the year, all of us worked from dawn
to dusk, six days a week, and we enjoyed the small private
parties that became an integral part of our lives. Sometimes
we would come home long after midnight, take a short nap,
study and teach our Sunday school lessons, and then sleep
during the afternoon, getting ready for another week of
work. On occasion, we had bitter arguments, based on jealousy or mutual criticism of behavior at parties. By this
time, we had been married for ten years.

Throughout our marriage, despite different interests,
the imperfection of both partners, mistakes made, even
irresolvable differences of opinion, love has prevailed.
There have been a number of times when we were angry at
each other and I had to teach a Bible lesson with Rosalynn
in the class. It is hardly possible for a quarrel to survive
when I am teaching a Scripture such as "Love suffers long,
and is kind; love envies not; love vaunts not itself, is
not puffed up, does not behave itself unseemly, seeks not
her own, is not easily provoked, thinks no evil; rejoices
not in iniquity, but rejoices in the truth; bears all things,
believes all things, hopes all things, endures all things"
(1 Corinthians 13:4–7).

We have not been immune from the problems that
threaten most couples. There is no doubt that some of
these family conflicts would have been serious enough to
threaten our marriage were it not for the sustaining religious faith that we have shared. We have never been to

counselors or psychiatrists, or even discussed our differences with a close friend or our pastor. But for both me and Rosalynn there have been religious and spiritual criteria by which we could assess our own actions and honor our marriage vows. Also, there has always been a third party, Jesus Christ, with whom we could share our most troubling crises through prayer—often individually, sometimes together.

In 1987, Rosalynn and I wrote a book as coauthors called *Everything to Gain*. It dealt with the traumatic events of my presidential reelection loss in 1980, finding ourselves in debt, and returning after ten years to an empty house with our last child, Amy, soon to leave home. We attempted to describe our experiences and offer advice to others who face similar difficult passages in their lives.

Writing this book was one of the most severe threats to the harmony of our forty-one-year marriage. It was fairly easy for Rosalynn and me to agree on 97 percent of the text, but we found the other 3 percent impossible. In our struggles to describe precisely what had happened and how we had reacted to each event, we simply could not concur on language. The adjectives and adverbs were particularly difficult. It soon became impossible for us to communicate directly, so we exchanged increasingly unpleasant comments through our word processors.

In addition, we had different writing methods. I write quite rapidly, while Rosalynn labors over each paragraph. She always considered my writing as a rough draft, while I accused her of acting as though every portion of her text had been delivered on stone tablets from Mount Sinai.

It was only the last-minute refereeing of our editor that saved the book, and, as we said only somewhat jokingly, perhaps our marriage. We finally accepted his suggestion that we divide up the paragraphs on which we could not agree, with mine marked with a "J" and hers with an "R."

We breathed a sigh of relief when our book was published shortly before Christmas, and we began to pull our lives back together. However, we soon found other sources of irritation. One that was particularly troubling was that during each of the increasingly cold winter nights we argued about the temperature of our electric blanket. Whenever I said it was too warm, Rosalynn said it was too cold, and vice versa.

One morning I returned from an overnight trip to New York, and she met me at the front door with a warm hug and a smile. "I think our marriage is saved," she said. "I just discovered that our dual blanket controls have been on the wrong sides of the bed, and each of us was changing the temperature on the other's side."

Over the years, Rosalynn and I have tried a lot of new things together, each of us expanding our interests to include those of the other. We have taken up downhill skiing (when I was sixty-two years old), tennis, mountain climbing, fly-fishing, biking, and Spanish as a second language. We have now had a lot of experience in resolving family disputes, and the proven lack of fragility in our long-term relationship helps us to address even the most unpleasant and difficult subjects with frankness (although sometimes with a high degree of anger). We've certainly never been bored, and on occasion we have found innovative ways to resolve problems.

One of my best gifts to Rosalynn was to resolve a recurring argument. I was very busy at the time, putting the final touches on a book. I went into my study early one morning, turned on my computer, and hit a button that automatically put the date on the screen. There it was: August 18, her birthday, and I hadn't gotten her a present! Rosalynn was still in bed. So I started wondering what I could give her that I didn't have to go down to my cousin Hugh's antiques store to buy. In desperation, I tried to analyze the things that caused trouble in our marriage—in addition to my forgetting anniversaries and birthdays.

One of the things that had created a problem for us for thirty-five years or more was punctuality. I was affected by my training in the navy and, I think, inherited the trait from my father. Whether to meet a train, to attend a baseball game, or to keep an appointment, he was always there long ahead of time. If someone kept him waiting, he had no patience. He would stalk out of a doctor's office if his appointment was delayed for more than ten minutes. Unfortunately, I, too, am uncomfortable if someone keeps me waiting, and if I'm late and inconvenience someone else, I get even more uptight. To the surprise of my campaign workers and some audiences, I even kept to a strict schedule during my political campaigns, in the governor's office, and in the White House.

And so Rosalynn and I had a lot of arguments about being on time. She always claimed that she was never late, and this would be true if judged by the standards of a reasonable person. What should two or three minutes matter between a husband and wife preparing to go to a movie or a party? But I was not reasonable, holding Rosalynn to a standard of absolute precision. Even before our appointed time for departure, I would remind her of the need to leave and would often produce at least a dirty look if I had to wait at the door.

So, reflecting on all this on that morning of her birthday, I wrote a note to her: "Rosalynn, I promise you that for the rest of our marriage, I will never make an unfavorable remark about tardiness." I signed it and gave it to her for a present. So far I've pretty well kept my promise, and she still agrees that it was the best birthday present I ever gave her.

When a man and woman first meet and there seems to be the potential for a bond between them, they explore each other in a cautious, perhaps uncertain way. Maybe the relationship develops into intimacy, families become involved, and a marriage proposal is accepted and consummated. This sounds like a happy ending to a delightful story, but it's just the introduction to a marriage.

What makes a marriage? Is a personal union built or strengthened mainly by dramatic events? I would say no. It's the year-by-year, dozen-times-a-day demonstration of the little things that can destroy a marriage or make it successful. The ability to communicate is most important. In almost every marriage, times arise when the husband and wife look on the same event with different perspectives. If they can talk about their views with honesty and mutual respect—a big if—many problems can be avoided.

We have to be willing to forgive, because mistakes are going to be made. There is going to be anger and even, at times, deliberately hurtful words, so understanding and flexibility are required. And it is crucial during times of crisis to maintain an overriding sense of permanence. For Rosalynn and me, the marriage vows have been a powerful stabilizing force. Largely because we consider these pledges inviolable, we have survived our differences now for fifty years.

Rosalynn and I share a page or a chapter in the Bible each night. In addition to what we learn about religion and life, there is an element of self-discipline about this ritual that is beneficial. It also brings us closer together, helping to reconcile a lot of small arguments that would otherwise have carried over until the next day. We alternate reading aloud, most often from a modern Spanish version, with the English text alongside. This gives us the additional benefit of practicing our second language; on occasion I have been able to deliver a fairly comprehensible Sunday morning message from the pulpit in a Latin American country. Even when we are not together, we continue our reading, and we enjoy knowing that we are reading the same Scripture passage.

If we outline the basic elements of a marriage, we see that the same things apply in our relationship with Christ: love, forgiveness, loyalty, flexibility, the admission of mistakes; looking inward; the ability to ask, What is there about my own life that is not acceptable to Christ, and am I willing to change, to repent?

Christians have, in effect, gone through a marriage pledge with Jesus, and it is a form of adultery to violate this pledge by putting anything above the relationship with him. I was reminded of my military and political oaths when I put on my navy uniform or walked by the Rose Garden to the Oval Office each morning. And of course being with Rosalynn is a constant reminder of my pledge and obligations to her. I want to continue developing the same awareness of my commitment to Christ.

Of course, being faithful to God is a way to strengthen ties within my family, in military service, and in political office. It is good for me to remember that I took my oaths "before God" to fulfill all those obligations to the best of my ability.

The way Rosalynn and I have dealt with our children has not been so naturally self-corrective. One of the most difficult challenges for me has been the questioning of my dominant role and the realization of as much equality as possible among all members of the family. My father instilled in me a respect for strict discipline, and, either genetically or through my home environment, I inherited his approach to the raising of children.

I never really questioned this approach to parenthood until our oldest son, Jack, became an adult. One day, while he and I walked through our fields hunting quail, he began to describe to me his deep resentment of the way I had treated him as a growing boy. I was shocked and immediately became defensive. We stopped walking and exchanged heated words about some specific events that he recalled tearfully but that I hardly remembered. I could tell that this was a subject he had discussed with his wife and that his decision to confront me had been very difficult. But I couldn't acknowledge that I had been mistaken in my basic approach all those years—or that my own father had also been overly domineering.

We returned home, unreconciled and extremely uncomfortable. I immediately told Rosalynn what had happened, emphasizing Jack's lack of appreciation for all we had done for him. But together we soon came to realize the legitimacy of much of what Jack had said. When I brought myself to analyze the bonds that existed between my father, me, and my three sons more honestly, I still found it impossible to express them except through a poem.

I Wanted to Share My Father's World

This is a pain I mostly hide,
but ties of blood, or seed, endure,
and even now I feel inside
the hunger for his outstretched hand,
a man's embrace to take me in,
the need for just a word of praise.

I despised the discipline
he used to shape what I should be,
not owning up that he might feel

his own pain when he punished me.
I didn't show my need to him,
since his response to an appeal
would not have meant as much to me,
or been as real.

From those rare times when we did cross
the bridge between us, the pure joy
survives.

                I never put aside
the past resentments of the boy
until, with my own sons, I shared
his final hours, and came to see
what he'd become, or always was—
the father who will never cease to be
alive in me.

I was a lot like my father, probably even as a child, and did not find it easy to demonstrate my feelings toward him. As an adult and a father myself, I finally realized that I had a similar relationship with my own sons. Since Jack and his family lived near Chicago, we didn't see them very often after our confrontation in the field, and it was only over a period of several months that we exchanged some brutally frank letters, made some visits, and took a few initiatives toward reconciliation, including my acknowledgment that my level of discipline in raising our boys may have been too high.

In retrospect, I can see that instinctively emulating this autocratic father-son relationship a generation later was a mistake. Times had changed, and growing boys expected and needed more freedom in an age of television and automobiles of their own.

It is not easy for us to give freedom to those we love. Most of us want to be able to rely on an intimate relationship, and we fear that liberation of a spouse or child will destroy our closeness and interdependence. This may mean that ours is a self-centered love, perhaps even relying on psychological domination to hold others close.

As my father dominated my mother, I had the same relationship with Rosalynn in our early years, but during the last forty or more years, we have evolved what is an almost purely equal partnership. This change has come about not from any decision of mine but as a result of Rosalynn's natural strength and ability. In my marriage and in that of my parents, I can see quite clearly the advantages of personal freedom and an absence of subordination of one person by another.

Sometimes the guidance of religious principles is even more valuable within the intimacy of a family than outside. With a spouse, especially one with a strong will, there is a mandatory give-and-take that tends to force frank assessments—and adjustments. Particularly since leaving the political world, where we all faced common challenges together, our family has learned to resolve difficult interpersonal issues by communicating. We have sometimes resorted to frank and disturbing letters, but on most occasions we find some way to approach difficult issues face to face. On a few occasions when it was not possible for me to relate directly to our sons, our daughters-in-law and Rosalynn have been able to resolve potential problems.

When possible during the year, Rosalynn and I try to take a few of our family members with us on interesting trips involving our work, and during each Christmas–New Year's season, we have a family vacation together—all eighteen of us! One or two telephone calls a week also help. Our sons have good and solid families, we have mutual trust and love among us, and so far this has worked.

However, everything is not perfect. Even though we always have a blessing together at mealtimes and take our grandchildren to church when they are visiting us, I can't say that we have been an effective influence on our children with respect to their religious lives. They acknowledge their Christian faith but are not regular members of a church.

Although we feel responsible, we realize that our children must have freedom to run their own lives. Since college, they haven't lived near us or in a close-knit community like ours, where everyone is expected to be active in a church. Also, they dislike the constant squabbling about doctrine and church politics among many Baptists and disagree strongly with some of the more fundamentalist positions of famous preachers. It may be that we were too demanding concerning church attendance when they were children, their suburban lives may have too many other enticements on Sundays, or our personal examples may not have been attractive. We realize that Rosalynn and I had the same slack habits about worship while I was in the navy, and it was only when we came back to Plains that we found church life attractive and gratifying.

All of us feel alone when we disagree with others or face the death of someone we love. I have felt the distress of losing all the members of my childhood family, and have seen two of my sons suffer through the emotional torment of divorce. In such times, the thing that has never changed as a sustaining force has been our religious faith, within which we have been able to find guidance on how best to face a crisis.

With increasing maturity, I have seen more clearly that I must adapt to differences among people, learn to accept the imperfect, understand the fallibilities of ourselves and others, and have mercy—in other words, forgive. Forgiveness is not easy, but it is a goal to be sought, a process that should continue throughout our lives.

More and more, I've come to realize that forgiveness is a basic foundation of my faith. Without the knowledge that I can be forgiven, it would not be possible to face my own shortcomings frankly. Without forgiveness, I could not confess to a God whose standards embody perfection, or learn how to forgive others or myself.

How can I believe God's promises of complete forgiveness? By remembering the teachings of Jesus, and by looking at the lives of biblical characters whose transgressions involved the most terrible of crimes, both against God and against human law.

King David was a poet, a musician, a courageous warrior, and a fine political leader, greatly blessed. But he was
also a terrible sinner who did almost everything we can
think of to violate the Ten Commandments. Yet he was
completely reconciled with God. How was that possible?
Through his confession and his turning to God for understanding and repentance: "And David said to the prophet
Nathan, 'I have sinned against the Lord.' And Nathan said
to David, 'The Lord has put away your sin; you shall not
die' " (2 Samuel 12:13).

In the Thirty-second Psalm, David writes, "Happy
are those to whom the Lord imputes no iniquity and in
whose spirit there is no deceit." David is giving us the
lesson he learned in going through the extremes of life,
from doubt to faith, from sin to forgiveness, and from guilt
to joy.

The most convincing proof of Jesus' forgiveness
involved Peter, perhaps the most intriguing disciple, whose
life with Christ went through wild swings from approba-
tion to condemnation.

When Jesus asked his disciples who they thought he
was, "Simon Peter said, 'You are the Christ, the Son of the
living God' " (Matthew 16:16). Just a few minutes later,
Peter rejected the idea that his master would have to suffer
death on the cross. Jesus turned to him and said, "Get
behind me, Satan! You are a stumbling block to me "
(Matt. 16:23).

Despite his weakness, his equivocation, and, later, his
cowardly betrayal of Christ, Peter was never finally

rejected but repeatedly forgiven and reconciled with Jesus. As Jesus prophesied, "You are Peter, the rock on which I will build my church" (Matthew 16:18).

God offers us a mixture of gentleness and discipline, not unlike that of a caring parent. Jesus said, "I did not come to judge the world, but to save the world" (John 12:47).

If we commit a crime or make a serious mistake, we are naturally reluctant to confess, fearing punishment or the condemnation of others. For a Christian, assured of God's mercy, this reluctance need not exist. However, the Bible says that confession and repentance are necessary before we can receive this total forgiveness.

Every now and then, one of my Sunday school lessons is about forgiveness, and it is a difficult subject for me to teach. Almost invariably, a feeling of hypocrisy gnaws at me as I remember people against whom I still hold a grudge. Most of my lingering resentments relate to our time in Washington. In some cases, I have said, "I can't forgive that jerk!" But when I forced myself to consider the original altercations more thoroughly, they usually came to seem somewhat silly—some I couldn't even remember.

Is lasting resentment *ever* justified? Not according to the standards set for us by Christ, who said, "Judge not, that you be not judged" (Matthew 7:1) and "But if you do not forgive others, then your Father will not forgive your transgressions" (Matt. 6:15). In the Lord's Prayer, God's forgiveness of us is conditional: "And forgive us our trespasses, as [or provided] we forgive those who trespass against us" (Matt. 6:12). Peter once asked Jesus, "Lord, how often shall my brother sin against me and I forgive him? Up to seven times?" Jesus responded, "No, seventy times seven" (Matt. 18:21–22).

Teaching these lessons has induced me to correct some of my mistakes. On a few occasions, I have written letters to the people involved, saying that I hoped we could be reconciled. Most of the time this has worked, and I've shared some of the responses with my classes.

There's another step, though, beyond my forgiving another person and being forgiven by God, and that is forgiveness of myself. If God can forgive us, why can't we forgive ourselves? A lot of us feel that this promise of total reconciliation is too good to be true.

Even aside from religion, to be forgiven is extremely important. Nowadays, many people are, in effect, willing to pay to have their feelings of guilt explained or forgiven. A psychiatrist will try to help us comprehend the reasons for even our grossest behavior, often because of something our parents did or failed to do when we were little children. Early mistreatment is sometimes even considered in our legal system to be an excuse for crimes, including murder. We may or may not be able to shift blame to our parents, but at least we can ease our pain or suffering by forgiving ourselves.

If we live with a permanent feeling of guilt, we are spiritually and emotionally crippled. The extreme case is someone who becomes depressed and commits suicide— an almost incomprehensible tragedy. A few years ago, my best friend in Atlanta took his own life, and just as I have been writing this, a distinguished navy leader took the same action, apparently because he wore on his chest some small symbols of personal valor in combat that he did not deserve.

We really need someone who can be judgmental but forgiving, able to accept our warts, our defects. Rosalynn, for instance, doesn't hesitate to provide me with suggestions to do better: "You didn't take enough questions in Sunday school" or "I believe you were too harsh with our son" or "You forgot to thank so-and-so for what she did for us." I cherish having a relationship with Rosalynn that is based on faith and mutual trust and is so intimate that I can reveal myself to her.

I would go a step further and say that if we are not willing to share ourselves with others enough to get beneficial suggestions from them, then we have lost a wonderful way to have better, more exciting, and more fruitful lives. It's through this exchange of criticism, based on mutual understanding and forgiveness, that we are able to grow.

Even among people who are closest, there is a need for repetitive forgiveness. Rosalynn and I are both strong willed and frequently have disagreements, some of them lasting for several days. It is difficult for either of us to admit being at fault. Recently, after a particularly disturbing argument, I decided that we should never let another day end with us angry with each other. I went to my wood shop and cut out a thin sheet of walnut, a little smaller than a bank check. I then carved on it:

*Each evening, forever, this is good for an apology—or forgiveness—
as you desire. Jimmy.*

So far, I have been able to honor it each time Rosalynn
has presented it to me. And she has!

CHAPTER FOUR

Leadership and Faith

I served in the U.S. Navy for eleven years, between the ages of eighteen and twenty-nine. These years had a profound influence on me and on the course of my life. In particular, during this time I thought frequently and learned much about the art and discipline of leadership as I rose through the ranks from a sailor obeying the commands of others to a position of authority, responsible for the safety and military effectiveness of many other men.

In the years since then, I have often compared my life as a Christian, as a naval officer, and as a political leader. I find my navy duty and my religious faith to be most closely related. Although I may be idealizing the navy example, I can see a relationship between my service on my first submarine, the USS *Pomfret*, for instance, and my idea of proper service as a Christian. Among the crew of this ship, because of the leadership of the captain, there was eagerness to measure up to strong and firm standards, repentance for mistakes, but confidence in forgiveness—qualities for which people of faith should also strive.

Later, of course, as president and commander in chief, I bore the ultimate military authority in our nation. (Although, as President Harry Truman said, one of the biggest surprises to him was that often when he gave an order from the Oval Office to the government bureaucracy, nothing happened. This is a significant difference between military and civilian authority!) In the White House, I tried to apply the lessons I'd learned about leadership from my varied experiences during the navy years.

As a young midshipman, I was instructed meticulously in a demanding code of conduct. According to my aging copy of *The Bluejackets' Manual*, in the performance of our duties we were "expected to exhibit obedience, knowledge, fighting spirit, reliability, loyalty, initiative, self-control, energy, courage, justice, faith in ourselves, honor, and cheerfulness." But the overarching criterion was truth—absolute truth, which was described as "the *final* test of a man." Any form of lying or dishonesty was justification for immediate dismissal from the Naval Academy. During every one of my eleven years in the U.S. Navy, I knew that my superior officers were judging my compliance with these standards.

Although the navy's image has been tarnished by recent

scandals, such as the Tailhook incident, basic military standards have not changed. One of the advantages of living in our democratic society is that such problems are most often revealed and then corrected. As a young officer, I saw the first break in widespread racial segregation occur at the Naval Academy and on ships; now, perhaps, reports of sexual abuse among naval aviators will help to expose and correct another problem that is much more pervasive in America than was previously acknowledged.

I looked upon the navy rules and regulations as a framework for my performance as an officer, one tried and tested for hundreds of years as the best means to ensure effective roles for my ship and crew. However, there were two limitations on the application of these regulations in my life. One was that they did not extend to my role as a Christian husband and father. The second was that the navy code was sometimes misinterpreted or distorted by the administration and enforcement of my commanding officers.

I had many opportunities to take on additional responsibilities that would contribute to the overall quality of my service. At first, I was an extremely eager officer, taking on as many volunteer duties as I could, including extra study about naval strategy, navigation, astronomy, seamanship, and the more intricate details of the ship's electronic system.

However, my continued zeal in performing these voluntary chores was determined by the satisfaction I derived from them and my respect for those who observed my performance. As we strive to go beyond the "letter of the law" and live up to higher standards of conduct and behavior, the quality of the leadership, guidance, and inspiration we receive becomes especially important.

As a naval officer, I served on four ships and under six captains. The good ships were governed with strict but fair discipline. However, my second captain was a martinet, who exercised his authority in an arbitrary and vindictive way. When the ship approached a port, we never knew whether or when we would be permitted to go ashore to see our families. If some member of the large crew had displeased the captain, there might be several hours of unexplained delay before anyone except the top officers could leave the ship. Morale was extremely low, and there was a smoldering resentment against the captain.

I was on this ship when the 1948 presidential primary election was approaching, and I was interested in politics, studying the news about the Democratic candidates who were challenging the incumbent, Harry Truman, whom I admired. We junior officers had some friendly but heated discussions about the campaign in the wardroom. One day, I was told to report to the captain immediately. When I found him, he was making an inspection of the ship. He didn't speak to me but motioned for me to follow his entourage. I did so for more than an hour, and finally we approached his living quarters. He paused outside his door, called me forward, thrust his flashlight forcefully into my chest, and said, "Either choose the navy or politics." Then he turned and left me standing there.

So far as I remember, these were the only words this

commanding officer ever spoke to me, and this insulting treatment—failing to explain the problem and prodding me physically and with obvious displeasure in front of several other people—I considered to be inexcusable. Less embarrassing but equally important was his condemnation and apparent prohibition of discussing the presidential election.

Life under this commander quickly eroded my sense of commitment to naval service. I soon came to believe that I had made a dreadful mistake in choosing a military career and resolved to resign as soon as my legal obligations were fulfilled. I hung a sign on the bulkhead of my tiny cabin that said, SO WHAT? For me, there were no remaining incentives—not the hope for future rewards, the threat of a negative fitness report, or the approval of the captain—for performance beyond my required duties.

However, before the end of the year, my application for service in submarines was accepted. This was elite duty. Standards of performance were high, and there was a degree of intimacy among the officers and crew members that I had not known before.

On one submarine, I had a captain who created a problem of a different kind. He was always friendly and forgiving, but he seemed more at ease dealing with all his subordinates as equals than with exercising real authority as our commander. This was nice at first, but we soon realized that his apparent benevolence came from a lack of interest in or knowledge about details. He treated all of us as he would wish to be treated by a forgiving superior who knew he didn't perform his duties well. As a result, a general lackadaisical attitude evolved, to the extent that we were not confident of the safety of the submarine, where our lives depended on the proper performance of all members of the crew. Eventually, some of us junior officers discussed the problem with the executive officer, who was second in command. In effect, for the remainder of this captain's tour onboard, he was quietly bypassed in the exercise of discipline.

I had two other fine officers as submarine commanders, but the best captain under whom I ever served was J. B. Williams, Jr., a natural leader. It was he who inspired me as an officer. He was bold and aggressive, pushing our relatively old submarine, the USS *Pomfret*, to its limit with quick dives, fast and deep runs, and steep eruptions to the surface. During war games with Canadian and British destroyers off the shore of China, he would have us emerge from the depths in the midst of their ship formations, taunting them with the realization that we had approached without being detected. He was also a kind and gentle man, and the junior officers and lowliest enlisted men felt a sense of his friendship and knew the captain was protective of their interests. He was strict and clear in his demands on the crew but always ready to forgive mistakes when we made them. Our punishment for errors lay in our remorse for having let him down.

As I've mentioned before, my final commanding officer in the navy was Adm. Hyman Rickover, the father of nuclear power. Rickover was intensely demanding of everyone who worked for him. Anything short of perfection brought severe castigation, but there was never any comment when he could find no fault with our work.

No matter how he drove us, though, we all realized that he demanded even more of himself. During the early 1950s, I would sometimes fly with him from the East Coast to visit nuclear reactors in Arco, Idaho, or the Hanford plant near Richland, Washington, where nuclear fuel was refined. Determined to make a good impression, I would resolve to work all the way, a trip that in prejet days required about ten hours. But despite my best efforts, I would have to take a nap or at least rest my eyes, something that Rickover never did.

I admired and respected him without reservation, and believe him to have been the finest engineer who has ever lived. If moored end to end, the nuclear-powered ships built under his close supervision would have stretched for ten miles. Despite being highly innovative in design, none of them ever experienced damage or loss of life because of a failure or defect in the nuclear power systems, for whose design, construction, and operation Admiral Rickover was responsible.

It should be obvious that my service on the *Pomfret* was what I consider to be ideal. In my own career, I have tried to conform my role as a leader to the standards of Captain Williams. It causes me concern that some of those who have worked for me see a closer likeness to Admiral Rickover. I recently overheard one of my associates remark, "When we make a decision to do something, we begin looking for a calendar. Jimmy looks at his watch." I can't deny that I am a demanding superior; my only

explanation—not excuse—is that I try to equal the effort of
those who work with me.

Whether within a church, among a crew of workers
building a house, in a family, or in a nation, I have noticed
that isolation comes with increasing power or prestige.
This can breed arrogance, as truth and sharing suffer when
others are not willing to speak up to us or to correct our
errors. This is true in military organizations and in governments, including democracies like ours, except that in a
free society even the top officials can expect criticism, both
constructive and otherwise, from political adversaries and
the news media. Appreciated or not, this provides a very
beneficial self-corrective influence.

These restraints are not available within a dictatorship,
where the leaders are surrounded by sycophants and never
hear frank criticism or receive strong advice. The all-
powerful shah of Iran was facing vocal but relatively
peaceful opposition to some of his policies in 1977, when
he came to visit me in Washington. He scoffed at my warn-
ings about the excessively brutal reaction of his secret
police, SAVAK, to some demonstrations in the city streets.
The next year, after a full-fledged revolution erupted, one
of his closest advisers came to the Oval Office to tell me
that for several years the shah had completely isolated himself from anyone who might question his decisions. He
would not even permit Iran's top commanders of the army,
navy, and air force to consult with one another. The consequences are well known: Despite strong support from the

United States and other allies, in January 1979 the shah was forced to leave his country and live in exile until his death.

There are special scriptural admonitions concerning those who hold high public office, and I was reminded of them throughout my terms as governor and president. I remembered Paul's urging Timothy to pray for "kings, and for all that are in authority, that we may lead a quiet and peaceable life in all godliness and honesty" (1 Timothy 2:2). I realized that any moral responsibilities I had as a Christian were greatly magnified when millions of people could be affected by my actions and my example.

I enjoyed being president, but during that time I felt a special burden. The questions that had to be answered in the Oval Office were the most difficult ones our nation faced, those that could not be resolved in the offices of mayors or governors or in corporate boardrooms. Knowing how many lives could be affected by my decisions, I felt a special need for wisdom and a sense of God's presence. Although I had a lot of advice from all sides, it was a lonely job during times of crisis or when the issues were especially controversial.

I prayed more during those four years than at any other time in my life, just asking for God's guidance in making the right decisions on behalf of the American people. There was a small private office a few steps from the Oval Office where I kept my personal books, papers, photographs, and mementos. I would go back to this place for my most serious prayers. Also, I started each day by reciting one or two brief thoughts while walking past the Rose Garden on the way from our living quarters in the White House to my office. One of them was a verse from the Nineteenth Psalm: "Let the words of my mouth and the meditation of my heart be acceptable in Thy sight, O Lord, my strength and my redeemer." The effort to maintain a partnership with God was reassuring to me and, at the same time, a humbling experience, helping me in my effort to resist the temptations of isolation and arrogance that all leaders face.

Some of the loneliest and most difficult decisions in government involve the use of military force. The president, as commander in chief, can cause or prevent the massive loss of human life.

Nowadays, one of the most hotly debated historical questions is whether President Truman made the right decision in ordering the atomic bomb to be dropped on Hiroshima. I vividly remember sitting on the steel deck of an old battleship in the North Atlantic on August 5, 1945, assembled with all the crew to hear an important announcement from our commander in chief. The ship's loudspeaker system and the intervening wireless transmission made the president's flat Missouri voice seem even more surreal. The message itself was just as otherworldly. Truman had authorized the use of "an atomic bomb," a weapon of indescribable power, against Japan.

All of us knew about the enormous casualties it had cost

the United States to take Okinawa from the sea. American troops had fought their way from landing ships to shore, and then foot by foot forward, from trench to trench and cave to cave, against ferocious opposition from the Japanese defenders. There were almost 50,000 U.S. casualties, with 12,000 dead. Ten times as many Japanese were killed, along with a third of the island's civilian population. Everyone in the military forces made mental projections about losses to be expected in an attempt to conquer the Japanese homeland. We heard estimates of up to a million American casualties, plus many more Japanese. Therefore, we were relieved and elated at the prospect of an early end of the war through a Japanese surrender. We all agreed that President Truman had made the right decision.

Now, more than fifty years later, that decision is still the subject of painful reappraisals. The horrors of a nuclear attack are being compared with what might have happened during weeks of massive bombing with conventional force, followed by the mainland invasion. In 1984, I was the first senior American statesman to visit Hiroshima, and I was deeply moved by the remaining evidence of destruction, and the estimates of 66,000 deaths from the attack. Clearly this was a devastating military blow with horrific human consequences.

Still, I believe that Truman's decision to use the bomb was correct. Remember, we were in a declared war, defending democracy, our nation, and our citizens. In wartime, a commander in chief cannot make protecting the enemy his preeminent concern; the lives of his own troops and citizens are more important. This is the nature of warfare.

Truman's decision has to be kept in perspective, not only about casualties that might have been avoided but about those experienced with the use of conventional weapons. In British raids on Hamburg, Germany, in July 1943, 50,000 civilians were killed; about 7 million perished in the German attacks on Stalingrad; and the total casualties of World War II were 55 million, 30 million of them civilians.

Although most Japanese strongly disagree, it seems to me that this difficult decision had two overriding benefits. Much greater invasion casualties were avoided, and the terrible evidence of atomic power has proved to be a major deterrent to its subsequent use. Thus, in the context of the vast, almost unimaginable evil of a world war, the lesser evil of using the first atomic weapon may have benefited humanity in the long run—though at an awful price.

Unlike some people of faith, I don't believe that pacifism is a necessary element of Christianity. This is a choice I made when I joined the navy. I knew there would be times, during war, when I might have to take human life in defense of my country. I accepted that. Had my Christianity been of the type that the Quakers and some others espouse, I would have been a conscientious objector rather than serve in the military. (I might also never have accepted political office, since this could have required me, as president, to send soldiers to their deaths.) But pacifism was not my choice.

Sacrificing lives in defense of our nation is sometimes necessary, and as a submarine office and then as commander in chief during the Cold War years, I was prepared to use the weapons at our disposal to destroy a Soviet submarine or respond to a nuclear missile or any other military attack that threatened our nation. This decision applied to a direct nuclear response against Soviet targets, most of which had been carefully designated since the administration of Dwight Eisenhower.

Even before my inauguration as president, I was thoroughly briefed about our military forces, and I consulted then and throughout my term with wise and knowledgeable people who shared my cautious approach to the use of our military power. My primary commitment was to protect America's interests while living peacefully with the Soviet Union. If peacekeeping efforts failed, as happened before World Wars I and II, I was prepared to use force if necessary. In addition, the mutual know-ledge of our mighty response capability was the greatest possible deterrence to an enemy attack and the destructiveness of the alternative—a third world war. Thus, although the life-and-death power I held as commander in chief was sobering, I was and am convinced of the moral rightness of maintaining America's military strength.

My ability to defend American interests without engulfing our nation or the world in war was most severely tested during my last fourteen months in office. First, Soviet troops invaded Afghanistan and threatened to move farther, into either Pakistan or Iran. This was the major

strategic problem for me, but there was a more highly pub-
licized and emotional crisis. In the aftermath of the revolution in Iran, Islamic forces led by the Ayatollah Khomeini
overthrew the shah. In November of 1979, Iranian militants invaded the U.S. embassy and seized sixty-six Americans as hostages. Our nation has seldom suffered such
anguish or uncertainty. I had few clear options during
those fourteen months. Because of the symbolic importance of our failure to bring the hostages home, the intense
interest among our own citizens and throughout the world,
and the lack of a clearly preferable response to the crisis,
this was the worst experience of my political life.

There was hardly a person in our country who had any
access to me or to the news media who didn't advocate
some response. Some quietly recommended that we
submit to Iranian blackmail by apologizing for our nation's
historic support for the now exiled shah. The Iranian
militants demanded that he be delivered to them for trial
and likely execution in Tehran. Much stronger voices
demanded that we launch a military attack against Iran.
These issues were hotly debated, both in the public
arena and among those who came to see me in the Oval
Office.

From the beginning of the crisis, I had two preeminent
goals: to protect the interests and honor of my country and
to bring all the hostages back home to safety and freedom.
I never deviated from these commitments. We seriously
considered military action, which would have been quite
popular and easy for me to order. However, I was con-

cerned that if I punished Iran in this way, the hostages would be brutalized or killed. Instead, I quickly sent the ayatollah an unpublicized warning, using multiple channels to be sure he received it. In essence, it said, "If you abuse a hostage, we will interrupt all trade between Iran and the outside world. If you kill one, we will respond militarily." In addition, I applied economic pressure by seizing more than $12 billion of Iranian deposits and urging our allies and supporters to refrain from trading with Iran.

Although a number of hostages were soon released, fifty-two were held captive throughout the balance of my term, an apparent reflection on my strength as a leader and, for many, on the power and prestige of the United States.

In April 1980, we made an unsuccessful effort to rescue the hostages. My orders were, if possible, to avoid any military confrontation or bloodshed, but eight Americans were killed in a tragic accident. Finally, through intense negotiations during the last three days and nights of my administration, during which time I never went to bed, we were able to achieve all our long-sought goals. At 10:00 A.M. on January 20, 1981, all the hostages were in a plane on the Tehran runway, waiting to leave Iran. The Ayatollah Khomeini finally permitted them to depart two hours later, a few minutes after my term ended, and two days later I met them when they arrived in Wiesbaden, Germany.

Not only did we secure the release of the hostages but

we retained enough Iranian assets to pay all claims by Americans who had suffered financial losses as a result of the Iranian revolution.

Although the hostage crisis was profoundly troubling, I have faced different but equally difficult personal challenges, as have almost all other people. As mentioned in this book, I have had to confront physical danger, financial despair, family tragedy, political failure, and quandaries concerning my career. In all such crises, self-analysis, self-questioning, and prayer have been the heart of my approach.

Prayer is the most essential element here. Even when I was reluctant to share my problems and my unanswered questions with any other human being, including Rosalynn, I was always able to share them with God. Prayer helps me to analyze the problem I face and to understand myself, including those things that are buried deep within me. This opens up a very important healing process. Unfortunately, the assurance my Christian faith promises to me is a treasure I don't always tap. Sometimes I go a long way down the road in a quandary, suffering inside, before finally I ask myself, "Why don't I talk to God about it?"

When I pray in such times, I try to ask myself three key questions: Are the goals I am pursuing appropriate? Am I doing the right thing, based on my personal moral code, my Christian faith, and the duties of my current position?

And, finally, have I done my best, based on the alternatives open to me? If I present all these issues to God, and then make the best possible decisions I can, things often work out well. But if I've tried everything I can and still fail, I find that I can say, "So be it." Putting the problem in God's hands gives me a degree of peace that lets me live with the outcome, whatever it may be.

Not that this comes naturally to me. I return frequently to a favorite lesson from the Epistle of James: Adversity and failure can lead not to hopelessness or despair but to new opportunity, perhaps to the pursuit of new goals that God has in mind for us, which may be greater than those we set for ourselves. I can never be certain of the wisdom of my decisions, but reliance on my faith gives me a greater level of assurance and equanimity.

I have reconsidered my decisions as president many times since leaving office, and a number of books have been written about the Iranian revolution and the seizure of the hostages. I have no doubt that the fact that our diplomats were still being held on election day was the major factor in my failure to win another term, but I cannot think of anything I could have done differently that would have achieved the same successful result.

Sixteen years later, I remain convinced that the wisest course for a mighty nation when confronted with a challenge like the hostage crisis is one of caution and restraint. For a person of faith, in particular, I believe that all decisions of war and peace must be made with the awareness that human life is never to be lightly sacrificed. Although as president I was prepared to use our powerful force if necessary, I have always been thankful that, in concluding my presidential memoirs, I could quote Thomas Jefferson: "I have the consolation to reflect that during the period of my administration not a drop of the blood of a single citizen was shed by the sword of war."

CHAPTER FIVE

To Establish Justice

Most Americans are committed to do what is right and just, to be concerned about others, to be champions of peace, to bridge the chasm between ourselves and the needy, to alleviate their suffering, to keep our environment clean, and to try to comprehend and demonstrate that in God's sight others are as worthy as we are. These are moral, even spiritual commitments, yet Americans have historically used our social institutions—including government—for help in pursuing them. Despite the justifiable criticism of and sometimes disillusionment with political processes, it is often government, and not the Christian churches, that is in the forefront of the struggle to "bring good news to the poor, to proclaim freedom for the prisoners, recovery of sight for the blind, and to release the oppressed," to use the words of Jesus as he announced his own ministry (Luke 4:18).

As a Christian who has served our nation as a statesman and political leader, I've frequently pondered the relationship between religious beliefs and the duties of a citizen. One of my most challenging and enjoyable tasks is lecturing at Emory University. During my first year of teaching, I was asked to discuss my life as a politician and as a church member—to compare politics and religion, or churches and governments I have known.

It surprised my religion and theology students when I said that the majority of church members are more self-satisfied, more committed to the status quo, and more exclusive of nonsimilar people than are most political officeholders I have known. Some congregations are more like spectators than participants, depending on the pastor and a professional staff to provide the program. Officeholders must be involved in the action. In political arenas there is an inherent and unavoidable mechanism for public assessment of performance against a standard of excellence, a degree of rivalry in dealing with human problems in the most dedicated and effective manner, and severe consequences for those who are seen to fail.

Whether campaigning or serving in office, a politician cannot avoid the most difficult and controversial subjects. They are the ones on which the news reporters focus and on which judgments will be made on election day.

When I was serving on a county school board, in the

Georgia senate, in the governor's office, and in the White House, I spent a major portion of my time exploring how I might resolve the difficult issues. How could I join with others in feeding the hungry, clothing the naked, providing homes for the homeless, educating the illiterate, eliminating the stigma of poverty or racial discrimination, making peace and resolving differences between people, preventing crime, rehabilitating prisoners, and ensuring justice? These were not just occasional concerns but were constant preoccupations for me and for most others who served with me in political office.

The same degree of commitment and willingness to address the problems of society is rare in our religious congregations. I have been a member of some good churches, at home in Plains and near where we lived in Atlanta and Washington. Our men's classes have included some of the finest and most dedicated community leaders, and we have been proud in the practice of our Christian faith. It was common for us, as Thanksgiving or Christmas approached, to do something especially benevolent for the poor people near our place of worship. After we'd taken up a nice collection, a frequent remark was, "Why don't we call the welfare office and get the names and addresses of a few poor families, so we can take them what they need for a fine holiday meal?" But this was a special seasonal interest in the needy, not one that prevailed throughout the year.

Our governments are obviously fallible, and they deserve criticism for many defects and failures. Moral standards are often ignored or circumvented. There are embarrassing revelations of malfeasance among office-holders, and some of them have been convicted of crimes. But some of the same problems afflict the religious world.

It is interesting to compare the moral standards of government and religion. Without going into the more esoteric aspects of the question, let me make the point with a somewhat humorous example. When Rev. Pat Robertson announced his candidacy for president in 1988, he meticulously went down a long list of claims he had made as a religious leader and television evangelist and publicly corrected them as he prepared to enter the more demanding and carefully scrutinized world of politics.

At its highest, government aspires to embody and defend values that are shared with religion. The great twentieth-century theologian Reinhold Niebuhr said, "To establish justice in a sinful world is the whole sad duty of the political order. There has never been justice without law; and all laws are the stabilization of certain social equilibria, brought about by pressures and counter-pressures in society, and expressed in the structures of government" (*Reinhold Niebuhr on Politics*, p. 180). Niebuhr's point is that the highest possible goal of a government or a society is justice: to treat people fairly, to guarantee their individual rights, to guard against discrimination, to try to resolve arguments peacefully. That's beautiful, isn't it? That's what a government should do.

However, any government, even the most benevolent, has inherent limitations. The best it can do is strive to establish a society that enhances freedom, equality, and justice. There are deeper religious values, such as atonement, forgiveness, and love, that transcend what government can achieve. When governments reach their limits, the teachings of Jesus Christ and of the prophets of other faiths must prevail: "You shall love the Lord your God—and your neighbor as yourself." We have a much greater opportunity beyond government to have our hearts united, to reach out personally to those in need, and to expand our lives in demonstrating self-sacrificing love, love for the unlovable.

There have been times when government was generally trusted to stand for some of the transcendent values that represent the best in humankind. Today, however, American attitudes toward government seem to be dominated by cynicism and pessimism. Tragically, American governments at all levels are seen to have gotten away from the concepts of forgiveness and reconciliation. Our society is steadily growing more racially and economically polarized. One reason is that many poor and minority Americans are convinced, with good reason, that the basic system of justice and law enforcement is not fair.

Though this problem is becoming increasingly serious, it is not new. When my three sons were in college, I realized that they might be experimenting with marijuana. This was of concern to me, but I was confident that an arrest would not destroy their lives. Ours was a prominent family, and I knew the sheriff and judge well. I always felt that they would not want to send "one of the Carter boys" to the state penitentiary. My promise to enroll them in a military school or to guarantee their future actions most likely would have substituted for prison. I also realized, at least subliminally, that if arrested on the same charge, our

poor and noninfluential neighbors would not have fared
so well.

This was the same era when the most distinguished
lawyers (including a majority of U.S. Supreme Court justices) maintained that "separate but equal" should be the
law of the land. Many white church leaders "proved,"
through selected Bible verses, that God had ordained the
superiority of whites.

In attempting to control crime, there has been an alternating emphasis on rehabilitation and punishment. During
the early 1970s, reacting against the ravages of racial segregation, there was a common desire, even competition,
among us state governors to reform injustices in the penal
system. In 1971, as a new governor, I visited the peniten-
tiaries with Georgia's enlightened prison director, Dr. Ellis
MacDougall, and met with the incarcerated men and
women. We found abominable conditions, with some
prisoners having been in solitary confinement for more
than five years. Almost invariably, the inmates were relatively defenseless, disproportionately poor and black, and
35 percent of them were mentally retarded.

We uncovered many cases of convictions on false accu-
sations, trials with inadequate or nonexistent legal counsel,
and confessions obtained under duress or with false
promises of leniency. There was an unwholesome traffic in
pardons and paroles by some lawyers, even by state legisla-
tors who had no legal training. They would charge relatively ignorant family members exorbitant monthly fees in
return for helping to obtain what were actually routine
paroles of penitentiary inmates.

When the laws are written and administered by the most powerful leaders in a society, it is human nature for them to understand, justify, and protect the interests of themselves and people like them. Many injustices arise from this natural human failing. In a Law Day speech as governor, I delineated some of these abuses to startled alumni of the University of Georgia Law School. My son, Jack, a law school student, was in the audience, and later I wrote a poem about the disagreement we had on this topic.

To a Young Lawyer, My Son

One day I lashed out at my lawyer friends,
and you were there
to hear me ask why legal ways are often
so unfair;
why, instead of what is just and right,
time and again
money, shrewd delays, and courtroom skills
seem to win.
I listened later to your angry claim
that you, with your
more legal mind, could understand their needs
and do much more
than I to help the cheerless poor and weak,
who rarely can
rely on laws designed by us to keep
the power in hand.
The problem's not that on the law we have
a different view—

> *it's how to shield our way of life, and share*
> *with others too.*

In Georgia, we established early release and work release programs. I personally recruited and helped train volunteer probation officers, who were Lions, Rotarians, Kiwanians, and members of other service organizations. We established a program of giving thorough examinations to all incoming inmates to determine their existing and potential skills, and helped them plan their careers for the years in prison and after release.

Many governors embraced this approach, and it resulted in a substantial decrease in the number of prisoners. My own experience in Georgia was that recidivism was reduced. Records show that a 9 percent *annual* increase in the U.S. prison population since 1980 has paralleled a dramatic 48 percent increase in violent crime from 1979 to 1992. Clearly, filling the prisons has not reduced crime as promised.

In 1977, the U.S. Supreme Court ended a thirteen-year prohibition on the death penalty. There is no proof that capital punishment deters capital crimes; in fact, statistics indicate just the opposite. In California, for instance, there was a 4.8 percent annual increase in murders before this ruling. With more than six executions per year during the next decade and a half, the murder rate increased 10.0 percent annually. There are now more than 3,000 Americans on death row, almost all of them poor, often mentally retarded, and disproportionately African-American. It is sobering to know that 50 have been freed since 1976 because they were proven innocent after having been sentenced to die.

The days of prison reform and rehabilitation of inmates are gone. One of the most effective campaign themes among political demagogues today is the harshness of their treatment of offenders. It is more popular for a governor to boast of building prison cells than schoolrooms. The range of capital crimes has skyrocketed at the state and federal level, and death penalties are executed with a literal vengeance. America now has more than 1 million prison inmates, a higher proportion of citizens incarcerated than any other industrialized country on earth. (Russia ranks second to us.)

One of the most dramatic changes, initiated in California, is the "three strikes and you're out" sentencing requirement, which eliminates any possibility of freedom for a repeat felon. The government of my own state, Georgia, trumped this by imposing "*two* strikes and you're out," and the governor is now attempting to limit physical exercise, library use, and similar "privileges" for inmates. Once again, shackled prisoners are working along the roads in Alabama, and visitors who come to enjoy the sight can buy "chain gang" hats and other souvenirs.

These changes have been made because harsh treatment is popular with voters, but there is no evidence that it deters crime. With little chance for rehabilitation, hopelessness prevails in prisons, where, early in 1996, the rising sense of injustice and despair led to an epidemic of revolts.

As these data show, the choices made by our leaders in

government can have a profound effect on the social and
spiritual well-being of millions of citizens. In political life,
the principles I followed were established partially in
laws, partially in the general platform of the Democratic
party, and partially through my personal interests and commitments. They involved such hotly debated issues as environmental quality, affirmative action, the nature of the tax
system, a general support for workers' rights versus those
of big business, and a concern for the poor and elderly. I
also believed in a strong defense system, minimal deficits,
and maximum transfer of authority from the federal government to local officials and individuals. Although something of a mixed bag, the array of platform commitments I
made was fairly complete, and extrapolating from them
helped me decide how to address unexpected issues. The
values embodied in my political positions spelled out, in
effect, how I defined *justice* and chose to strive for it as governor and president.

There is never hope of infallibility, because the future
can't be predicted accurately, and there are always arguments, even among leaders in the same party, concerning
the application of general principles to specific questions
or local communities. In no case is it possible to embody
the pure ideals of justice in a system of laws. This is what
Reinhold Niebuhr meant by justice as the highest *goal* of a
group, a society, or a government. His definition of justice
is quite complicated, requiring many pages to express.
However, in brief, it involves the proper juxtaposition of
order, equality, and freedom. A just system of government

must be designed to arbitrate and adjudicate competing claims and conflicting rights.

The Bible is ambiguous concerning our duties in regard to secular authority. Paul told the Romans, "Let every person be subject to the governing authorities . . . those who resist will incur judgment" (Romans 13:1–2). But the Hebrew prophets did not hesitate to denounce those in power when they did not act justly in the eyes of God. Their demand, in the words of Amos, was that rulers should "Let justice roll down like waters, and righteousness like an everflowing stream" (Amos 5:24). When justice is denied because of unfair laws or misguided or corrupt leaders, it is our duty as citizens to struggle for changes in the laws and the system that enforces them. But what should we do, as people of faith, when the laws support acts that are evil according to the religious values we hold? Jesus, Paul, and the disciples all gave the answer to this question. Civil disobedience is in order when human laws are contrary to God's commands to us. Jesus went to his death and Paul spent his final years in prison rather than conform to religious and secular laws which they could not accept. In our own century, civil rights activists in America and Mahatma Gandhi in India demonstrated the necessity and effectiveness of such action.

We are not required to submit to the domination of authority without assessing whether it is contrary to our faith or our beliefs. Even in a democracy like ours, each of us must confront and examine our national policies. When I was in the White House, I disagreed with some of the laws I was sworn to enforce, such as those concerning energy, the environment, and abortion, and I attempted in every legitimate way to change or minimize what I considered to be their adverse effect.

When governments fail to defend real justice in Niebuhr's sense, it is a duty for citizens informed by religious faith and a sense of morality to challenge the powerful and demand change. In the 1960s, when my sons were of college age, the young people used peaceful demonstrations and other forms of protest to change American policies in three of the most important issues that faced our government: civil rights, the environment, and the Vietnam War. Civil disobedience, of course, includes a willingness to accept the penalty for breaking the law one opposes. Later, in the 1980s, our daughter, Amy, was arrested on three occasions for participating in student demonstrations against apartheid in South Africa and once for condemning the policies of the CIA during the Contra war in Nicaragua.

Gandhi, Martin Luther King, Jr., and the biblical heroes made it clear that nonviolence and tolerance are the necessary hallmarks of effective civil disobedience. Understood in this way, this action is the prerogative of any private citizen.

A notably successful mixture of religion and politics was the civil rights crusade of the 1950s and 1960s. The segregation and abuse of African-Americans was a gross violation of both the spirit of our Constitution and the basic teachings of Jesus. The movement led by Dr. Martin Luther King, Jr., in the black churches and such organizations as the National Association for the Advancement of Colored People and the Congress of Racial Equality was watched closely by Southern segregationists, who soon judged them not likely to succeed in breaking down racial barriers.

However, a radical change occurred when the young black and white civil rights activists of the Student Nonviolent Coordinating Committee began sitting down at white-only lunch counters, daring to disrupt normal commercial and legal proceedings. They aroused even more concern and condemnation when they attempted to enter church sanctuaries in order to worship with white Christians.

Those forces merged, slowly and inexorably, always with the core of their support and their major forum in the black religious congregations. It was this full coalition, and ultimately the politicians and federal courts, that broke down the racial barriers of our segregated society—most often with white congregations opposing the change. Despite setbacks, arrests, and physical abuse, the leaders were inspired and strengthened by the conviction that their cause was just and that God was with them. Their adoption of peace, nonviolence, and the symbols and trappings of religion in their rallies, sermons, and songs shook the convictions of white Christians who believed that segregation was compatible with biblical teachings. I saw this within my own church and community.

Many white Americans in all regions during slavery and

segregation times were willing to accept these evils without questioning them, and many of our black neighbors were reluctant to challenge the racist system. Its violation of basic religious values seems clear now, but, during the era of "separate but equal" laws, it was the way of life for us. When civil rights emerged in the early 1950s as a major political issue, respected religious leaders were invited to speak to the members of our Plains Baptist brotherhood. Most of our church leaders nodded approvingly while, with carefully selected verses, the speakers "proved" that segregation was condoned or even mandated by God. Their reassuring testimony was corroborated by our nation's distinguished "constitutional lawyers," including Supreme Court justices, who maintained that racial segregation was acceptable under the U.S. Constitution.

Even during these times, however, there was an evolutionary, unpublicized conversion of most white Southerners by the civil rights leaders concerning the compatibility of their cause with the teachings of Jesus. But this was a slow process. When the issue of accepting black worshipers was addressed by our congregation in Plains in 1963, I spoke in favor of welcoming them and any others who came in good faith. We usually had about fifty members attend our monthly conferences, but on this occasion every pew was filled. When a vote was taken, only one other person voted with our family to admit everyone, while fifty opposed the motion. The significant thing was that almost two hundred others abstained.

A year later, in 1964, the Georgia legislature voted on the Twenty-fourth Amendment to the U.S. Constitution, which prohibited poll taxes as a prerequisite to voting. Although we no longer collected such taxes in our state, this amendment was considered an important civil rights proposal, since poll taxes were still used in some states to prevent voting by black citizens. Formerly in Georgia and then in other states, the tax had been allowed to accumulate each year, beginning at age twenty-one, so that a payment exceeding forty-five dollars was required to permit some older people to cast a ballot. When we were debating this issue, I received my only telephone calls from Georgia's congressional leaders in Washington, urging me and other state senators to oppose the measure. Despite these efforts, we voted overwhelmingly to ratify the amendment.

It is well known that during segregation days many white Southerners respected and often loved individual Negroes who were our neighbors. We didn't have to introduce ourselves to our black friends when legal integration came. Nowadays, secular life in most schools, businesses, and governments is legally integrated. Maranatha Baptist Church warmly welcomes all visitors who come to attend our services, and we are proud of a few interracial worship events in Plains, such as joint choir services on Easter.

Even when they are welcomed in our own and other predominantly white churches, however, few black Christians choose to join these congregations. They may feel that the welcome is not genuine; there are ties to family and friends that are binding on Sundays; or it may be that our rigid two-hour periods for both Sunday school and a sermon, ending at noon, are not attractive to worshipers accustomed to a more leisurely and unstructured session that often extends far into the afternoon.

Unfortunately, all too few congregations make an enthusiastic and effective effort to break down the racial and social barriers that still divide us. One of the finest programs to pursue this goal is Habitat for Humanity, a Christian-based organization that builds homes in partnership with homeless families or those living in substandard housing. Although the primary purpose of Habitat is to improve the lives of needy families by providing them with shelter and the dignity of decent housing, an equal benefit is to bring together people from widely differing backgrounds who might otherwise never meet, enriching us all with a reminder of our common humanity.

Not everyone understands this. When Habitat began serving poor families in our county, one of the wealthiest local women called Millard Fuller, the founder. "Why don't you build a house for my maid?" she demanded angrily. "She needs a new home as much as anyone." Millard explained the criteria for choosing homeowners, pulled out a standard form, and began to ask a few questions.

"How long has she worked for you?"

"Twenty-three years."

"Is she a good and reliable worker?"

"Of course. She comes every day, without fail."

"What is her name?"

"I don't know her last name, but her first one is Maude."

Like Maude's employer, many of us do not know or really care about our next-door neighbors. One obstacle to breaking down racial barriers is that we don't quite know what to do. How many of us actually know a poor family well enough to have a cup of coffee in their living room or kitchen? Or know the names of their teenage sons? Or take their kids to a movie or baseball game with our children? Or, God forbid, invite them to our house?

Those of us who have everything we need and, in general, make all the decisions about our society simply do not know those who are living in poverty, alienation, and despair. The families who find it difficult to get good jobs, decent homes, safe neighborhoods, and good medical care and education do not know or trust their privileged neighbors, the court system, or the police to care about their plight. The prisoners, drug addicts, alcoholics, homeless, teenage mothers, and school dropouts have little hope or confidence in the system. I think this incompatibility between the rich and powerful and the poor and weak is the root cause of the worst problems our country faces.

In announcing his ministry, Jesus spoke to this very point: "The Spirit of the Lord is on me, because he has anointed me to preach good news to the poor. He has sent me to proclaim freedom for the prisoners and recovery of sight for the blind, to release the oppressed" (Luke 4:18). He went on for three years to fulfill this commitment—and to give Christians the same goals.

As president, I tried to make human rights a core value of my administration. This emphasis was derived from my experience growing up in the South, and from the guilt I shared with others over the way we deprived our black neighbors of their human rights. I find it incredible to recall the social customs we took for granted in the South in decades past. I now ask, as almost all white Southerners do, "How could this have been? Why did we not see that racial segregation was a millstone around our necks as well as those of our black neighbors? How could we reconcile the way we acted with the teachings of Jesus Christ?" By the time I was elected president, most Southerners saw the evil of this very clearly.

My concern about relations between the races was based on a lifetime of experience and was more a personal commitment than a political stance. But I had also accumulated a broad base of support among black Georgians while I was governor, and they participated fully in my presidential campaign. Early in 1976, then-Congressman Andrew Young took me to meet with the members of the Congressional Black Caucus. The other Democratic presidential candidates were better known in Washington than I was; I'd only met two of the two dozen or so black congressmen.

Andy reported that all the candidates who'd previously met with the group had seemed ill at ease and had been quick to agree with virtually every policy suggestion the caucus members made. At the end of each meeting, there was a final, routine question: How many black people do you have on your campaign staff? Most of them had one or two, and one had three. The most politically liberal of the candidates replied that he was currently interviewing people in hopes of hiring one.

When it was my turn to meet with the caucus, I felt at

home, and I was not reluctant to disagree with many things they said about mandatory quotas, costly social programs, and other topics. It was a frank and unrestrained discussion of some major political issues. But when they asked me, "How many blacks do you have on your campaign staff?" I didn't have the slightest idea. So I started naming them aloud to count them up, and when I was finished, I realized that I had twenty-two. I left the room while Andy Young stayed behind, and he later told me that, although I'd disagreed with the congressmen on most issues, there was a positive attitude toward me in the room. With the strong support of Andy, Martin Luther King, Sr., and many other black leaders who knew me personally, I later received 85 percent of the black vote.

I have often been asked if there were many serious conflicts between my religious beliefs and my duties as an elected official. There were very few occasions when I felt torn between my own faith and my obligation to comply with my oath to "preserve, protect, and defend the Constitution of the United States." There is probably not a great incompatibility between our patriotic ideals for America and Judeo-Christian values. Justice, equal opportunity, human rights, freedom, democracy, truth—those are the kinds of things that were spelled out by Thomas Jefferson and others in the founding days of our country, and we still would like to preserve them.

However, there were some harshly debated interpretations of the law that confronted me with difficult choices. I was thankful that there were no executions of criminals while I was governor or president. One of my fundamental political beliefs is that we should avoid modifying the Constitution in response to cyclical changes in American public opinion. Therefore, I opposed constitutional amendments that would have permitted mandatory prayer in public schools or totally prohibited abortions. However, the latter issue was one over which I had great concern. I have never been able to believe that Jesus would have approved the taking of a human life, but the difficult question then remained: When does a fetus become a human being? My duty was to comply with the rulings of the Supreme Court, but I did everything possible to minimize the need for and attractiveness of abortions.

Some of the simple parables of Jesus have to be interpreted flexibly to fit complex and unpredictable situations. One of these is his use of a Roman coin to draw a line between secular and religious authorities: "Render to Caesar the things that are Caesar's and to God the things that are God's" (Mark 12:17). My father interpreted this counsel strictly and extended it to the premise that the government should not be involved either in religion or in his personal affairs. Although Georgia overwhelmingly supported the three reelections of President Franklin Roosevelt, Daddy never supported him after 1935, when a New Deal program required farmers to plow up knee-high cotton and kill young pigs in order to lower production and increase prices.

I inherited my own support for the separation of church

and state from my father, I guess, but I came to realize while holding public office how ambiguous is the line between the secular and the sacred.

I know from sad experience the dangers of mixing my religious faith with my political career. An attempt to explain my religious beliefs to a large audience almost prevented my becoming president. This is one of the best-known events in U.S. political history, but until now I have tried to explain it only in my Sunday school classes.

During the late summer of 1976, I was far ahead of President Gerald Ford in public opinion polls and holding a steady lead. Wanting as much publicity as possible, and particularly interested in attracting support from young voters, my overconfident staff and I agreed to the entreaties of *Playboy* magazine to do a series of short interviews, mostly while flying from one campaign stop to another, that would become a definitive cover story. We insisted that the final text of the article be submitted to my press secretary for editing, at least for accuracy, before it could be published. The *Playboy* editors agreed, but I still answered their questions carefully with everything recorded on tape.

The final interview was in the living room of my home, and it went well. The reporter thanked me and turned off his tape recorder, and we moved to the front door to say good-bye. He said, apparently off the record, "Governor, there is still one thing that really concerns me. You are a farmer, living in a small town, who has pledged never to lie to the American people. You also claim to be a born-again Christian. The citizens of our country and other public officials are not perfect. How will you be able to relate to them, when you consider yourself to be so much better than they are?"

This took me aback, and I tried to describe my real feelings. I explained that Jesus was particularly concerned with human pride and a sense of superiority over others, and condemned those who judged others. I then moved to the Sermon on the Mount, in an attempt to explain further. If you hate your brother, the sin is like murder. It is necessary to love your enemies, not just your friends. Public prayer is its own reward. You should fast and give alms in secret. And then I quoted the crucial words of Jesus: "You have heard that it was said, 'You shall not commit adultery'; but I say to you, that everyone who looks on a woman to lust for her has committed adultery with her already in his heart" (Matthew 5:27–28).

The reporter asked me if I had ever been guilty of adultery, and his next question was predictable. I replied truthfully, "Yes, I have lusted. . . ."

The reporter left, and I felt quite pleased with the entire interview, not realizing that he had surreptitiously restarted the tape recorder as we stood at the door. What he had recorded was too good to be submitted for our review.

Several weeks later, while I was emulating Harry Truman on a whistle-stop railway campaign across Pennsylvania, I found that dozens of reporters on the train were absorbed with the new issue of *Playboy*. To my amazement,

I was besieged with questions about my sex life. At first I thought this was just a passing joke, but I was wrong. It became the dominant news story of my candidacy, and my popularity dropped precipitously. Any attempts to explain the Christian theology behind my answers only served to keep the issue alive. Reporters became instant students of religion and rushed to interview famous pastors and television evangelists. Almost all of them denied fervently that they had ever had sexual thoughts in their minds or hearts—except, of course, for their wives.

Rosalynn has always told me that she saw this as merely another unpredictable political crisis that would have to be faced and overcome. When asked by reporters for her reaction, she responded that she was certain of my love, that she was familiar with the Bible verses and understood my explanation of them. My three sons, all in their twenties, were particularly angry at the preachers who professed their total innocence. Most of my campaign workers were distressed that we had made such a foolish mistake. I guess all of us felt that way. I was finally elected, but only by a narrow margin.

Having attained the White House, Rosalynn and I faced a different set of issues regarding our faith.

We had observed that my predecessors had invited Billy Graham and other famous preachers to conduct well-publicized worship services in the White House. We respected their right to do so, but we felt that for us to do the same would violate our concept of the church and state being kept separate. At the same time, we didn't want to let holding political office prevent our worshiping as normally as possible.

After I was elected governor, Rosalynn and I had visited a friend who was dying with cancer and had assured her that we intended to continue as members of the Baptist church congregation in Plains. We thought our friend would be pleased, but she immediately replied, "My mama always said that when you move your cookstove, you should move your church membership." Because of this remark, we became active members of the Baptist church nearest the governor's mansion in Atlanta and, later, the White House in Washington. I was a deacon in Atlanta's Northside Drive Baptist Church while governor, and I taught Sunday school several times a year at First Baptist Church while we were in Washington.

Whenever possible, Rosalynn and I went to Camp David for the weekends, and we were able to worship there in almost complete privacy. Our Sunday services were conducted by a chaplain from a nearby army base, early enough in the morning for him to return for his regular sermon to his troops. A few of our staff members and some of the navy personnel stationed there would attend with us, in a room set aside for this purpose. In 1978, during the thirteen days of Camp David negotiations between Israel and Egypt, we were able to convert the same little room each weekend to accommodate the religious services of the Jews, the Muslims, and the Christians. Now a chapel has been built on the grounds, with donations received while President Ronald Reagan was in office.

* * *

Americans are rightly sensitive about clashes between church and state, but conflicts between religion and government are not the only questions. There is also the issue of too much melding of the two. In Norway and Finland, for instance, a fixed portion of the taxes collected by the federal government goes to support the religious programs of officially accepted churches. There is debate among Christians in those countries about whether this is good or bad. We always have to struggle in our own Baptist church to meet our budget, so we can expand our church if our congregation grows, support our missionary family in Togo, give our preacher an adequate salary, and do other desirable things. To varying degrees, of course, all members feel that we have a direct involvement in the character and actions of the entire congregation. Being called upon for financial support is part of this involvement. I believe that forgoing our own financial responsibility and depending on government support would sap the vigor of the church.

Separation of church and state doesn't just protect religion from government meddling. It is also a positive good, encouraging Americans to support hundreds of varied and active religious denominations, worshiping God in churches, synagogues, mosques, and temples of every size and type.

How can diversity among sincere religious beliefs be a powerful unifying influence among us? Historically, this is not a strange concept. The signers of the Declaration of

Independence said that our people had the right "to assume among the Powers of the Earth the separate and equal Station to which the Laws of Nature and of Nature's God entitle them." They went on to remind the world that the people were "endowed by their Creator with certain unalienable Rights." In closing, they wrote, "And for the support of this declaration, with a firm Reliance on the Protection of Divine Providence, we mutually pledge to each other our lives, our Fortunes, and our sacred Honor." Thus, despite their varied faiths—Puritans, Quakers, - Catholics, Baptists, and Deists—our founders joined together in invoking the aid of one creator and the shared values they derived from their belief in God.

However, to be certain that references to God, Creator, and Divine Providence did not imply any encroachment by a powerful government on religious freedom, the First Amendment of the Constitution stated clearly, "Congress shall make no law respecting an establishment of religion, or prohibiting the free exercise thereof." This was a burning issue among our nation's founders, since so many American families had come to this continent to escape religious persecution and to worship freely. For more than 200 years, the church-state relationship has been debated, but our Constitution has prevailed.

The fact is that the basic political principles of America are compatible with our deepest religious beliefs. With the exception of atheists, Jehovah's Witnesses, and a few others whose consciences do not permit it, we citizens can address our flag and pledge allegiance without qualms to "one nation, under God."

I grew up in a community that was racially, economically, and socially diverse. However, all of us—black and white, rich and poor, merchants and farmers—were Protestant Christians, and Democrats. It was only later, as a naval officer, governor, and president, that I had the responsibility of respecting the different religious faiths—and political beliefs—of others. World history has taught us that it is not easy for authoritarian leaders with deep religious beliefs to be tolerant of the divergent views of others.

It is obvious that the ways Americans deal with some of these issues have evolved with the passage of time. When I grew up in Plains, for instance, we had mandatory chapel every morning in school. We sang religious songs, had prayer, and recited memorized Bible verses. This can be justified in retrospect by the fact that we all shared the same faith. But nowadays, even if we have an overwhelming majority of Protestants but just a few Catholics, Jews, Muslims, or atheists in the classroom, it would not be proper for a teacher to force all the kids to worship the same way, or at all.

Even then, we were living in a changing world, and we had to accommodate evolving customs and standards, including different interpretations of the Scriptures and how rigidly they were to be observed. It was a surprise to me to learn that, before World War I, the running of trains was restricted in the United States on Sundays. Until after the Second World War, there were no baseball games played on Sunday, and I remember the blue law debate when I was in the Georgia Senate, which finally resulted in stores being legally open throughout the weekend.

There has been a metamorphosis in our lifestyles, and it continues at an ever more rapid pace. How can we deal with it successfully? The best advice I've ever known came from my former teacher Miss Julia Coleman, whom I quoted in my presidential inaugural address: "We must adjust to changing times and still hold to unchanging principles." For her, changing times meant the advent of gramophones, school buses, electricity, talking movies, and radio programs. For us, it means supersonic jets, genetic engineering, personal computers, and the Internet. Yet Miss Coleman's wisdom still holds true.

Searching for Peace

A fter I was defeated for reelection in 1980, it was a real temptation for Rosalynn and me simply to stay close to our home in Plains and care for our farmland. But we decided instead to embark on a new career. We wanted my presidential library to be more than just a repository for my official records, so we began plans for The Carter Center, an international peacemaking organization to be headquartered in Atlanta.

Our early vision of The Carter Center was just a vague hope that we could combine our secular and religious interests in worthwhile projects. At the time, I was still deeply concerned about the Middle East peace process, which my administration had helped begin at Camp David, and frustrated that the effort to follow up with the Palestinians, Jordan, and Syria had been largely abandoned by the Reagan administration. My hope was that, in some way, I could use my knowledge and experience in addressing this and other conflicts in the world and, with approval from Washington, perhaps Rosalynn and I could become involved in some mediation efforts. In the early 1980s, our visits to the Middle East were officially encouraged, and I always gave full reports to the secretary of state and the White House. On occasion, I would also meet secretly with Palestinian leaders.

I soon began to realize that there were many needs other than peacemaking that could not be met by the U.S. government or other official agencies. Increasingly, our center became a neutral forum within which diverse and even hostile groups could meet to explore common approaches to problems.

Since then, the scope of our interests has continued to expand, and we now see the inseparability of peace, justice, freedom, democracy, human rights, environmental protection, and the alleviation of physical suffering. Our work is almost entirely among the poorest and most needy people, in this country and in many foreign nations. In every Carter Center program, Rosalynn is a full partner with me, and she has been in charge of our efforts in the field of mental health. Under her leadership, more than sixty formerly uncooperative organizations now come together annually to share their common ideas and goals.

When we decided to establish The Carter Center, we sought help and advice from many sources. I visited more than fifty benevolent foundations, occasionally receiving financial support and always benefiting from information about needs we might fill that other organizations were not addressing. We also brought in former associates from my administration, experts from Harvard and George Mason Universities, and peacekeepers from the United Nations to give us advice on mediation techniques and ways of learning about the many relatively unpublicized conflicts in the world.

We wanted to involve the faith communities in some of our causes, and we assembled leaders from different religious groups to discuss how our center might serve them and act as a catalyst to expand our combined work. At one large meeting, we hosted representatives from about twenty Christian denominations, plus groups of Jews, Muslims, Hindus, Buddhists, Baha'is, and members of other faiths. Despite the many differences among us, there were two issues on which we could all agree: one was peace, and the other was the prevention and alleviation of suffering. From this has grown our Interfaith Health Program, within which many faith groups now share ideas and experiences through regional meetings, periodicals, and World Wide Web pages on the Internet.

The Carter Center has been operating in an especially interesting and important time on the international scene. With the end of the Cold War, we in the United States no longer face intense competition with a powerful Soviet Union for hegemony or influence in almost every region of the world. There is a void in international leadership, which offers us a comparatively blank slate on which to imprint the finest aspects of our nation's ideals. As a Christian, I think we can prove that it is possible to support the religious or spiritual values of compassion, sharing, and peace along with the democratic principles of freedom, equality, human rights, and self-rule.

When given the opportunity, though, our country has not always chosen to adopt the option of peace. During the last few years, the United States has been involved in many wars, one way or another. We gave at least tacit approval to Israel's disastrous invasion of Lebanon in 1982, then sent in U.S. Marines and bombed and strafed the villages around Beirut. We invaded and defeated Grenada. We invaded and destroyed a good portion of Panama. And on a more massive scale, we orchestrated the Persian Gulf War. In none of these cases did we first exhaust the opportunities for peaceful resolution of the dispute.

We Americans are proud of our military achievements, and war almost invariably brings instant popularity to the president, who changes in the public perception from a beleaguered civilian administrator to a dynamic commander in chief when our brave young men and women go into combat.

Yet with a deep and consistent commitment to peace, a powerful and admired America could have a tremendously beneficial influence on troubled regions of the world and could help both to resolve and to prevent needless wars. Many political (but not necessarily military) leaders disagree with these ideas and consider them weak, naïve, and overly idealistic. But in our work for The Carter Center, we witness firsthand the eagerness of people in war-torn or suffering nations for the peaceful interposition of American power. Such involvement would often be unsuccessful and frustrating, at times even politically unpopular. But peace efforts are closely related to all our ideals and moral values: human rights, freedom, democracy, and the alleviation of human suffering. Even when such efforts end in failure, they can greatly improve the reputation and influence of our country in areas of the world that do not share our own high opinion of America.

For some reason, Americans tend to see conflicts in terms of friend/enemy, angel/devil. This view is one of the major impediments to realizing our global potential as a champion of peace.

Consider a few well-known names on the international scene, including Anwar Sadat, Yasir Arafat, Kim Il Sung, Emile Jonassaint, Fidel Castro, and Hafiz al-Assad. These are, or were, all powerful, famous, nondemocratic rulers. Their names are "foreign," not Anglo-Saxon. All these men have at times been misunderstood, ridiculed, and totally condemned by the American public, and some of them deserve it. But like it or not, someone must be willing to deal with these kinds of leaders if we are to avert future wars and human suffering.

Most Americans now think of Egypt's Anwar Sadat quite favorably, but I remember that when he visited us in the White House for the first time in 1977, the vast majority of Americans looked upon almost all Arabs, including the Egyptian president, with great suspicion or animosity. Later, with his historic visit to Jerusalem, his agreement to the Camp David Accords, and the treaty with

Israel, he became a heroic peacemaker—and finally a
martyr to peace.

All too often, conflicts and wars arise when we fail to
consider the views of others or to communicate with them
about differences between us.

In my personal life, I sometimes find it difficult to
understand those with whom I disagree or those who con-
tradict me. Strangely, I find it easier to put myself in the
position of an adversary when I am involved in negotiations as a mediator or even as an antagonist. It seems
natural in those circumstances for me to attune my mind
away from myself and to a more objective point of view. As
president during the intense days of the Cold War, for
instance, I would sit in the Oval Office, glance at a big
globe, and try to view the world as Soviet President Leonid
Brezhnev did—living in a closed society, surrounded by
frozen seas, powerfully armed enemies, and doubtful allies.
The insights gained from this reflection helped me in
negotiating, when I tried to alleviate his concerns while
still pursuing the goals of my own country.

I used to argue vociferously with the Russian leaders
about human rights. It was disturbing for me, as president,
to hear Andrei Gromyko, the foreign minister of the Soviet
Union, say, "We don't have any human rights violations in
our country. Everybody in the Soviet Union has a place to
sleep, adequate medical care, and a job." I couldn't argue
when he quoted our own statistics about the number of

Americans who were homeless, lacked adequate health care, or were unemployed. Gromyko's argument was that these were examples of our failure to recognize our citizens' human rights.

Obviously, the Soviet citizens were assigned jobs, they had to live where they were told, and they didn't have the right to voice their opinions, choose their own leaders, avoid summary convictions and punishment, move to another country, or even know the facts about their own society or the outside world. These are gross violations of human rights as Americans define them. But it was not easy for either Gromyko or me to accept an expanded definition of human rights. We each had a convenient definition, one that caused us few twinges of conscience. Differences like these must be recognized and understood when negotiating with adversaries—without abandoning our own beliefs and principles.

Over the past fifteen years, we at The Carter Center have adopted a number of principles for making and keeping peace within and between nations. One of the most basic is that in political, military, moral, and spiritual confrontations, there should be an honest attempt at the reconciliation of differences before resorting to combat. The fact is that in most cases—though not all—there is enough common ground between adversaries to avoid violence and to permit people to live as neighbors, even if their differences are not resolved. However, there must be a basic desire for peace, enough respect for opponents to communicate with them, a willingness to reexamine one's own beliefs, and the personal and political courage to employ the principles of dispute resolution.

Provided I can obtain permission from our top government officials and believe that my efforts might be helpful, I feel no reluctance about having personal contact with people who have been branded as oppressive, dishonest, or even guilty of launching wars of aggression.

A typical but troubling example of these experiences came when I was asked by the International Red Cross and the UN High Commissioner for Refugees to help resolve a problem with the Ethiopian communist dictator, President Mengistu Haile Mariam. Tens of thousands of Somalian and Sudanese refugees had filled camps in Ethiopia, and the relief agencies reported that Mengistu was not permitting them to deliver food, water, and medicine. Since I was already in East Africa on Carter Center projects, I traveled to Addis Ababa, the capital of Ethiopia. At the time, the United States rightly had withdrawn its ambassador from the country in protest against the government's policies.

Mengistu welcomed Rosalynn and me to Addis and invited us to stay at the palace of the late emperor Haile Selassie. (It was generally believed that the eighty-three-year-old emperor had been smothered in bed by Mengistu's revolutionary forces in 1975.) So far as we knew, no American officials had ever visited Mengistu, but we found him to be frank with us and apparently willing to resolve the impasse with the international organizations. Through an interpreter, he explained that he was quite willing to see supplies go to the refugees but that the agencies had refused to permit deliveries by Ethiopians. It took only a brief discussion for him to accept our suggestion that his troops carry the supplies but that representatives of the international agencies monitor the procedure. This solution proved acceptable to all parties.

While there, I also suggested that peace talks be commenced between the Ethiopian government and their chief adversaries, revolutionaries from Eritrea and Tigre, in a war that had lasted more than two decades and caused more than a million deaths. Mengistu agreed, and extensive discussions were later conducted, with Italian officials mediating the Ethiopia-Tigre dispute and The Carter Center negotiating between the Eritreans and Mengistu's officials.

Later I was asked by Israeli officials to intercede with Mengistu to secure emigration permits for about 3,500 Ethiopian Jews, known as Falasha, or "exiles," who were being prohibited from leaving Ethiopia to go to Israel. I learned what I could about them before approaching the Ethiopian leader. This was the remainder of a group of about 15,000, the others having been transported to Israel some years earlier. The Falasha claim to be descendants of Menelik I, son of the biblical King Solomon and the queen of Sheba, and many of their worship practices have remained unchanged since the times of the prophets. Their Scriptures are not in Hebrew but in another ancient Semitic tongue, and the Falasha still offer animal sacrifices. When I broached the subject of the Falasha's emigration with Mengistu, he agreed to release them provided the government of Israel made a direct request. Eventually this was done, and the Falasha were united in the Holy Land.

I knew that Mengistu was well educated and had received some of his training in the United States, but he always insisted on speaking Amharic, conversing with me through an interpreter. Later an American told me about an interesting event that occurred when he was visiting Mengistu. When a waiter came into the office to take orders for refreshments, the interpreter and the president both requested "chi," while the Westerner, desiring the same drink, said "tea." The visitor wondered aloud about the difference, and Mengistu said casually in English, "Well, there must be an etymological explanation."

When the Tigrean guerrillas took Addis Ababa in 1991, Mengistu fled to Zimbabwe, where he still lives in exile despite unsuccessful attempts by his successors to extradite him to be tried for murder.

I have been willing to deal with Mengistu and others considered international pariahs, since government officials would not communicate directly with them and they are often the only ones who can resolve a serious problem. In most cases, they are eager to have some contact with the Western world, and their status as international outcasts makes them quite reluctant to alienate me by lying.

Certainly some of the people with whom I've dealt have been dictators, killers, and violators of human rights. No one could defend the moral codes of such people, or claim that ethical distinctions among governments cannot or should not be drawn. I realize that the primary "code" of some political leaders is simply to continue enjoying the benefits of power.

The question is, what do we do about it? Do we refuse to talk to such oppressors and simply impose sanctions or trade embargoes on their nations in an effort to apply pressure on them? If so, we deprive the children in those countries of food and medicine, causing needless suffering of innocents. The dictator himself doesn't suffer, and his children and grandchildren get all the food and medicine they need. One unwanted result of such trade embargoes is that we sometimes make a hero of the dictator who is defying the American giant, while he blames his nation's ills on the embargo itself. This has been the result of our unfortunate and counter-productive policy toward Cuba.

The alternative is to focus on pragmatic goals: to prevent war, to reduce suffering, and to open up and bring positive change to cruel or repressive regimes. Often this can be done only if we are willing to communicate with the people in power, however unsavory they may be. Only our willingness to have a dialogue enables us to find room for compromises that can save lives and even, in some cases, induce the dictators to mend their ways.

Sometimes I find that leaders we brand as "evil" are willing to work seriously with us for the sake of peace. North Korean President Kim Il Sung was such a person. When I was serving on a submarine in the Pacific Ocean during the Korean War, I blamed him as the one who had caused the conflict. I approached our meeting in 1994 with trepidation and some degree of animosity, but I found him to be a man who wanted to end the nuclear crisis and begin a fruitful series of discussions with the United States.

Much the same situation existed with Gen. Raoul Cedras in Haiti. He was seeking a way out of a political and military quagmire. But because he and his political associates had been branded as totally evil and excluded from direct communication with the U.S. government, he had no way to redeem himself or to correct an evil situation.

I can't claim that I changed the hearts of Kim or Cedras, or that I "redeemed" them in any spiritual sense. That is not the point of our peacemaking efforts. The point is to change their approach to a problem, their behavior.

Although forgiveness is taught in the Bible, I don't draw a parallel between this religious principle and these activities of The Carter Center. We are not in the business of forgiving anyone. We only attempt to resolve crises and prevent the repetition or continuation of illicit acts.

I am sometimes asked, "How can you trust the word of these men?" The unusual position I hold gives me significant leverage over the leaders of certain pariah states. Today, for example, President Mobutu Sese Seko in Zaire is something of an outcast, forbidden to enter the United States or most of the European nations. Yet his cooperation is vital in resolving problems of war and refugee flight in neighboring Rwanda and Burundi. Since I am one of the few Westerners who is willing to meet with Mobutu, he now views me—as Mengistu and Cedras did—as one of the few means through which potentially beneficial negotiations can be conducted. If we at The Carter Center were to announce that Mobutu is unwilling to negotiate seriously or to move toward democracy in Zaire, it would be a serious blow to his remaining credibility on the world scene.

Many times I assume that a person is untrustworthy, since he is known to have broken promises in the past. In these cases, I attempt to understand what is in his best interest, analyze our own goals, and then try to connect the two. If I can convince the leader that what we want to achieve is also best for him, then we have a good chance for agreement. In my experience few leaders have broken the promises they have finally made.

One of the most intense negotiations in which I have been involved occurred when, with approval from the White House, I went to Haiti on Saturday, September 17, 1994, with Sen. Sam Nunn and Gen. Colin Powell to try to prevent an armed invasion of the island by 30,000 U.S. troops who were poised for action. Haitian military leaders, headed by Gen. Cedras, had overthrown the elected president, Jean-Bertrand Aristide, who was living in exile in the United States. An old and distinguished man, Emile Jonassaint, was serving temporarily as president.

It was the policy of the United States to communicate only with Haitian leaders whom we recognized, and this meant that, officially, Aristide and his cabinet (all in exile) were the sole official government. The U.S. ambassador in

Port-au-Prince was prohibited from exchanging a written note or even indirect messages with Jonassaint and members of his cabinet. But we were free to discuss the issues with anyone in Haiti.

The key issue was whether the acting president, his cabinet, Cedras and his top staff, and the head of the state police would all resign from office and allow the return to power of the elected president. A previously negotiated agreement plus two UN Security Council resolutions spelled out the precise terms, and all had to be honored. We negotiated for hours with General Cedras and the other military and political leaders, but there were always remaining obstacles to a final agreement. We reached deadlock on several key issues. Cedras was willing to resign voluntarily the following year, but not immediately or under pressure. The top military officials also demanded that Aristide officially issue a bill of amnesty. None was willing to leave the country, maintaining that sending any citizen into exile was a violation of the Haitian constitution. At about 3:00 Sunday morning, we decided to adjourn our session, to get some rest and reconsider our proposals.

I find it helpful to establish some kind of personal relationship with key adversaries, so I made a point of engaging Cedras in a more relaxed conversation. As our small group was leaving the room, he told me that he had not been home for several days, and that he had missed the tenth birthday of his youngest son. I sympathized with his inability to act as a proper father, and we recalled that Rosalynn and I had met him and some of his children four years earlier, when we served as monitors of the election in which Aristide became president. At that time, Colonel Cedras was in charge of security for the election.

Although we were never informed of exactly when the military attack would be launched, everyone knew that an American invasion was imminent. I thought it would not come before Monday evening. Quite early Sunday morning I called Rosalynn just to tell her that I was OK but that we were not making any progress in the negotiations. She said, "Jimmy, you need to talk with General Cedras's wife, because she has a great influence on him." So we made arrangements to visit their home, and our negotiating team arrived there at eight o'clock.

We were introduced to the Cedras's seventeen-year-old son, I autographed a photograph of me and their thirteen-year-old daughter taken during the 1990 election, and I gave a pocketknife as a birthday present to their youngest son. Then the general's wife dismissed the children. It was immediately obvious to us that the petite Yannick Cedras was a powerful force in their family.

While we and her husband remained silent, Mrs. Cedras told us that she had been up all night getting ready for our visit. She complained fervently that Americans didn't acknowledge the grandeur of Haiti. She pointed out that Haiti was the oldest black republic on earth; that it had become independent in 1804 when a small group of slaves under inspired leadership defeated the French army, the finest in the world, and drove the French from Haiti. She deplored the poverty of her country and the divisions that had created strife among the people. She said that her father and grandfather had been offered the presidency of Haiti but had refused to go into politics; they wanted to serve the people in other ways. She also said that the Haitians have great pride, and there was no way that foreign invaders could come into their country without any self-respecting Haitian offering his or her life in defense.

She had seen an American special forces team surreptitiously surveying their house and believed that it would be one of the first targets when the invasion came. Mrs. Cedras told us that the previous night she had brought her three children to the room where we were sitting, and they had taken an oath that they would not leave their home but would stay there and die. Finally she said, "There is no way that we will yield." Her presence was overwhelming, and when she finished speaking, all of us remained silent for a minute or two.

Obviously, we thought our mission had failed. I thanked Mrs. Cedras for her frankness and her forceful presentation, and then nodded to General Powell. As the former chairman of the U.S. Joint Chiefs of Staff, he was highly respected by the Haitian military leaders. He said that there were two choices a commander could make when facing overwhelming forces. Either he could commit suicide, in effect, by sacrificing his life and the lives of all those who trusted him, or he could exercise judgment and wisdom by yielding to the superior forces and preserving his life and his troops for another day.

Then I pointed out the difference between waging

peace and waging war. Peace is much more difficult, I said, because it is more uncertain, continuing, and complex. It is easier to say, once and for all, "I know that the forces we face are overwhelmingly superior, but I will give my life for my country, and I'll also permit my family and many of those who look to me for leadership to die with me." I assured General Cedras that he and his military associates would be treated with respect, as we had promised in the written document over which we had been negotiating.

There was a long and very uncomfortable silence, but Mrs. Cedras finally looked at her husband and nodded silently. Then he said, "OK, we'll meet you in our head-quarters in about an hour." This was just one step toward success, but it was a crucial one. I'll never understand completely, but I believe the key factors in the Haitians' decision to resume talks were the inexorability of a massive invasion, their desire to prevent bloodshed, and our pledge that the top military officers would be treated fairly and permitted to work with the leaders of the invading force until the time specified for President Aristide's return to Haiti.

However, back with the military leaders, we were still unable to reach agreement after several hours. Then, Cedras's key assistant burst into the room and announced that U.S. paratroopers were boarding planes to attack Haiti. This news was astonishing to us. The Haitian generals accused us of having misled them by preventing their preparations for an invasion while we professed to be talking peace. Cedras and his associates said that they were breaking off the discussions and leaving to marshal their troops. As a last, desperate ploy, I suggested that we lay the issues before Acting President Jonassaint, so that the civilian leaders could make the final decision.

They reluctantly agreed, and we quickly left through a back door of the large building and entered several armored cars. We drove around an enormous square, filled with thousands of angry demonstrators, to the presidential palace.

Emile Jonassaint was universally ridiculed in America as an aged puppet of Haiti's military dictators. But Rosalynn and I had met him when we had been in Haiti to help monitor two elections, and we knew him as the longtime chief justice of the Haitian Supreme Court and the author of the nation's first democratic constitution. He obviously had the respect of both the civilian and military leaders of the "provisional" government. I explained to Jonassaint and his key cabinet leaders the issues on which we had not been able to agree, while General Cedras and his military associates listened attentively. Knowing that the invasion had already been launched, Jonassaint said simply, "The decision has been made. Haiti chooses peace, not war." Some of his cabinet officers objected strongly and threatened to resign, but he was firm in his commitment. It was his personal courage that prevented a massive military confrontation in Haiti.

By telephone, President Clinton and other top U.S. officials approved our faxed agreement and cleared it with President Aristide, who was in Washington. Finally, after sixty-one planes loaded with paratroopers had been on the way to attack for more than an hour, Emile Jonassaint and I signed the agreement. President Clinton then aborted the operation and ordered the U.S. planes and paratroopers to return to their base.

The next morning, after our team had returned to Washington, a massive military force entered Haiti peacefully, with General Cedras assisting the U.S. commanders to preserve order in the country. Subsequently, I helped to arrange for the Cedras family to move to Panama before President Aristide was scheduled to return. We also ensured that proper compensation was made for the property that the Cedras family agreed to abandon.

The crisis was resolved, and the elected leaders returned to Haiti the following month to assume office.

Earlier in 1994, a serious problem had developed halfway around the world when North Korea persisted in plans to process high-grade uranium, which could be used for warheads in nuclear weapons. When inspectors of the International Atomic Energy Agency were expelled from the country, the global community became deeply concerned, and the United States initiated an effort in the UN Security Council to impose sanctions against North Korea.

For three years, North Korea's President Kim Il Sung had been asking me to come to Pyongyang so that he could explain his position. Now I was informed by Chinese and other experts that North Korea was likely to go to war if the sanctions resolution was approved. They could not accept the branding of their country as an outlaw nation and of their revered, almost worshiped, president as a criminal. The U.S. State Department had been unwilling to approve my intercession, but President Clinton finally gave me permission to make the effort.

Rosalynn and I went first to Seoul to reassure the South Korean leaders about our intentions; then we crossed the demilitarized zone, went to Pyongyang to meet with Kim and other leaders, and returned to South Korea. We were the first people in forty-three years to make this round trip.

During our hours of private conversation in Pyongyang, it was obvious that President Kim was willing to find a way to resolve the differences that had caused the crisis. We knew him as a communist dictator who had precipitated the Korean War and kept his people almost completely isolated from the outside world for more than forty years. But now we heard him extol the virtues of the Christian missionaries who had saved his life when he was a prisoner of the Japanese, promise to cease processing nuclear fuel, express a strong desire for good relations with the United States, and offer to return the remains of all Americans buried in his country during the Korean War.

Although at the time I had no way to confirm his sincerity, I knew that all these commitments would soon be put to the test through Kim's own actions and official U.S.–North Korea negotiations. In addition to being transmitted to Washington, the agreements were announced to the world in a CNN International telecast. It seemed that our mission was completely successful. Not only did the North Koreans agree to cease processing nuclear fuel and to permit the international inspectors to return, but the North Korean president also authorized me to invite South Korean President Kim Young Sam to an unprecedented summit meeting.

Unfortunately, within a month, Kim Il Sung was dead, and, with uncertainty in North Korea about his successor, some of his personal commitments have not been fulfilled. Despite this setback, steady progress has been made to resolve the nuclear issue and some other urgent problems. However, North Korea is still a closed society, and memories of the Korean War leave bitter resentments among those on the Korean peninsula, in the United States, and elsewhere who suffered grave losses during the conflict.

Sometimes our peace efforts involve situations in which the leaders refuse to deal with government officials. Another problem is that almost all of the major wars now taking place in the world are civil conflicts, not hostilities between sovereign nations. It is often unfeasible for U.S. officials or UN representatives to communicate with a revolutionary group attempting to change or overthrow a regime to which our ambassador is accredited or which is a member of the United Nations. So it falls to representatives of The Carter Center or other nongovernmental organizations to serve as the contact point between the warring parties. Since we maintain our unofficial status, representing only The Carter Center, we are generally acceptable even to the most sensitive or suspicious groups.

Obviously, it is important to be careful not to disturb sensitive political situations, and to avoid any encouragement of human rights abuses or violations of peace. It is a firm policy of The Carter Center not to duplicate or compete with efforts by others, and I obtain personal approval from the president of the United States before initiating a peace effort in which our nation is involved. We always make clear to adversaries that our goal is simply to resolve the issue, and we seek commitments from them to cease all activities that violate human rights or international law.

There are more wars today than ever before. At The Carter Center we monitor them all—usually about 110 conflicts at any given time. Some are fairly dormant, but about seventy erupt into violence each year. Thirty are what we call major wars, in which more than 1,000 deaths have occurred on the battlefield. In modern times, there are almost ten civilian deaths, including many women and children, for each soldier killed. The casualties can be horrendous, as we have observed in Bosnia. Many Americans don't realize that in a number of other countries—including Cambodia, Sudan, Ethiopia, Liberia, Burundi, and Rwanda—they have been much greater.

Experiences like the ones we had in Haiti and Korea illustrate, in successes and in shortcomings, some of the peacemaking principles we have developed over the past decade or so at The Carter Center.

PRINCIPLES FOR PEACEMAKERS

1.   Strive to have the international community and all sides in any conflict agree to the basic premise that military force should be used only as a last resort.

2.   Do not interfere with other ongoing negotiation efforts, but offer intercession as an independent mediator when an unofficial presence is the only viable option.

3.   Study the history and causes of the dispute thoroughly. Take advantage of any earlier personal involvement with key leaders and citizens of a troubled nation as a basis for building confidence and trust.

4.   Seek help from other mediators, especially those who know the region and are known and respected there. (In Africa, for instance, we join forces with distinguished leaders from that continent.)

5.   Be prepared to go back and forth between adversaries who cannot or will not confront each other.

6.   Explore all possible beneficial influences on those who have created the problem. Use the news media to bring pressure on recalcitrant parties.

7.   Be willing to deal with the key people in any dispute, even if they have been isolated or condemned by other parties or organizations.

8.   With sensitive international issues, obtain approval from the White House before sending any Americans to take part in negotiations.

9. Insist that human rights be protected, that international law be honored, and that the parties be prepared to uphold mutual commitments.

10. Be willing to listen to detailed explanations and demands from both sides, even when they seem unreasonable or unrealistic.

11. Ensure that each concession is equaled or exceeded by benefits. Both sides must be able to feel that they have gained a victory.

12. Tell the truth, even when it may not contribute to a quick agreement. Only by total honesty can a mediator earn the trust and confidence of both sides.

13. Be prepared for criticism, no matter what the final result may be.

14. Be willing to risk the embarrassment of failure.

15. Never despair, even when the situation seems hopeless.

We work with many others not only to seek peaceful resolution of conflicts but also to attempt to resolve the root causes of despair by increasing the production of basic food grains, improving health care, and supporting the growth of democracy. At The Carter Center, we don't believe that any peace effort, even if it is successful, will be lasting unless people have some control or influence over their own government. If dictators continue to be in charge, they are very likely to persecute their people and deprive them of equal treatment under the law. Eventually, another war will break out. In many countries, we have helped monitor democratic elections, to assure that they are honest, fair, and safe, and that the results are trusted and accepted by the people.

Often military adversaries vying for political power are so filled with hatred that they cannot bring themselves to seek peace through direct or indirect communication. Even when both sides come to realize that they can't prevail on the battlefield, they still reject our offers to shuttle back and forth between them. In a few cases, free elections provide an alternative. When proposing this, we often rely on self-delusion—a major factor in politics. Almost anyone seeking an elective office is convinced: "If the process is honest and the voters know me and these other jokers who are candidates, *surely* they will vote for *me*."

The Carter Center has developed a reputation for ensuring either that an election will be completely fair or that any fraud will be exposed and condemned. Our initial invitation to serve as monitors often comes from a ruling party that has achieved office through military force and wants us to authenticate its democratic victory, which it usually assumes will be inevitable. Sometimes the initiative comes from adversaries who suspect that the incumbents will try to steal the election. When all the major parties want us to monitor the procedure and we feel that our services are needed, we agree to participate. Although we never seek any legal authority, we gain great influence to correct problems as they develop because both sides soon realize that our public condemnation of their improprieties can be quite damaging and that our judgment on the legitimacy of the election will be accepted as final by the international community.

I consider this service vital in many cases, either to prevent or resolve a conflict or to assure that, with freedom in a new democracy, the will of the people will improve the policies of a formerly authoritarian and abusive government. Only in a democratic country can real, lasting peace take root.

CHAPTER SEVEN

Faith in Action

All of us wonder about our real purpose in life. For a few, this question can become a profound source of anxiety. When we have inner turmoil that needs healing, uncertainty about the meaning of life can grow into an obsession with self-pity or depression. For many people, the best solution is to think of something we can do for someone else.

The Bible says that God will wipe away our tears (Revelation 21:4). Wiping away someone else's tears is sometimes necessary to help us dispel our own. No matter what we seek in life, we are more likely to find it if we are not self-centered but concentrate on something or someone outside ourselves.

In many ways, Rosalynn and I were devastated after my

defeat for reelection as president in 1980. We had really wanted another four years in the White House and had many plans for ourselves and our nation. Now all these hopes were shattered. And, at the age of fifty-six, I was too young to consider retirement.

After a few days of considering other possibilities that didn't appeal to either of us, we decided definitely to return home. We still had no idea what to do, but we learned from our financial trustees that our warehouse business had suffered heavy losses while we were away, and we were almost a million dollars in debt. It seemed that we might have to sell all our farmland to pay what we owed. In about three months, however, a large agricultural corporation decided to enter the peanut market, and they bought our warehouse and six others in the Southeast to give them an adequate supply of this crop. The sale price was almost enough to pay our debts.

When my term in office expired, we moved with Amy back to Plains, where she enrolled in the public school and we became, once again, full and active members of our local church. As we repaired our house and grounds, put a floor in the attic to store possessions accumulated during the past nine years of public service and campaigning, became reacquainted with our farms and woodlands, and settled our urgent business affairs, we also tried to inventory what we might have to invest in a productive future life. We would build The Carter Center and write our memoirs. We also became involved with another interesting and challenging project: Habitat for Humanity.

Working with Habitat for Humanity has changed our

attitude about how we can relate to those who really need help. In building homes with "God's people in need," we follow a few simple rules. Volunteers work side by side with families who have been living in subhuman dwellings. The future homeowners are chosen and most other decisions made by a committee formed within the local community. There is no charity involved, if "free handouts" is the meaning of *charity*. The homeowners must contribute about 500 hours of work on their own and neighbors' houses, and they must also repay the full price of their homes, to which they will then have clear title. This is possible because the houses built by Habitat are relatively inexpensive: much of the construction work is done by volunteers, and Habitat's policy is not to charge interest. This makes monthly payments possible from a very low income, even from a welfare check.

One of the greatest benefits of a decent home is that it gives its owners, often for the first time, a sense of success and fulfillment. Working with other volunteers on tasks ranging from clearing a lot to hanging curtains, laying carpets, sodding a lawn, and planting a garden, the new homeowners come to realize that they can take on difficult tasks and perform them. When they have moved into their own new houses, they are full-fledged citizens, with a new status and additional responsibilities. They must pay taxes, maintain their homes, and seek jobs. Although Habitat cannot guarantee our homeowners employment, some of the volunteers observe their good qualities and often guide them to jobs that can support a new and self-sufficient life.

Habitat for Humanity was founded by Millard and

Linda Fuller. Millard is a dynamic and charismatic lawyer; he and Linda are two of our closest friends. As students at the University of Alabama, Millard and a partner, Morris Dees, set up a number of imaginative entrepreneurial ventures. For example, they collected the best recipes from the mothers of other students and published them in fast-selling books. In addition, they obtained from university records information about every student and sought orders from their parents to deliver cakes or flowers on their children's birthdays. (Morris Dees later became a famous civil rights lawyer and the founder of the Southern Poverty Law Center in Montgomery, Alabama.)

As a young lawyer and entrepreneur, Millard continued to be innovative and enthusiastic, and he was soon a millionaire, with so much money coming in from his business ventures that he gave up his law practice. One day, much to Millard's shock, Linda told him that she was leaving him and going to New York for marriage counseling because he was neglecting his family and seemed interested only in getting rich. Millard followed her and begged her to come back to him. Finally, in desperation, he declared that he would give away all his money and join Linda in any work that they could share.

He kept his promise, and they soon settled on the biracial Koinonia Farm. There, for five years, the Fullers joined in building houses for destitute black families. Then they and their four children spent three years in Zaire as missionaries supported by several Christian denominations and continued to develop the idea of organizing Habitat for Humanity.

The Fullers say that Habitat uses the "theology of the hammer" or the "economics of Jesus." By the time this book is published, Habitat will have completed homes for more than 50,000 needy families in about 1,500 communities in the United States and in forty-five foreign countries.

Now Rosalynn and I send out a large number of fundraising letters for Habitat, spend occasional days on projects near our home, and join with others for a week each year to build a number of complete homes. To date, we have done this in more than a dozen communities, including New York City; Tijuana, Mexico; the Cheyenne River Sioux reservation in South Dakota; Liberty City in Miami; Philadelphia; Chicago; Winnipeg, Manitoba; Atlanta; Charlotte, North Carolina; and the Watts area in Los Angeles. In 1996, our project site was near Budapest in Hungary, and we plan to be in the Appalachian Mountain region in Kentucky in 1997.

Rosalynn and I enjoy vacations, and we could go to Hawaii or on a Caribbean cruise every summer for about the same amount it costs us to travel to one of the Habitat building sites. But when I look back on the last twelve years or so, I see that some of my most memorable and gratifying experiences were when I joined other volunteers and worked to exhaustion building a house alongside the family who would live there. These exhilarating occasions have been rare in my life, but I have learned that the opportunities are always there, for any of us.

It is difficult to describe the emotions of our Habitat workdays. We see extraordinary commitments and lives changed among formerly forgotten people. On our first

project, a nineteen-apartment dwelling in Lower Man-
hattan, one of our homeowners, a former chef named Roosevelt, was sleeping on the street when we met him. He
worked with us on this large and difficult project, and when
it was finished he lived on the first floor. Because of his fine
character and good work, he became the building superintendent. One day while we were installing the roof, I finished a cold drink and began to crumple the aluminum can.
Roosevelt startled me by shouting, "Don't bend the can!" I
discovered that this was part of his livelihood; he supported
himself and began making his monthly payments by collecting empty cans and bottles.

Later, at one of our projects in Puno, Peru, on the shore
of Lake Titicaca, Rosalynn and I observed the local people
building their homes far above the tree line, at an altitude
of about 13,000 feet. There seemed to be an unspoken
assignment of tasks, with the men doing most of the laying
of concrete blocks and carpentry work on the homes. The
women, some with babies strapped on their backs, were
using small chisels and tin cans to dig a channel several
hundred yards through solid rock to bring water from a
small spring to the new dwellings.

In northwest Nicaragua, we visited a Habitat project
with President Daniel Ortega and other Sandinista leaders.
There, in an area with an almost pure clay soil too poor for
farming, people were living in wide open, three-sided
shacks built of limbs and grass. The clay, however, made
excellent bricks and roof tiles, and the homeowners and
their families were molding thousands of them by hand. A
small power saw was used to cut a few boards from the local

trees (which happened to be mahogany), to create roof
trusses held together by twisted strands of used barbed
wire. Only some mortar mix and a few nails had to be pur-
chased, so the cash needed for a house for ten people was
only the equivalent of $300 in U.S. currency. When homes
were completed for every family in the village, the people
continued their new industry: manufacturing and selling
high-quality bricks and roofing tiles to other villages.

I asked a woman who lived in a Habitat home in
Philadelphia what kind of dwelling she had had before. She
replied, "There were just two good things in that old place:
me and my husband." Another woman standing nearby
said, "I've got two teenage sons, whom I rarely saw in the
evenings in my other place. Every time the phone rang, I
thought it was the police calling about my boys. Now,
they're home every night, and they bring their friends to
watch television, play games, or study. They said the other
day that they used to be too ashamed to let anyone know
where they lived."

A Habitat family in Olympia, Washington, had been
living in an abandoned automobile. One of their children
was an eight-year-old boy, who was very excited about getting a new house. When the family was chosen, he jumped
up and down and shouted, "We won! We won! We won!"
After the Habitat home was finished and the family moved
in, the little boy attended a different school. He had always
been in the "slow learners'" class, but when he moved his
records were lost and he was put in a regular class by mistake. No one noticed the error, and at the end of the first
half year, his lowest grade was a B. Now he is still learning

with the smartest students. This is what having a decent home for the first time in life can do.

As I said earlier, Rosalynn's and my primary responsibility is to The Carter Center. One of the bases for this work is to avoid duplicating or competing with what others are doing. This means that if the World Bank, UN agencies, the U.S. government, or Harvard University is dealing effectively with a problem, we turn our attention to other issues. Almost by default, then, much of our overseas work is in Latin America and Africa—regions that tend to be neglected by other governmental and social agencies.

As in Habitat, working on common projects as equals tends to forge almost instantaneous and binding ties among people, regardless of geographic separation or other differences. In the ghetto areas of great cities, on American Indian reservations, and in the villages of Chad, Haiti, Ethiopia, and Sudan, I have seen the emotional effect of sharing an opportunity for a better home, an increased yield of food grains, or relief from a devastating disease. There is an instant and overwhelming melding of cultures, languages, and interests into a spirit of friendship and love.

Much more than when I was president, I now understand the potential benefits from programs among some of the world's poorest people. Unfortunately, relatively little attention is given to these opportunities for our country to demonstrate world leadership by sharing a small portion of our great wealth. For some reason, the words "foreign aid" have become dirty words in politics, to be avoided by any candidate for public office.

There is a dramatic difference between what American citizens believe and want and what our government is doing. A 1995 public opinion poll showed that almost two-thirds of Americans agree that economic growth in poor foreign countries helps us, and that the United States should use part of our wealth to assist less fortunate people abroad. Those surveyed also thought that our foreign aid was, on average, 18 percent of the U.S. budget. The actual figure is less than 1 percent. Norway gives almost 3 percent of its gross national income to humanitarian causes, while the United States gives only one-sixth of 1 percent. Of all the industrialized nations, we are by far the stingiest in sharing our wealth with others. And today the U.S. Congress is making further large reductions in USAID funds for Africa, which are used for food, medicine, the control of AIDS and polio, and the promotion of democracy and peace. This selfish policy betrays the concept of greatness for the world's only superpower.

Despite our government's attitudes, Americans always have been a generous people. Privately, we give more than $4 billion to humanitarian causes in other countries. The work of CARE, Save the Children, and other secular relief organizations is well known. Religious groups, including missionary organizations, play a powerful role as well.

Too often we think about evangelism only as preaching the Gospel, but there is also a powerful ministry in the alleviation of suffering, reaching out in harmony, respect, and partnership to others, and sharing life. One of the most significant aspects of the ministry of Jesus was the combination of his religious witnessing with his personal service to those he encountered. His spirit lives on today in the work of people like Jerome and Joann Ethredge.

In 1976, Jerome Ethredge was an agronomist at the experiment station near Plains. Always active in the work of our church congregation, Jerome eventually realized that he had more to offer than just his service on Sundays among relatively self-sufficient farmers and neighbors. With no previous religious experience except as lay members of our church, he and Joann volunteered for full-time service as Baptist missionaries. After receiving basic religious instruction and French language training, they were assigned to Togo, in West Africa. The ministry of Jerome and Joann provides a vivid demonstration of the inseparability of faith and works.

For seven years the Ethredges served in the large town of Sokodé, where they offered language and other education courses to young people who were willing to visit their small Christian library. Hundreds learned to read and write, but few had any interest in the religious aspect of the center. In time, Jerome and Joann decided they wanted to move deeper into the agricultural regions, where the needs were greater and they could use Jerome's experience in agronomy.

When a new missionary came to Sokodé, the Ethredges moved to the small village of Moretan, in the East Mono area of Togo, where most of the people worshiped various aspects of nature. All attempts by both Muslim and Christian evangelists in this region had failed. Within sixty miles of their new home, there were only five small Muslim and two Catholic congregations. Jerome and Joann decided to combine Christian witnessing with attempts to alleviate the people's urgent physical needs.

One of the most obvious needs was for drinking water. Some lucky villagers had a water hole even during the dry season, but many lived miles from any supply. In one village, half the women had to walk sixteen miles each day to fetch clay jars of water, alternating this duty with others who cared for all the children and performed the rest of the community chores. With financial support from some Baptists in North Carolina, Jerome began to seek water supplies with a truck-mounted diesel drill. He had to penetrate a regional layer of granite at or near the surface, making the operation slow and tedious. Assisted only by the local residents, he went to every village within eighty miles of his home base and drilled 167 wells, 130 successful and capped with hand pumps. Now every village has a clean and healthy water supply.

During this time, Jerome also used his agronomy skills to increase greatly the production of basic food crops. Recognizing the shortage of protein in the villagers' diets, he acquired a bulldozer and constructed twenty-one deep ponds that fill during the rainy seasons. Located to serve as many villages as possible, the ponds were stocked with fish, and they now provide a continuing new source of food.

While Jerome was busy with these and other projects, Joann worked with families on intensive health and education projects. She has helped to build a pharmacy in Moretan and arranges transportation to a distant regional hospital for people too ill to be treated locally.

The greatest problem of the East Mono people was that they were isolated from the rest of Togo during four months of the rainy season, when the Mono River became an impassable torrent. Only one small dugout canoe, hewn from a tree trunk, was available to cross the stream in emergencies. Working again with local people and his Baptist friends from North Carolina, some of whom came to Togo as volunteers, Jerome designed and eventually built a bridge across the river. Rosalynn and I were amazed when we visited the Ethredges to find a 230-foot concrete span. It was hard to believe that this vital transportation link had been built by one missionary and a few volunteers.

All this work has been done in a quiet and self-effacing way, in complete cooperation with the Togolese people, and always in the name of Christ. The Ethredges demonstrate their religious faith by their work in classrooms and health clinics, behind ox-drawn plows, on hospital trips in a dilapidated van, on a bulldozer, or operating a borehole drill.

Most of the evangelistic work is now being done by new Togolese Christians. Each group has a recognized leader who preaches and organizes Bible teaching and other church activities. The oldest is just thirty-five years old. This has been the religious result of the Ethredges' work as the only Christian missionaries in the region. There are now eighty-one church congregations in East Mono, with a total of 5,000 active members, more than one-third of the Baptists in the nation!

Most of The Carter Center's humanitarian programs are in Africa, involved directly with health care and the production of food by small farmers.

A few years ago, leaders of the World Health Organization, UNICEF, the World Bank, the UN Development Program, and the Rockefeller Foundation were all striving in their own ways to immunize children throughout the world. However, they were never able to reach more than 20 percent of the total, primarily because they were not cooperating with one another. The Task Force for Child Survival was created and located at The Carter Center so that all five organizations could work as a team. Within only five years, with no appreciable increase in funding or personnel, 80 percent of the world's children were immunized against polio, measles, and other contagious diseases.

The Carter Center has also formed a task force on disease eradication, which is continually analyzing human ailments to ascertain which ones might be totally eradicated. Two—polio and dracunculiasis (guinea worm)—have already been targeted, and others—like measles, yaws, and leprosy—will probably join the list in the near future.

The key to all these efforts is Dr. Bill Foege, a tall, lanky Iowan and devout Lutheran who has combined his deep religious faith with humanitarian work. He is one of the most effective medical doctors on earth in preventing dis-

eases, having been instrumental in the eradication of
smallpox in 1977, head of the Centers for Disease Control
for almost ten years, and later executive director of The
Carter Center. The opportunities for our involvement in
health programs come from his inspirational work. He has
forgone a high income so that he could continue to serve
people in the most remote, seriously afflicted, and often
unknown communities in the developing world. Many
other health experts are willing to make similar sacrifices
just to work with Dr. Foege.

He is a fine companion, with wonderful stories to tell of
his experiences in the battle against disease. Once he was in
the deep jungle of Biafra during the final stages of smallpox
eradication. The challenge was to immunize hundreds of
people scattered in small, isolated villages. He went to see
the regional chief, explained the program, and asked for a
guide to take him to the widespread communities. The
chief looked up at the six-foot, seven-inch American and
replied, "No, it will be easier if we bring them all here." He
directed his drummer to commence sending a message,
and the next morning a stream of people crowded into the
village square. After they were all immunized, Dr. Foege
asked the chief, "How in the world did you induce them to
come here just for an immunization program?" The chief
replied, "I told them to come if they wanted to see the
tallest man in the world."

The opportunity to perform neighborly service for
needy people is not limited to individuals, and not all cor-

porate leaders are as hardened toward human illness and death as are the tobacco company executives. It may be a surprise to many readers to learn that American corporations are deeply involved in some of the most effective humanitarian programs in the Third World. I have found that, when corporate leaders understand a problem, they are often quite generous, and their employees are proud and enthusiastic.

Guinea worm is a terrible disease that, until recently, afflicted people in India, Pakistan, Yemen, and nineteen nations across the continent of Africa. Villagers who drink water from stagnant ponds ingest the minuscule eggs that, within a year, grow into worms more than two feet long. These parasites then sting the skin from the inside and emerge, over a period of weeks, through the festering sore. As the sufferer wades into the pond for pain relief or to secure more water, the worms lay thousands of eggs, and the cycle is repeated. There are several ways to eradicate the disease. One is to drill borehole wells that provide pure water, as Jerome Ethredge did in Togo. Another is to put into the water a chemical called Abate, which kills the eggs.

In tests in Pakistan, we learned that using a filter cloth, finely woven and resistant to rot, would be the most effective technique for providing safe, potable water. However, such fibers and fabric did not exist, and even inferior substitutes were very expensive. I went to see Edgar Bronfman, then one of the major owners of the DuPont Company, and described our problem. He soon brought the issue to DuPont's board of directors, and they agreed to develop a special fiber and provide enough of the cloth, at no cost to us, for our entire effort. President Lanty Smith and other executives of Precision Fabrics Group volunteered to have their production facility weave the fabric. Later, American Cyanamid Company offered to give us a worldwide supply of Abate so that we could attack the problem by treating the water in some smaller ponds.

In 1988, when we began our eradication program, we found 3.5 million people suffering from guinea worm. As of the end of 1995, there were only 130,000 cases, with more than half the total in an area of southern Sudan where a thirteen-year war has prevented health workers from getting access to many villages.

I went to DuPont headquarters to report on our progress, where President Ed Woolard and about 600 top managers, scientists, and salesmen were assembled under a large tent. When I thanked them for their gift and showed a brief film demonstrating its almost miraculous results, most of them were weeping—and so was I.

One of the most profitable medicines marketed by Merck & Company, the large pharmaceutical firm, is Mectizan, used to prevent heartworm in dogs and other animals. A few years ago, one of their research scientists discovered that the same drug was effective for humans. Just one tablet each year could stop the development of onchocerciasis, or river blindness. For people living alongside rapidly flowing streams in thirty-six African and Latin American countries, the sting of a little black fly first causes a terrible rash like permanent poison ivy. Later there are splotches on the skin that resemble leprosy, and nodules— puffed-up places as big as golf balls—develop on the body. After twelve years, total blindness results.

The chief executive officer of Merck, Dr. Roy Vagelos, came to The Carter Center and met with Dr. Foege to tell him about this discovery. He learned that there were more than 30 million people who needed the treatment. Dr. Vagelos said that if The Carter Center could develop a procedure to deliver the Mectizan tablets, Merck would provide them to all the affected villages in the world, free of charge.

To meet this challenge, a very modest but successful young businessman from Texas, John Moores, established and personally financed the River Blindness Foundation, which has helped to distribute a total of 50 million Mectizan tablets, reaching more than $14^{1}/_{2}$ million people in 1995.

Rosalynn and I recently accompanied Dr. Vagelos to a small village in southern Chad where every person had river blindness; many of them were totally blind. Although lost sight cannot be restored with the annual tablets, for those not yet blind the illness will not progress further, and for everyone in the village, the terrible itching and sores have disappeared. Onchocerciasis is not a further threat to them, and they can now move back into the productive bottomlands near the stream, which they had abandoned to escape the flies.

These are examples of business executives who, because of their personal interest, have helped to make possible the kind of healing that Christ himself exhibited. This corporate generosity has been extremely gratifying, not only for top executives but for all employees. In the main lobby of Merck's headquarters in New Jersey, there is a bigger-than-life statue of a little boy holding one end of a stick, the other end held by his blind father. Everyone who works in this company knows that millions of Africans will never be blind because of their generosity in contributing Mectizan tablets. There are similar opportunities for other leaders in the corporate world.

What was the main thrust of Christ's ministry? Did he just sit under a fig tree telling stories, or stand on a mountain explaining his theology? No. His ministry was tangible proof of his love for everyone, including the sick, the ostracized, and even those who were believed by their neighbors to be suffering the punishment of God for their sins. This was a powerful witness. Christ was a doer, one whose faith took the form of action, not merely words.

It is a real challenge to correlate our religious faith with what we actually do. In his epistle, James says, "For as the body without the spirit is dead, so faith without works is dead also" (James 2:26). James is not suggesting that we should ignore faith and sharing the Good News with others. He is saying that if we have faith, then we must show it by how we live, what we do.

Even in a personal way, we cannot separate faith or belief from our actions or works. When I offered Rosalynn an engagement ring, we both realized that her simple acceptance of it implied the commitment of a lifetime. Similarly, when we accept the free gift of salvation through God's grace, it imposes an obligation—a pleasant one—to serve by striving to live in harmony with his teachings.

Jesus made it plain that he had not come to change "one jot or tittle" of the law (Matthew 5:18), but he went out of his way to demonstrate that a narrow, legalistic interpretation of the Scriptures should not obscure the real meaning of faith in God. He repeatedly forgave and healed people on the Sabbath, reached out to the despised Samaritans and to Roman soldiers and other gentiles, touched lepers and a bleeding woman without considering himself unclean, and condemned merely superficial compliance with the law. These differences with the religious authorities helped lead to his arrest, trial, and crucifixion.

Christ wants us today to follow his example by expanding the meaning of forgiveness, service, and love—all in a practical way. And he goes on to teach that this is the avenue toward personal peace and freedom. We're not putting ourselves in a cage by reaching out to other people—we're doing just the opposite. To me, Christianity is not a submission to restraints; the essence of Christ's teaching is to liberate us and give us peace.

A few blocks from The Carter Center in Atlanta is a place known as Café 458. There, homeless people can get a hug and a warm welcome, sit down at a table, select the meal they prefer, and order it from an attentive waiter. Many of them have serious problems, including addiction to drugs or alcohol. The eleven volunteers, who live next door, get to know the "guests" well enough to refer them to treatment centers or to work with them directly.

A salesman, A. B. Short, and his wife, Ann Conner, a nurse-practitioner, opened the café in 1988, knowing that many people needed help but also realizing that standing in soup lines every day offered little permanent benefit.

The guests make table reservations for a month at a time, with extensions provided they are working steadily toward the goals they have set for improving their lives. More than 1,600 people have passed through Café 458, in the process regaining some of their dignity as human beings, and many of them now help as volunteers. Among those who have been through the drug rehabilitation program, only 8 percent have relapsed.

One man named Roy said he had slept in a Dunkin' Donuts Dumpster for ten years before being welcomed at Café 458. He then stopped selling cocaine, took a job with a landscaping company, made foreman in six months, and began to believe in God. He finally met his daughter, and he no longer lives in an enormous trash container. Treated with care and respect, Roy has found a new life.

Many of the people mentioned in this book are fairly well known, but publicity is not necessary for an inspirational life. We recognize Mother Teresa, Billy Graham, Pope John Paul II, and others who have become famous because, in their own ways, they have demonstrated their Christian faith. But Rosalynn and I have had many friends,

most of them unknown except among their close neighbors, who have been able to live their faith by combining
the apparently conflicting elements of strength and gentleness. These are the people who have motivated us and
helped to transform our lives.

When I was growing up in Archery, a fine young woman
named Annie Mae Hollis worked for my parents. After I
left home for college, she moved to Albany, Georgia, where
she married a man named Rhodes and got a job helping in
a wealthy woman's house.

When my father was terminally ill, Mother called Annie
Mae and said, "I can't nurse Earl and take care of all the
family at the same time. Could you come back and help
me?" So Annie Mae moved back to Plains to be with our
family. I will never forget that when my father breathed his
last breath on July 22, 1953, Annie Mae Rhodes was
holding him in her arms.

Annie Mae had a good life. Because of her sterling
qualities, she never lacked a job, and she became almost a
full member in the families she served as a maid. She was a
stalwart member of her church and a counselor to others in
her congregation. She owned her small but attractive
home, which was a focal point for socializing, especially
among her family. Her handicapped brother lived with her,
able to move around, mostly in his wheelchair, and even
assist in the household chores.

In July 1994, Annie Mae was sleeping when, in the
middle of the night, her brother woke her and said, "It's
been raining for hours, and the radio says the water's
coming." She said, "The water's not coming. I've been here

thirty-seven years, and water's never come in my house."
But he insisted, so she got up, found her Bible, and tried to
pull her old dog out of the house. Before she could get to
the car, the water was waist deep, so she clung to the car
door handle until some rescue workers picked her and her
brother up in a boat. Her dog drowned, and her car, her
house, and everything in it were destroyed. Annie Mae lost
all she had, except a Bible and the small and now water-
ravaged lot where her house had stood.

Rosalynn and I were in Japan when we heard about the
flood, and we didn't know anything about Annie Mae's
plight. Two women from Atlanta went down to Albany
within a couple of days to help in the relief work, and they
met this extraordinary seventy-seven-year-old woman,
who was hobbling around trying to see what was left of her
community. She was helping to rejuvenate everybody's
spirits by saying, "We need not be concerned. The Lord
will take care of us. We have to have faith in God and in
ourselves."

The two women were so impressed with Annie Mae
Rhodes' faith that they asked about her life. She mentioned
in passing that she had worked for our family about forty
years ago, but she said, "Don't bother Mr. Jimmy. I don't
want to be a burden to him." Nonetheless, the women
wrote me a letter and described what had happened.

Some of us volunteers with Habitat for Humanity
helped Annie Mae build a small new house on her lot, for
which she will have a clear title by making monthly payments. She has decided, since she's elderly and doesn't have
any children, and since her brother is also quite old, that

she's going to deed the house back to Habitat when she passes away.

Annie Mae's simple faith, expressed in works, is what James describes in his New Testament epistle: "My brothers and sisters, whenever you face trials of any kind, consider it nothing but joy, because you know that the testing of your faith produces endurance; and let endurance have its full effect, so that you may be mature and complete, lacking in nothing" (James 1:2–4). Most of us don't know from personal experience how people like Annie Mae Rhodes live in potential flood plains, the ghettos of America's cities, or the Third World nations of Sierra Leone, Ethiopia, Haiti, Niger, or Chad. But James tells us to let our religious faith inspire us to help alleviate their suffering.

People like the Ethredges, Bill Foege, Roy Vagelos, A. B. Short, Ann Conner, and Annie Mae Rhodes show that simple acts can be transforming and highly significant. Life is made up of an accumulation of habits, shaped by the day-by-day, hour-by-hour decisions that we make. There's a need for me, as a Christian, to take a look at myself and my relationship to others, and ask whenever I make a decision, "What would Christ do?" When I remember and act accordingly, my life can be made more resistant to worry, fear, frustration—and boredom!

"Enduring faith" describes Annie Mae Rhodes, who survived the flood that destroyed her home. But what would I do under the stress of a terrible loss? Could I be equally resilient, forceful, courageous, and innovative, not based on my own physical strength or intelligence or ability to borrow money or to buy another house, but based upon my faith in God? What was Annie Mae's most important possession—an automobile that has now been hauled off and crushed, an old dog, a modest house that is now just a pile of splintered lumber, or her religious faith, which sustained her in a crisis? Hundreds of flood victims and rescue workers were inspired by the quiet faith of a stooped, confident, quiet seventy-seven-year-old woman.

CHAPTER EIGHT

Crossing Barriers

It is perfectly legitimate and even admirable for Americans to promote their personal values through either religious or political processes. As I have said elsewhere in this book, the role of spiritual leaders in America's civil rights movement is a wonderful example of the healing role faith can play in our national life. But when we attempt to use our government to force others to worship as we do, or treat those who differ as second-class citizens, then we are violating the basic tenets of a democracy.

Unfortunately, many people of faith today focus more on the quarrels that divide us than on the values that unite us. As a traditional Baptist, I am deeply concerned about arguments that have driven wedges between members of our denomination. I know and respect many devout believers who accept every word in the Bible as literally true. In a number of American school systems, in state legislatures, and in the federal courts, the debate rages about whether creationism should be taught in high school science classes. Even though some people are obsessed with both sides of these issues, arguing them is fruitless.

Christians can buttress their arguments on almost any subject by emphasizing certain selected Scripture verses and then claiming that they should be applied universally. But when we do this, we're using the Bible as a rationalization for our personal preferences, which we assume are correct. The resulting divisions are usually based on the presumption of preeminence by one group over others: "God and I are right, and anyone who disagrees with us is wrong." I'm always concerned about such "true believers."

About twenty years ago, some of these Christians began to forge a political union with the more conservative wing of the Republican party. This wedding between the political and the religious would have conflicted with my belief in separation of church and state even if it had been with Democrats.

Now leaders of the highly organized Christian Right have successfully injected into America's political debate some divisive questions. The most vivid examples involve sexual preference, which obviously has highly personal and emotional overtones. The focus seems to be colored by political considerations. For example, almost all Protestants, including many allied with the Christian Right, will now acknowledge divorce as an acceptable choice for unhappy couples, and they rarely speak out against "fornication" or adultery, although Jesus repeatedly condemned these acts. It is much easier and more convenient for heterosexual Christians to attack homosexuals, based primarily on selected verses in the Old Testament. They fail to acknowledge that homosexuality was never mentioned by Jesus.

Some prominent Christian leaders even claim that AIDS is God's special punishment on sinners and that AIDS victims should be treated accordingly. In the time of Jesus, many thought this way about people with leprosy, who were also looked upon as condemned by God and capable of contaminating their neighbors. Jesus set an example for us by reaching out to them, loving and healing them.

Other Christians and the general public must not condone, even by silence, the judgmental attitudes promoted by a few demagogic religious and political leaders. That a premise originates within the religious community tends to authenticate it among those who want to justify their personal prejudices. It would be a tragedy if a platform of "I hate gay men and women" proved to be a route to political office in the United States of America.

The Gospels make it clear that dividing and despising people according to sexual behavior, religious or ethnic background, or other personal traits was never Jesus' way. The fourth chapter of John's Gospel describes a significant encounter between Jesus and a Samaritan woman. She was known as promiscuous, having lived with five "husbands" in succession, and was condemned by her own people. She never went to the well during the cooler hours of the day with the other women but went at noon, by herself. We can imagine that the other women walked together, exchanged the gossip of the village, and talked about their children or grandchildren while she watched from her window until they came back to their homes.

Furthermore, this woman was a Samaritan. The Samaritans were Jews whose ancestors were Abraham, Isaac, and Jacob and who worshiped the same Almighty God as all other Jews. However, the Samaritans were convinced that only five books belonged in the Bible, and they recognized Moses as the only prophet. They looked upon Mt. Gerizim, not Jerusalem, as their holy place. When the Israelites returned home from exile, some of those who had stayed in Samaria had intermarried with gentiles, and these were excluded from rebuilding Jerusalem.

Subsequently, the Samaritans were despised outcasts who were considered to have betrayed their religion. An Israelite on whom a Samaritan's shadow had fallen required ceremonial cleansing before he or she could enter the temple to worship.

One day, while his disciples were away buying food, Jesus approached the Samaritan woman and said, "Will you give me a drink?" Although its significance may not be obvious at first, this simple act was a startling demonstration against racial or religious prejudice. All Southerners who lived during the time of racial segregation can recognize its bold nature. As a child, when my parents were away on a trip, I lived, ate, and slept with our African-American neighbors, Jack and Rachel Clark. My black boyhood friends and I played and went fishing together, plowed with mules side by side, and played on the same baseball team.

But when I carried water to a group of people working in the field, it would have been inconceivable for black workers and white ones, including me, to drink out of the same dipper. For Jesus to drink from the Samaritan woman's cup was a powerful symbolic act of acceptance and friendship.

Amazed by Jesus' openness to her, the Samaritan woman engaged him in conversation, and, after just a few minutes of simple talk, she became convinced that Jesus was the Messiah.

During her brief encounter with Jesus, a miracle occurred—not a physical miracle but a spiritual one. Because Jesus broke down all the racial, social, and religious barriers between them, this woman became a messenger around whom the villagers gathered to hear the Good News about a man whom they soon knew as "truly the Savior of the world." The encounter between Christ and the Samaritan woman is one of the most gratifying examples of salvation in the Bible. This woman was given what she needed most: acceptance, forgiveness, and a new life.

Unfortunately, we are usually quite comfortable with our prejudices. In my book *Turning Point* I described the racial discrimination that existed over thirty years ago in the Deep South. At that time segregation was legally enforced. But although the laws have changed, our society now is almost as segregated as it was then, not just in the South but in Boston, Chicago, Los Angeles, and New York City.

Christians and believers of every faith have a responsibility to help break down barriers based on race, sex, religion, and other differences. Jesus used just one cup of water to demonstrate the overcoming of prejudice. We have opportunities to do the same.

When Paul wrote, "There is no longer Jew or Greek, there is no longer slave or free, there is no longer male and female; for all of you are one in Christ Jesus" (Galatians 3:28), he was expressing a revolutionary tenet of Christianity. This was a leveling of the ground, an uplifting of those who felt despised, and a warning to those who considered themselves superior. Notice that Paul included gender as one of the distinctions no longer to be recognized by believers. Most people don't claim publicly the right to discriminate against those who are poor, those who come from Asia or South America, or those whose skin is black or brown. But many still maintain the right to discriminate against people because they are female.

There was gross discrimination against women in ancient times. They were often treated as chattel, or worse. Demosthenes, a famous Greek orator and writer, described the attitude of the men who belonged to one of the competitive religious cults that worshiped a goddess: "Our mistresses are for pleasure. Our concubines are to meet our day-to-day bodily needs. Our wives are to produce legitimate children and to be trusted guardians of our homes."

By contrast, Jesus ministered to women, even to prostitutes, and exalted them in general to be equal with men in his service. We know from the New Testament that it was the women who helped care for Jesus during his ministry.

Unlike the male disciples, who fled in fear of their lives, the women were there when he was crucified: "There were also women looking on afar off: among whom was Mary Magdalene, and Mary the mother of James, and Salome; who also, when he was in Galilee followed him, and ministered unto him, and many other women which came up with him unto Jerusalem" (Mark 15:40, 41). Not only that, but we know from Paul and Peter, as they wrote their epistles, that after Christ's death, women played the roles of preachers, missionaries, disciples, and leaders in the Church.

Many early translators of the biblical texts chose words that prescribed a lesser role for women, expressing the male-dominant attitudes that prevailed in their societies at the time. The same prejudice continues today, with some contemporary religious leaders even extrapolating from the temptation of Eve in Genesis to a condemnation of all women as responsible for original sin.

In some states today, the official Baptist policy is to expel from the convention any church that ordains a woman as pastor and to condemn those that have women serving as deacons. In one of our major seminaries, in fact, where I had made the graduation speech the previous year, the new fundamentalist president began firing all professors who believed that women should be permitted to serve as deacons or ministers.

Those who believe in repressing the aspirations of women like to find Bible verses that seem to support their position. It is true that, under certain local circumstances, the apostle Paul made statements that seem to restrict the activities of Christian women. Perhaps these ideas were derived from his background as a Pharisee or were designed to resolve specific social problems in a troubled New Testament church. In a letter to the Ephesians, Paul wrote, "Wives, submit yourselves unto your husbands, as unto the Lord. For the husband is the head of the wife, even as Christ is head of the church." But he added, "Husbands, love your wives, even as Christ also loved the church, and gave himself for it. . . . So ought men to love their wives as their own bodies. He that loves his wife loves himself. . . . Let every one of you in particular so love his wife even as himself; and the wife see that she reverence her husband" (Ephesians 5:23–33).

This prescription of *equal* love between husband and wife was a startling improvement over the way wives had been treated in ancient times. But for too long, and among all too many Christians, these and a few other verses have been selectively quoted by men to prevent equal opportunities for women to serve our Savior. Paul's admonition to women to "submit" is an anomaly among the attitudes of Jesus and other New Testament texts, including other more definitive writings of Paul.

In the sixteenth chapter of his epistle to the Romans, Paul mentions the people who played a significant role in the early church's ministry. Ten of the twenty-seven listed are women, and they were top leaders by any standard. He referred to Phoebe as a minister or deacon (not a "deaconess"), Junia as "outstanding among the apostles," and Priscilla and her husband as co-pastors of a church that worked with Paul, "laid down their own necks" for his life, and corrected the Christian beliefs of Apollos, himself a great preacher.

There are similar instances throughout the New Testament, demonstrating vividly that Jesus brought a revolutionary status of equality to women. One of the most remarkable examples is Mary Magdalene, who was cured of her afflictions by Jesus. She became one of the most valued helpers during his ministry, traveling with the disciples and raising money to pay expenses, and, as I noted before, she was extraordinarily loyal and courageous, even when the men abandoned Jesus. We know that Mary Magdalene was present when Jesus was crucified and accompanied his body to the tomb. Most dramatically, she was the first Christian witness after the resurrection of Jesus, who went and announced to the others, "I have seen the Lord."

Most Baptist men have long recognized the inspired leadership of women in our church congregations, in serving other members in countless ways, and in supporting missionary programs, fulfilling the highest commands of our Savior. In almost every case, the dedication and effectiveness of women as Christians have exceeded the contributions of men.

But this has had little effect on the fundamentalists who have taken control of the Southern Baptist Convention. In 1984, they pushed through a resolution denying the ordination of women because "man was first in creation and woman was first in the Edenic [Garden of Eden] fall." This ridiculous statement, based on a convoluted interpretation of some verses in the Book of Genesis, is now the official policy of Southern Baptists.

Although each church congregation is still considered to be autonomous, this decision has had a far-reaching effect. There are approximately 3,350 Baptist churches in Georgia, of which only one has a female pastor. A graduate of the Candler School of Theology at Emory University, she has been serving a small congregation just ten miles from Plains for about a year. During her brief ministry, eight new members have been added to her church, a 35 percent increase. Unfortunately, her church is not a member of our forty-five-church Friendship Association, having been denied membership seven years ago when they elected some women to serve as deacons.

Recently I told an audience about a neighbor of ours, a Methodist pastor assigned to a little church called Morningside. When Rev. Jackson-Adams came, there were only eighteen church members, with just one child in the whole congregation. The new pastor asked the district superintendent, "Why have you given me a church that's heavily in debt and only has a few older members, none of whom are financially able to meet our budget?" The district superintendent replied, "Well, you can't go wrong. Anything you can figure out to close down that church by next December, we will accept. And we will be proud of you because you did it harmoniously."

Rev. Jackson-Adams prayed about it and remembered that in the seminary graduating class there were some Korean students who were ordained as ministers. In Korea, each graduate of a seminary must go to a community and form a new congregation. So the pastor thought about it and decided, "Why don't we try, in effect, to start a church?" The members began visiting families in the community, and by December the church was out of debt. The sanctuary was now almost full. Within another year, Morningside had over 215 members, with even more attending the worship services. They soon had to have two morning services every Sunday and began planning a larger building.

Some local Baptists are discomfited because Rev. Jackson-Adams's first name is Virginia. But this pastor—Jenny, to us—has proven the great, and special, contribution that women have to make in a Christian church, even in a very conservative community like ours.

Although I am a member of Maranatha Baptist Church, which is affiliated with the Southern Baptist Convention, I don't feel exclusively loyal to a particular Christian denomination. In fact, looking back on my life, I remember most favorably the close interrelation among the churches in our hometown. My mother was a Methodist and my father a Baptist; Rosalynn was a Methodist, her mother a Baptist who joined the Methodists to be with her husband; Rosalynn's grandfather was a Baptist and his wife a Lutheran.

Until the mid-1950s, the Plains churches were part-time and our families alternated our church attendance: the first and third Sundays of the month, we went to the Baptist church; the second and fourth Sundays to the Methodist church; and some people, including Rosalynn's family, went to the Lutheran church on fifth Sundays.

Now, among those who attend my Sunday school class at Maranatha, only about 15 percent are Baptists. In addition, many Jews and other non-Christians join us in our Habitat work.

I feel especially sympathetic with the basic religious beliefs of the Mennonites and the Amish, two groups I know well. To me, the essential beliefs of all Christians, including Protestants, Catholics, and Orthodox Christians, are fundamentally compatible. Although a matter of controversy and concern to some, denominational divisions or distinctions are not important in my daily life and actions.

As we learn in the Book of Acts, the few and embattled believers in the early Christian church were united by their euphoric and inspirational sense of the presence of the Holy Spirit. Jesus had lived just a few years earlier and was still described in vivid terms by people who had actually known him. His disciples had walked the dusty streets of the Holy Land with him, had slept in fields with him, had been tried and persecuted with him, had abandoned him during the last few hours of his life, and had then been reunited and inspired by his resurrection. All this shared life experience was a powerful influence for harmony among the early Christians.

But as the church grew in numbers and influence, sharp divisions arose. People considered their own talents or spiritual gifts to be superior. There were ethnically based arguments between Jews and gentiles who had become followers of Christ, and the Christians squabbled over how to share wealth between the rich and poor. They argued about which of the apostles was most prestigious—Paul,

Peter, or Apollos. Some claimed that it was necessary first to be circumcised before becoming a Christian, others that it was not. Was it permissible to eat meat that had been offered to idols, even though the idols were only pieces of carved wood or metal? Questions like these divided the early church. These Christians had let the overarching concepts of faith, love, and forgiveness be obscured by arguments about exactly what was written or said or remembered about past history.

Unfortunately, after 2,000 years of studying and debating these kinds of issues, the Christian church now is probably divided worse than it was in those early days. In almost all denominations, various beliefs have torn us apart, and sometimes entire denominations have split permanently and officially. As a result, there are lawsuits in many states about who has control of a church building or which group has the authority to choose a pastor. There are "inerrantists," who think that every word in the Bible, preferably the King James Version, is literally true. To argue about matters of this kind is divisive and counterproductive, but they are still burning issues within the fundamentalist Christian community.

Looking at the experiences of today, I can imagine a hypothetical church in New Testament times, where 52 percent might have said Peter meant "so-and-so," 30 percent said the opposite, and 18 percent had no opinion. So the 52 percent took over, and then what happened? The 30 percent split off and formed their own congregation. That may have been the first Baptist church!

To outside observers, the divisions among Christians

are incomprehensible and scandalous. While we preach love for one another as a foundation of our faith, many of the leaders of our religious factions vituperate other groups of believers. There is no doubt that most Christians are also dismayed by these disputes.

Recently, I asked my Sunday school class members to list the items that now seem to be supported or condemned most enthusiastically within our various Christian denominations, and they quickly named abortion, homosexuality, mandatory prayer in public schools, use of public funds to support religious education, the ordination of women as priests or church officials, the inerrancy of the Bible, the priesthood of believers, the autonomy of local congregations, the glorification of pastors, and the breakdown of barriers between church and state. All these issues are important and worth debating, but none should become the basis of hatred and exclusion among believers.

I also disagree with Christians who promote the doctrine that God decides in advance who will be accepted—who will be the chosen or "the elect." There is an element of arrogance in making the claim "I have been chosen by God, others have not." The New Testament clearly states, "It is not the Lord's will for any to be lost, but for all to come to repentance" (2 Peter 3:9). And Jesus says, "I shall draw *all* people to myself" (John 12:32). If God is prepared to break down the barriers that divide us, shouldn't we try to do the same?

Noted American evangelist Tony Campolo tells of visiting an all-night diner in Hawaii while suffering from jet lag and being unable to sleep. From his booth, he overheard a conversation among several "ladies of the night." One said that the next day would be her thirty-ninth birthday, and, sadly, she confessed that she had never in her life had a birthday party. Tony secretly arranged with the manager of the diner to throw a surprise party for the woman. The next night, the woman and her friends were stunned and thrilled, and Tony led the group in prayer.

Later, the diner manager asked Tony, "What kind of church do you belong to?" He replied, "I belong to the kind of church that throws birthday parties for whores at three-thirty in the morning." This was Jesus' kind of church.

CHAPTER NINE

Reaching Out

It is not always easy to maintain religious faith when we are faced with tragedy or disappointment. Sometimes we are tempted to blame God or feel that we have been abandoned. Human nature apparently requires that we rationalize and concoct defenses, avoiding responsibility even when our mistakes and failures lead to suffering. We tend to feel that God should understand our secret motivations, our general good intentions, and the special circumstances that caused a problem. It is difficult to believe that tribulations are inevitable in life, much less that they can be used as an opportunity to grow.

In his epistle, James teaches us how to deal with the trials of life, including matters over which we have no control. It may be a limitation of talents and abilities that prevents our reaching cherished goals; it may be the loss of a loved one, or the necessity of facing our own deaths. And James says, surprisingly, that we are to face such trials with joy!

My sister Ruth was a successful author and an evangelist who inspired large audiences and ministered personally to countless troubled people. Even now, as I travel the world a decade after her death, people approach me to say, "Your sister Ruth changed my life."

Her faith was beautiful in every way. She loved people and devoted her ministry primarily to those who had lost hope in life. No matter what had happened to them, whether it was drug addiction, alcoholism, infidelity, or crime, she was able to convince them to place the affliction on the shoulders of Christ and in that way to overcome it. She persuaded people that, through simple faith, they could find a way to use their tribulations for the glory of God.

Ruth used a few verses from James as one of the foundations for her ministry: "Consider it pure joy, my brothers, whenever you face trials of many kinds, because you know that the testing of your faith develops perseverance. Perseverance must finish its work so that you may be mature and complete, not lacking anything. Blessed are those who persevere under trial, because when they have stood the test, they will receive the crown of life that God has promised to those who love him" (James 1:2–4, 12).

James' statement is almost impossible to believe, but I reluctantly have come to accept it as true. At one of the most difficult times in my life, Ruth shared her faith with me in a way I'll never forget. Up until 1966, I had been successful in reaching almost all my goals. But that year, after much prayer and soul-searching, I ran for governor of Georgia. When the returns came in, I had lost to Lester Maddox, an avowed segregationist, whose symbol was a pick handle that he used to drive potential black customers from the door of his restaurant in Atlanta. I could not believe that God would let this person beat me and become the governor of our state.

Afterward, I was not only very disappointed with the election but disillusioned about my religious faith. Ruth drove to Plains from her home in North Carolina and asked me to take a walk with her. We sat under a pine tree, and Ruth listened patiently while I bemoaned my misfortune, deplored the poor judgment and racist tendencies of my fellow Georgians, and vented my anger toward God. Then Ruth quoted the second verse of James, that the trials of life should be accepted with joy.

I said, "Ruth, my political life is over! It's not my goal in life just to grow peanuts, sell fertilizer, gin cotton, and build up a bank account. I have nowhere to go! God has rejected me through the people's vote."

Ruth replied, "Jimmy, you have to believe that out of this defeat can come a greater life."

I responded with bitterness, "Ruth, you and I both know that this is nonsense. There is no way I can build on such an embarrassing defeat."

Patiently, Ruth explained what James was saying. When we face trials with courage, we learn to endure and to pray for wisdom. Wisdom can lead us to put our dependence on things that don't change. Lives end, and our health, friends, careers, and financial status all change. We must cling instead to the things we can't buy, things that we can't count or measure but that are available to all through God's love. With faith, we can make the right choices—measured not by our peers or by societal standards but by unchanging priorities. In adversity, Christ can give us enough courage to take a chance on something new. We are not to be discouraged or selfish, not to exclude opportunities for adventure and excitement but to live constantly expanding lives.

If we take a Christian point of view, Ruth concluded, what seems tragic or fearful fades into relative insignificance. The permanent things that characterize the life of Christ become paramount.

Ruth advised me to do something extraordinary, something totally unrelated to my business or politics. I didn't know what this might be, but shortly afterward I was asked by the Baptist Brotherhood to go as a lay witness on a pioneer mission in Pennsylvania. I did, and it changed my religious life forever. But first, what does it mean to be a witness? What is a mission?

One of the most difficult assignments Jesus gave to me and other Christians is to be personal witnesses for our faith. The last command given to followers of Christ during his earthly ministry is clear and unmistakable: "Therefore go and make disciples of all nations. . . . And surely I am with you always, to the very end of the age" (Matthew 28:19, 20). Also in the Book of Acts: "But you will receive power when the Holy Spirit comes on you; and you will be my witnesses in Jerusalem, and in all Judea and Samaria, and to the ends of the earth" (Acts 1:8).

Even as a young boy, I had this mandate ingrained in me as a personal responsibility. Later I shared with other church members the duty of visiting every local family known to us who were not actively worshiping in one of the neighborhood churches. This task was especially empha- sized just before our annual summer revival, when the pastor and members of our brotherhood would ensure that all "unchurched" citizens in the Plains community were invited to attend the worship services. During our sessions with each family, usually in their front parlors, we would often explain the plan of salvation, but our primary goal was to have them join us for the services. We expected the evangelistic sermons of our visiting preacher to bring the "lost" to faith in Jesus Christ.

Another man and I were often assigned the names of some of my own farmer customers. To confront my friends in this way was embarrassing, but during revival times our congregation was permeated with a spirit of prayer, fellow- ship, and mutual commitment, and we never failed to per- form our duty. A number of the visits would prove successful, resulting in new attendees at our services, but some people I visited each year always rejected our efforts. Yet even this group seemed to welcome our visits. A few really liked to debate the biblical issues and were as well versed in the Scriptures as we. One of their predictable arguments was to name some of the members of our church whom they considered sinful. One older man always maintained that he was not worthy to enter a place of worship because of previous unnamed transgressions for which God, he believed, had never forgiven him. However, he did permit all his children to join the church, and both of his sons later became deacons.

Although the old-fashioned revival fervor is missing today in Plains, the members of our church, particularly we deacons, habitually comply with the command of Jesus by joining the pastor in visiting newcomers to our community to welcome them and invite them to join us at church.

Reaching out to others in an effort to help them understand the liberating message of Christ—that is, witnessing to Christ—is one of several ways that we Christians practice our faith. The degree of emphasis we place on each of these ways often causes debate or dissension among us.

One of these paths is a life of contemplation, based on prayer and regular communion with God. Monastic life is the classic example of this way of serving Christ. This can be very beneficial if used to search for more effective ways to strengthen and to demonstrate our faith. However, as James said, "Faith without works is dead" (James 2:26). Therefore, the contemplative Christian must be careful not to fall into a life devoid of service to others.

Another way of Christian living is to emphasize the avoidance of sin, striving for a virtuous or holy existence. Again, this is a worthy goal, but one that can lead to isolation from others, a highly subjective definition of what is sinful, and a sense of superiority. A person who chooses this path must live and work in close fellowship with others, so as not to become self-absorbed or judgmental.

The third path is to seek to be filled with the Holy Spirit, often called a charismatic life, sometimes exemplified by speaking in tongues. My sister Ruth had experiences of this kind, and I envied her for the intensity and powerful emotion of her spiritual life. There is a clear scriptural basis for this way of Christian living. Paul said that he spoke in tongues more than others, but he also reminded us that it is fruitless if we speak in tongues that have no relation or benefit to others (1 Corinthians 14:6).

Some Christians choose to emphasize compassion for others and a striving for social justice. Christians and others of faith have done much good in the world as a result of their commitment to service. However, service can become just another social program, or one designed to exalt ourselves. Jesus warns that we should perform acts of kindness secretly and always in the name of God rather than as a way of drawing attention or praise to ourselves. As do the other Christian paths, this one offers both opportunities and dangers.

Another way of Christian life is to witness through preaching about Christ. There are some dedicated and inspirational Christian leaders who speak with conviction and effectiveness. For many years, Billy Graham has been justifiably the most admired man in America. He reaches millions with his sermons, and his personal life is looked upon as compatible with what he preaches.

All of these can be effective ways of serving Christ. The problem comes when a Christian assumes one or two of these roles, emphasizes them as most important, and dero-gates the others. I, for instance, look on the more inner-directed ways of Christian life, such as the contemplative path, as less important than active witnessing by serving the poor and needy. This is why I derive so much satisfaction from The Carter Center's work in Africa or helping to build homes through Habitat for Humanity. Some major churches, in my opinion, overemphasize the importance of preaching as a means to increase membership and fail to reach out with compassion to their own neighbors in need.

The fact is that every Christian should attempt to adopt a strong element of all five ways to practice our faith, and not judge others who worship Christ differently. The important thing is that we take our Christian faith seriously and consider thoughtfully how best to express it in our lives.

Most of us Christians have a relationship with Christ that is fairly casual. The presence of the Holy Spirit in our lives is not total. I'm often filled with doubt; I lack courage, determination, commitment, and certainty. Yet I'd like to mold my life and my relationships to be more compatible with the examples set for us by Jesus and the early disciples who made a total commitment to their faith under the most difficult of circumstances.

Jesus, John the Baptist, and the Old Testament prophets all condemned those who publicly professed their faith, assumed a devout demeanor, and then betrayed the divine covenant they claimed to honor. This was a betrayal not only of God but of themselves.

A lukewarm faith is easy to practice but worth little.

Jesus spoke of it in surprisingly harsh terms: "I know your works; you are neither cold nor hot. I wish that you were either cold or hot. So, because you are lukewarm, and neither cold nor hot, I am about to spit you out of my mouth" (Revelation 3:15, 16). To me, these are some of the most disturbing words he ever spoke. They made little impression on me, a fairly proud and self-satisfied Christian, until one morning when our pastor at Plains Baptist Church preached a sermon with the title "If You Were Arrested for Being a Christian, Would There Be Enough Evidence to Convict You?"

I began to think about the questions the prosecutors might ask me: "What have you actually done for others in the name of Christ?" "Have you ever made sacrificial gifts of time or money?" "How many of the very poor families in Plains do you really know?" "Have you visited them in their homes?" "If you are not a Christian, why are you a member of the church?"

Defending myself against the charge of being a Christian wouldn't be hard. I could imagine explaining with great conviction that, except during the Thanksgiving and Christmas seasons, I had rarely associated with the really poor citizens of our community. I knew those who were my customers and employed a few of them to shovel peanuts, load fertilizer, or drive my trucks and tractors, but these relationships were strictly business. No evidence could be presented that I associated with them socially, and I certainly had never sacrificed the interests of my own family for the benefit of these people.

As far as my church membership was concerned, there

were obvious social and financial advantages in being part of the largest and most influential congregation in town. Many of my potential customers for insurance, fertilizer, seed, and other farm supplies were my fellow Baptists, and a non-Christian businessman would be almost an outcast in our small community. The pastor of our church was a sincere speaker who entertained us every week and made us feel contented with ourselves because we attended his services. Also, my family and I enjoyed our fellowship with other church members and the social events sponsored by the church.

I could admit that, as a good citizen, I obeyed the laws of my state and nation. But was I guilty of walking an extra mile? Turning the other cheek? Loving my enemies? Making gifts in secret? Rarely, or never! I certainly was not one of the extremists who tried to conform my life to the radical elements of the Sermon on the Mount.

All in all, there was little evidence that I was anything other than a lukewarm follower of Christ.

For many of us Christians, one of the old stories about St. Peter is applicable. A man approached the gates of heaven and was asked for his credentials. "Well," he said, "during the Depression years I saw a starving family on the street and gave them fifty cents. More recently, my neighbors' house burned down, and I gave them a table that cost me a half dollar." An angel checked the record and found the two reports accurate. The angel then asked what should be done, and St. Peter replied, "Give him his dollar back and tell him to go to hell."

We tend to define religion, Christ, and Christianity in

the most convenient way. It's much easier to discuss doctrine and the nuances of theology than to read and follow Jesus' words in the New Testament. C. S. Lewis suggested that our own devised religions inevitably stand in the way of our growth into true Christians. If our religion identifies God just with our own peace of mind and our social and economic welfare, our religious lives will be narrow and shallow, instead of broad and deep.

Some leaders of congregations tend to regard church attendance as a sufficient service to God and as an adequate repayment for his blessings. Reaching out to others in the name of Christ is of great importance only if it is not a superficial act. What is significant is the permanent impact on a person's way of living, continuing growth in relation to God—not just the name on a church roll.

Some of our most famous Protestant churches are growing by leaps and bounds, making membership so appealing to earthly ambitions that their pastors are almost exalted as little saviors. The implied message is, "Just look at the advantages of Christian fellowship. If you are an insurance salesman and you join our church, we've got 1,500 members who might need insurance. It's a natural thing, you know, to do business with a fellow worshiper."

We have seen the trend for some preeminent downtown congregations to sell their property in the increasingly troubled city neighborhoods and move into the suburbs, which have a more affluent and homogeneous population. Some spend millions of dollars installing recreation facilities that compete with the finest country clubs.

The "Doonesbury" comic strip once had a series about

some yuppies who were looking for a church to attend. They went from one church to another, and they rejected the ones that emphasized atonement for sin or the need to change the way they lived. "Oh, we can't accept that," they said. They went to another church that had a ministry in the inner-city neighborhoods, which would have required some of their time. No, they didn't want that. They finally chose a large and beautiful church—because it had a racquetball court. As Cecil Sherman, leader of the Cooperative Baptist Fellowship, would say, "This church was majoring in the minors."

When I was campaigning for president in 1976, I visited one of the most famous television evangelists. We drove through a large, ornate gate, with uniformed guards on duty, up a circuitous driveway through a beautifully landscaped woodland and garden area, and arrived in front of an ornate mansion—his home. When I politely mentioned the seclusion and luxury of the place, he replied that he needed some privacy from his many admirers, and that the entire estate had been "dedicated to the Lord." He and his family were just using it during their lifetimes. Strangely, I didn't feel that I was in the presence of Jesus.

A *living* Christian faith is both demanding and rewarding. My most memorable religious experiences have been when I reached out to others in personal witnessing efforts and in our annual Habitat for Humanity work projects. The common thread is the clear religious atmosphere, the opportunity for binding with others who are different, a deep and difficult challenge, a sense of selflessness, and the faith that our best efforts will be rewarded with success. Fundamentally, however, these euphoric moments have grown out of simple but meaningful acts of giving and sharing. The first of these was the pioneer mission I served on in Pennsylvania in 1967, following my electoral defeat and my pivotal conversation with Ruth.

With a small budget and a WATS line that could be used only at night and on weekends, a group of volunteers at Pennsylvania State University had called everyone in the telephone book of Lock Haven, a nearby city. Their purpose was to identify those who had no religious faith and would accept a visitor to discuss the subject. About a hundred were found, and my task was to visit these families and talk to them about my faith. My partner was a farmer from Texas named Milo Pennington, who had been on other missions of this kind. This was a new experience for me, and I was both nervous and somewhat embarrassed, but when I met Milo he tried to reassure me: "We don't have to worry about the reception we will get or the results of our efforts. We'll pray a lot, do our best, and depend on the presence of the Holy Spirit to determine the outcome." This attitude was foreign to me as someone with a strong sense of personal responsibility, usually determined to accomplish every task I set out to do. The idea of letting God have the responsibility puzzled me, and my nervousness was only partially alleviated.

Nevertheless, Milo and I found a three-dollar-a-day double room at the YMCA in Lock Haven, met a state game and fish ranger who was a Christian and would be our host and adviser, and embarked on our adventure in this strange city. Following addresses on a handful of three-by-five cards, we went from one home to another and offered a prayer before knocking on each door. With rare exceptions, after we explained our mission, we were invited in to meet with the family members.

Milo was tall and thin, and a simple, relatively uneducated man. I eagerly accepted his offer to do the primary witnessing, and he explained, in very basic terms, the plan of salvation: All of us fall short of the glory or perfection of God, and all deserve punishment. But God loves us, and through his grace, not because we have earned it, he offers us complete forgiveness. Jesus has taken on our punishment, and through repenting and accepting this forgiveness we are reconciled with God and can now have eternal life, with the Holy Spirit dwelling within us.

We found a surprising degree of welcome among the families we visited. Some said they were already Christians, others seemed amused, and still others seemed to have been eagerly awaiting our message and invitation. I admit I was uncomfortable with the fumbling way that Milo made his presentation. He would use simple examples from the lives of workers on his own farm and would tell about his own religious experiences. I was amazed, therefore, at the emotional response of many of the people we visited. We would join them in prayer, often in tears, as they pledged to change their lives and to accept the faith we offered them. I knew that the Holy Spirit was in the room.

One night that week, I called Rosalynn and described some of these extraordinary visits. I told her that I had no trepidation about our future encounters and, strangely, no sense of responsibility for the results of our fumbling presentations. I added, "I feel as if our lives are in the hands of God." This was the first time I'd ever been able to put myself totally in God's power, becoming completely free and letting the Spirit of God take over. And the results we achieved—the transforming experiences we shared with the people we visited—were my first encounter with the miraculous power of Christian faith.

Some of our efforts failed. Once we climbed some outside stairs to see a woman living in a small apartment. When we spoke about how all people fall short of the glory of God, she jumped up from her chair and shouted, "Not me! I don't transgress against God, and I certainly do not deserve any punishment." Despite our further efforts to explain, she ordered us out of her home.

Another memorable visit came later that week, in the poorest part of the city. When we asked a Salvation Army worker how to find our targeted address, she told us it was above some stores and then asked if we *really* wanted to go there.

As we entered an alley door, we heard a stream of invective coming from above—language I'd heard only a few times while in the navy—but this time it was in a female voice. Milo and I looked at each other and finally decided to continue. The woman received us with amusement and soon let us know that she was the madam of a small whorehouse, with three other "girls" working with her.

She obviously enjoyed arguing with us and asking leading questions, which we answered as effectively as possible. Eventually, we began to talk about her background and found her to be especially bitter toward her parents, on whom she blamed her present plight. Her father, she said, had made improper sexual advances toward her. As a teenager, she finally had the nerve to tell her mother. An angry and tearful family confrontation resulted, and both parents accused her of lying and being obsessed with sexual fantasies. She ran away from home and began her life as a prostitute "to support myself," she said. She had had no contact with her family for eight years.

We had been there almost two hours, when she said we would have to leave, but she invited us to come back the next day—our last in Lock Haven. We prayed for guidance that night, but our return brought no miracles. We read in John 8:2–11, where Jesus forgives the woman "taken in adultery" and says to her accusers and would-be executioners, "Let him that is without sin among you cast the first stone." He then tells the woman, "I do not condemn you. Go, and sin no more."

Despite our best efforts, this woman could not consider herself worthy of God's forgiveness—because at that time she was not willing to "sin no more." She did agree to call her parents, though, and actually dialed their number while we were there. When there was no answer, she promised to try again later. I have prayed often that she was reconciled with God and her parents.

Despite these apparent failures, more than forty people in Lock Haven agreed to start a new church, and we helped them rent an abandoned building near the end of the runway of Piper Aircraft Company. I came home from

Pennsylvania with a heightened sense of the intimacy possible between a human being and God.

The next year I went on a missionary trip to Springfield, Massachusetts, with five other men from Georgia. This was a real adventure for members of the Plains church, not only to go to a strange and somewhat foreboding new community but to test our knowledge of the Scriptures. My assignment was to witness to Spanish-speaking families, most of whom were from Puerto Rico. They were very poor and lived in ramshackle, almost abandoned apartment buildings near a large textile mill that had closed. Those who were lucky enough to find work would travel in buses to labor in nearby fields of vegetables and shade-grown tobacco.

We stayed in a YMCA and would go each day from one large building to another, visiting the families crowded together in it. My partner was a remarkable Cuban-American named Eloy Cruz, the pastor of a small church in Brooklyn, New York. I was quite proud when I was chosen for this task because I knew a foreign language. However, Reverend Cruz and I soon realized that the Spanish vocabulary I had known and used in the navy was quite different from the one we were now using to teach the Gospel!

Reverend Cruz did almost all the witnessing; my contribution was limited to reading the Bible verses that we chose in advance of each visit. I was amazed at how effective Reverend Cruz was in reaching people's hearts. They would become quite emotional when he explained to them some aspect of Jesus' ministry and how his life could relate to them.

Once a woman opened her door surrounded by five or six children. When we told them the reason for our visit, her husband, who was sitting across the cluttered room, immediately tried to hide a half-empty beer bottle behind his chair. As Eloy Cruz explained the story, I read from the Book of John about Lazarus, Mary, and Martha, three of Jesus' closest friends. Lazarus had died, and Jesus was preparing to restore him to life. This was a dramatic story, even with my inept reading of the Spanish Scripture. After Jesus wept, and then called to Lazarus, our listeners waited breathlessly. When the dead man came forth from the tomb, everyone broke into cheers. Later, they knelt with Reverend Cruz and me and accepted Christ as Savior.

I had wonderful experiences every day as I worked with this remarkable man. He always seemed to know exactly what to say and seemed to form an instant intimacy with the people whose homes we entered. With the simplest words, he could capture their imaginations and souls. I was as overwhelmed as they and several times had tears running down my cheeks.

I was embarrassed by the deference with which Eloy Cruz treated me. For one thing, I owned an automobile— something he'd never dreamed of having. Furthermore, I had been a state senator and even a candidate for governor (he seemed to ignore my defeat!). He considered himself "just" a Cuban, and a refugee, but I knew the opposite: He was a great man.

As we prepared to say good-bye at the end of the week, I asked him about what made him so gentle but so effective as a Christian witness, and he was quite disconcerted. He finally said, *"Pues, Nuestro Señor no puede hacer mucho con un hombre que es duro."* (Well, our Savior cannot do much with a man who is hard.) He noted that Christ himself, although the Son of God, was always gentle, especially with those who were poor or weak. He went on to say that he always tried to follow a simple rule: "You only have to have two loves in your life—for God, and for the person in front of you at any particular time."

Eloy Cruz's words express a profound and challenging theology. It requires courage and a lot of humility, because there has to be a sense of equality when you love someone else. To put myself on an equal basis with a homeless person, a drug addict, or someone who might be lonely or in need tends to make me feel uncomfortable. In fact, when I do this, I am ennobling them—and myself. This is not just an idealistic theory, because I know from a few such occasions in my life that it is true.

After these home mission experiences, when I was preparing to run for governor a second time, I was invited to speak to the men's brotherhood in a nearby church about my experiences as a Christian witness. I went to my front room to write my speech, very proud that they had recognized my performance in personal evangelism. I began to write down my achievements. I computed that in all my visits, in Pennsylvania, Massachusetts, Atlanta, and around my own community, I had witnessed successfully to 140 people.

I wrote down the figure, but I guess the Lord must have been looking over my shoulder, because I immediately remembered the frantic 1966 political campaign, when Rosalynn and I had gone throughout the state and shaken hands with 300,000 Georgians, extolled my good points, and asked them to support me for governor. The difference between the hundreds of thousands of personal visits on my own behalf in a few weeks and the small number over a lifetime for Christ was a reminder of how little I had done compared with the potential of my religious life.

But although my activities as a Christian witness have been relatively modest, they have given me both experiences of the power of the Holy Spirit that have shaped my life as a Christian and memories I'll never forget.

CHAPTER TEN

The Lord I've Come to Know

People in my Sunday school classes like to ask questions about religion and my own beliefs concerning God, Jesus, the Holy Spirit, and the church. There are a few extensively marked religious books in my library, and it has been useful for me to learn from them how some Christian theologians define religion.

Karl Barth said that religion is our search for God, and that this always results in our finding a god that is most convenient for our own purposes. He distinguishes this from faith, which results from God's seeking us through Christ.

Dietrich Bonhoeffer saw religion as "dividing life and

the world into two spheres, sacred and secular, or holy and profane."

Reinhold Niebuhr maintained that religion is the final battleground between God and man's pride. He also called it "a search for all of life's highest values."

Paul Tillich explained that through religion we seek our proper relation to the ultimate and to other humans. He insisted that we cannot receive answers to questions we do not ask. He said it is all right to be doubtful. "Doubt is not the opposite of faith; it is one element of faith."

Martin Luther said, "Men are not made religious by performing certain actions which are externally good, but they must first have righteous principles, and then they will not fail to perform virtuous actions."

What is meaningful to me is the application of religious ideas to life.

When I was young, my understanding of God was simple and naïve. There were times when I felt confident that all the biblical teachings were absolutely accurate messages to me, inspired by God and surviving almost verbatim in their original form. I knew that the original texts were written mostly in Hebrew and Greek, but I assumed that somehow the scholars who produced the King James Version of the Bible in 1611 were inspired to translate each thought into English with precise accuracy. I believed the legend that the forty-seven men chosen by the British monarch worked independently for several years and then found to their amazement that every word in each of their final texts was exactly the same as in the other forty-six.

At least I wasn't as certain in my beliefs as Miriam "Ma" Ferguson, who was elected governor of Texas in 1924, the year I was born. There was then, as now, an intense debate about whether Spanish should be used in the public schools by children who had recently moved to our country from Mexico. Governor Ferguson, who opposed the use of Spanish, concluded the argument by holding up a Holy Bible and saying, "If English was good enough for Jesus Christ, it's good enough for Texans!"

Except during my childhood, when I was probably influenced by Michelangelo's Sistine Chapel depiction of God with a flowing white beard, I have never tried to project the Creator in any kind of human likeness. The vociferous debates about whether God is male or female seem ridiculous to me. I think of God as an omnipotent and omniscient presence, a spirit that permeates the universe, the essence of truth, nature, being, and life. To me, these are profound and indescribable concepts that seem to be trivialized when expressed in words.

At the same time, I feel a need for a personal relationship and an ability to communicate with God. As a Christian, I have additional knowledge about God from New Testament Scripture: "God is love" (1 John 4:8) and what Jesus told his questioning disciples: "If you have seen me, you have seen the Father" (John 14:9). It seems fruitless for me to go any further in trying to analyze the exact character of God.

* * *

My Sunday school students sometimes want to know about the Jesus Seminar, a group of liberal academics who meet annually in their search for "the historical Jesus." It seems that they consider any biblical statement about Jesus fallacious if they can't prove it to their own satisfaction based on the examination of existing records, computer analysis of the Gospel texts, group assessment of the psychological pressures on and attitudes of the disciples, and some fragments of the Dead Sea Scrolls and other ancient scripts. Their stated purpose is to discover the "real" Jesus.

Some of the more radical of the group claim that Paul, Peter, John, Matthew, and others had visions of a risen Christ after his death, perhaps based on guilt about abandoning Jesus or self-hypnosis caused by their urgent psychological need to see a resurrected Savior. One of these scholars' many books states that the more than 500 believers described by Paul were caught up in a "mass ecstasy" that caused them to see Jesus in a vision like those caused by LSD. A scholar from Chicago, John Dominic Crossan, writes that Jesus' body, after having been removed from the cross and left in a sealed tomb, did not rise from the dead but was eaten by wild dogs. An Australian author, Barbara Thiering, claims that Jesus was buried by mistake in a cave by the Dead Sea, not dead but just drugged, and later was revived with a purgative, married Mary Magdalene, had three children, was divorced and remarried, and finally died in Rome.

These scholars have "voted" collectively that only one sentence in Mark's Gospel is authentic, that the Book of John should be completely disregarded, and that only a few phrases in the Sermon on the Mount are authentic. They attempt to write their own individual Gospels, claiming to have more knowledge about the events of the time than did those who knew Jesus, including Paul, who began writing only about fifteen years after the crucifixion. Although there is dispute about dates because of the lack of direct evidence, it is thought that Mark wrote his Gospel about twenty years later and that the other Gospels came soon thereafter. The skeptical scholars use these time intervals to cast doubt on the Scriptures, tending to ignore the accuracy of oral history traditions and claiming that memories thirty to fifty years old are bound to be incorrect. Yet, in fact, I can remember vividly some of the acts and words of my father before I left home for the navy more than fifty years ago.

How could the diminished Jesus they describe, a failed prophet who made no notable statements, who did not rise from the dead, have transformed his timid and disloyal disciples into historic giants willing to become martyrs for their faith? Where would there be a basis for today's worldwide church, with 1.5 billion believers, many of whose lives have been deeply affected by their faith? How could Jesus still be alive to me and other Christians, his life a perfect model for admiration and emulation? How could so many hearts be touched and minds stimulated by Jesus to seek ultimate truths about life? If these naysayers are right and either the Gospel writers and Paul were all liars or their words were largely subverted by later revisionists, then what is the basis for the Christian faith?

Like most other Christians, I read and study the historical evidence about Jesus from archaeology, textual analyses, and sociological and anthropological studies of the Palestine of 2,000 years ago. But when the theories conflict with my basic beliefs and my living experience of Christ, I prefer to rely on faith, confident that further discoveries of ancient texts and other evidence will never disprove what I believe that makes the impact of Jesus on my own life so profound. After all, it is the role of Jesus in reshaping the lives of believers today that matters most.

A crucial stage in the growth of my faith came when I began to see that the teachings of Christ could be applied to a secular existence. Previously, I'd focused my daily activities on ambitions as a naval officer and then as a young, aspiring farmer and businessman: to excel on my ship, to develop the best seed peanuts in the world, to run a successful warehouse and cotton gin, to move into a nice home of our own, to raise a close and happy family, to win public office, and so on. All of these goals I achieved.

The first real defeat in my life had come in 1966, when I lost the governor's race to a racist opponent. As I've already explained, I felt that God had let me down. After all, I thought, I've done a pretty good job of being a Christian! Don't I deserve a better reward than this?

Religious faith helped me turn adversity into opportunities to work as a lay missionary with Milo Pennington and Eloy Cruz, my first exposures to the miraculous qualities of Christianity. But it also brought home to me in a stronger way than ever before the disparity between my secular ambitions and the example of Jesus Christ.

When I turned to the Gospels, the Jesus I met had a very different way of life from the one I was building for myself and my family. Jesus had no money, no possessions, no house; he turned away from his mother, brothers, and sisters; he was abandoned in time of trouble by his friends and followers; and he died when he was still a young man. How could this be my God?

I began to realize that when I envisioned a supreme being, he was more like Muhammad, the founder of Islam, a patently successful man in earthly terms: a powerful warrior, political leader, founder of a great institutional church. This was in many ways the opposite of the Jesus of the Gospels, or the image of the "suffering servant" in Isaiah, whom Christians identify with Christ: physically unattractive, uneloquent, scorned, rejected. The more I thought about the discrepancy between my image of God and the image in the Gospels, the more it tortured me, not for Jesus' sake but for mine—because I was so different from the divine human being I claimed to worship.

Jesus' rejection of earthly standards of success was a deliberate and essential aspect of his ministry. There is a remarkable description in the fourth chapter of the Gospel of Matthew of how Jesus was severely tempted by the devil just as he was commencing his earthly ministry. Jesus was not tempted to do something morally wrong; rather he was offered easy ways to achieve his own worthy goals.

The first temptation offered to Jesus, who had been fasting for forty days, was a seemingly innocent one: "If you are the Son of God, tell these stones to become bread." Every Jew knew the story of Moses and the Israelites in the desert, to whom manna was delivered each day—as a boy, I thought of this miraculous food as similar to Southern grits. One of the things expected of the promised Messiah was that he would at least have the powers that Moses had. How nice it would be for the nation of Israel if they didn't have to work for their supper anymore!

So this temptation was not illogical or ridiculous, nor was it obviously sinful. It would not only have assuaged Jesus' famished condition after forty days of fasting but also would have demonstrated that he was, indeed, the Messiah. What a quick way this might have been to Christ's ascendance as the supernatural, spiritual leader of the world! It might even have made unnecessary his crucifixion and death.

We can see the attractiveness of this temptation. But if Jesus had succumbed to it, he would have exalted himself and the transient needs of this life at the expense of the eternal. What happened to the Israelites when they got manna from God? Did they stay loyal? No, they took their blessings for granted. And they also came to feel that the alleviation of their human needs was the central point of their belief in God.

After Jesus rejected this temptation, another was offered: "Then the devil took him to the holy city and had him stand on the highest point of the temple. 'If you are the Son of God,' he said, 'throw yourself down, for the scriptures say God's angels will lift you up in their hands, so that you will not strike your foot against a stone.' " It would have been a convincing demonstration of Jesus' divinity if he had stood on top of the temple, leapt into space, stopped his fall just above the ground, walked into the sanctuary, and then preached his sermon! It would have made it much easier for us modern-day Christians to allay our doubts if we could read the Bible and say to ourselves, "If he wasn't the Son of God, how could he fly from the top of the temple?"

Jesus gave a clear and simple reason for rejecting this temptation: "It is written, you shall not tempt the Lord your God" (Matthew 4:7). He made it clear that the Creator's power will not be used for entertainment or to impress believers. Almost all Jesus' miracles were designed to alleviate human grief, loneliness, and physical suffering.

The devil's third and final temptation was his offer to allow Jesus to replace Caesar and other leaders as the ruler of the entire world. Again, the logic of the temptation is powerful. What a wonderful and benevolent government Jesus could have set up! How exemplary the justice would have been! Maybe there would have been Habitat projects all over Israel for anyone who needed a home. And the proud, the rich, and the powerful could not have dominated their fellow citizens.

It is easy to see the attractive nature of this offer. It would have not just exalted Jesus but also set an example for centuries of later rulers. As a twentieth-century governor and president, I would have had a perfect pattern to follow. I could have pointed to the Bible and told other government leaders, "This is what Jesus did 2,000 years ago in government. Why don't we do the same?"

But the devil stipulated fatal provisos: an abandonment of God, and an acknowledgment of earthly things as dominant. Jesus answered, "It is written, 'Worship the Lord your God, and serve only him' " (Matthew 4:10). Anyone who accepts kingship based on serving the devil rather than God will end up a tyrant, not a benevolent leader.

As the story of the temptations in the desert shows, Jesus refused to perform miracles in order to exalt himself or to demonstrate his own greatness. Instead, when he performed extraordinary acts of healing that would have increased his fame and recruited followers, most often he would say, "Don't tell anyone what I have done." There was always a lesson in what Jesus did, sometimes quite subtle, as when he first forgave the sins and only then healed the affliction of the crippled man whose conniving friends lowered him through a roof to gain access to Jesus (Mark 2:2–11). The Pharisees there understood the lesson: Forgiveness and reconciliation with God are more important than being able to walk.

My own attitude toward the miracles of Jesus has gradually changed. At times, they make me uncomfortable; it's not always easy for me to feel complete faith in their validity. But I now believe that, even if some of the more dramatic miracles recounted in the Gospels could be untrue, my faith in him would still be equally precious and unshaken. I am not a Christian because I think that belief in Christ will let me see my father again, or my brother, after I die. That's not a major consideration for me anymore, although it was for a long time. What is important is what Christ means to me as a personal savior, an avenue to God, an example, a guide, and a source of reassurance, strength, and wisdom.

If I could read only one book in the Bible, it would be the Gospel of John. To me, the first few verses, which refer to Jesus as the Word of God, are almost breathtaking, ending with "And the Word was made flesh, and dwelt among us, and we beheld his glory, the glory as of the only begotten of the Father, full of grace and truth" (John 1:14).

One of the most intriguing passages in John describes the relationship between Old Testament beliefs and the revolutionary message of Christ through a series of encounters between Jesus and Nicodemus, a distinguished Jewish leader of his day.

Nicodemus visited Jesus in the first place because of curiosity. He came at night, probably because he didn't want to be seen with Jesus. There was a reason for caution when someone who was, in effect, a member of the Supreme Court and a top law official came to visit a man considered guilty of blasphemy, a crime that could and would be punished by death.

Nicodemus was a devout religious leader who knew and obeyed the Jewish ritual law: how far one could walk on the Sabbath, how to cleanse oneself, what one could eat, how much to give in tithing, and exactly how to perform the religious services. He also knew how to be careful about the kinds of people he touched or even talked with to avoid becoming unclean. All this was delineated in his community's religious rules, and obeying them was an essential aspect of Nicodemus' faith.

However, this night he was willing to ask some troubling questions. Let me summarize his conversation with Jesus:

Nicodemus said, "Because of the miracles you have done, I know that you are a teacher from God."

Jesus replied, "To see God's kingdom, you must be born again."

Nicodemus: "How is it possible for an old man like me to go back into his mother's womb and be born a second time?"

Jesus: "You must be born of water and the spirit, which is like the wind that you can hear and feel but cannot see. How can you be a master of Israel and not understand? We have said what we know and see about earthly things, which you have rejected, so how will you believe heavenly things?"

And then Jesus made a brief statement that describes the foundation for Christianity: "For God so loved the world that he gave his only son, that whoever believes on him will not perish but will have everlasting life. For God sent his son not to condemn the world, but that the world through him might be saved" (John 3:16, 17).

Nicodemus did not grasp what this meant, both because of the strange and mysterious nature of the message and because he was clinging to the way his life had been shaped by his tradition, his family, his wealth, his power, and his privileged status in life. His exact response at that time is not recorded, but we know that he was profoundly affected by these words and continued to search for their meaning.

Later, Nicodemus was to play one of the most dramatic roles in biblical history. When his fellow Pharisees plotted to arrest Jesus, Nicodemus defended him by quoting the law and was even accused by his powerful peers of being a believer in Jesus. The final reference to Nicodemus in the Bible occurs after Jesus' body was removed from the cross, and Joseph of Arimathea had taken it to be buried with the approval of the Roman governor Pontius Pilate: "Nicodemus, who at first had gone to see Jesus at night, went with Joseph, taking with him about one hundred pounds of spices, a mixture of myrrh and aloes. The two men took Jesus' body and wrapped it in linen cloths with the spices, preparing it for burial" (John 19:39–40). Thus, Nicodemus' last appearance is in an act of mercy and generosity.

To emulate the perfect life of Jesus and to comply with his teachings is impossible. God, being perfect, cannot condone sinfulness, and the punishment for our violation of divine laws is separation from God. But through our faith in Christ, who was perfect and who personifies grace and truth, we can be totally forgiven and reconciled with God, for "the gift of God is eternal life through Jesus Christ our Lord" (Romans 6:23).

In my early life, the varied, even paradoxical qualities of Jesus were obstacles to my faith. Only over time, and through the powerful examples of people like Eloy Cruz, Bill Foege, Millard and Linda Fuller, and Jerome and Joann Ethredge, did I begin to comprehend what they meant. I came to realize that the apparent weaknesses of Christ are really what make him precious and give him a quality of authenticity that I now find convincing.

In his last encounter with the disciples before his death, Jesus clearly described his intimate relationship with God, and emphasized his status as the Messiah. It is perhaps the most self-exalting statement he ever made (John 2:44–50). But then he took off his clothes, wrapped himself in a towel, knelt down on the floor, and washed the disciples' feet. This kind of image is profoundly important to me as I try, in my own way, to follow Jesus' example: for instance, when I go with a Habitat team to build a house in Los Angeles or Chicago, inhabited by the poorest Americans, surrounded by drug addicts and criminals, sometimes with gunfire resounding on nearby streets. (One of our Habitat volunteers, a teenager, was actually hit by a pistol shot as we worked on a house in Miami.) The awareness that my God walked this way before me makes it possible to sustain such an effort.

To me personally, Jesus bridges the tremendous chasm between human beings and the seemingly remote and omnipotent God the Creator. The more I learn about Jesus, the more complex and challenging are his teachings, and the more closely connected are God the Father and God the Son. It really comforts and satisfies me to equate the almighty Creator with the humble but perfect Jesus, and to remember that "God is love."

People in my Sunday School class often ask what it

means to be a Christian. My best explanation is that a Christian is a person professing Jesus Christ as a personal savior, and striving to have the qualities demonstrated by Jesus.

God is committed to absolute purity and justice but also filled with grace, forgiveness, and love. For me, the indefinable character of God can be envisioned only through the mixture of these apparently incompatible characteristics in the life of Jesus. He was both God and man, all-powerful, all-knowing, gentle, compassionate, suffering, despised, burdened with the sin of others, abandoned by his followers, publicly executed; but resurrected, and now worshiped by hundreds of millions of believers throughout the world.

God's demand for obedience and an unwillingness to condone sin required some special means for reconciliation between fallible humans and the supreme being. But through God's only son, who was perfect and took the punishment for our sins, we have been given an insight into the nature of God.

True Christianity is a transcendent commitment. It cannot be achieved through our own desire to live right, to be good people, or to share what we have with others. It is not going to church or being baptized. Membership in a church congregation or a religious denomination is not enough. The personal relationship with Christ is the only core around which religious life can exist.

A more private question that I get, usually when a person is leaving my class, is "What can I get from these lessons about Jesus if I am not a Christian?" I explain that personal faith in Christ and a special reverence for him will help to reveal God's transcendent love. However, I have never found anything in the strictly human life of Jesus that was not admirable and inspirational. So whether or not a doubtful person can accept Jesus' divinity, there is in him a model of human existence to be studied and perhaps emulated.

Jesus' intriguing and often delightful experiences are fascinating, and they offer examples of how to deal with our afflictions and concerns in a reassuring and joyful way. They give us priorities or standards for living. Almost any of our most exalted ideals can be explained, clarified, and expanded by what Jesus said and did. Jesus' teachings can help to put us at peace with both our Creator and our neighbors. All of this can be gratifying and valuable, regardless of our public profession of faith.

Abundant Life

The most unforgettable funeral I've ever attended, maybe with the exception of those of my own family members, was the service for Mrs. Martin Luther King, Sr., mother of our nation's greatest civil rights leader. Her husband, Daddy King, and the whole family were close friends of ours. I and a number of other speakers made brief comments, but there was one truly memorable presentation. Rev. Otis Moss from Cleveland, Ohio, preached a brief but remarkable sermon about "the little dash in between." He said there would be a marker on Mrs. King's grave, with her name and a couple of dates—when she was born and when she died—and a little dash in between. He said he didn't want to talk about when she was born, or when she died, but about that little dash. He described Mrs. King's great life and then shifted his attention to the audience. He said that everybody has what might be considered just a tiny dash but that to us, with God, it is everything. The question is, What do we do with that little dash in between, which represents our life on earth?

Many people my age have cautionary phrases deeply ingrained in us: "A penny saved is a penny earned." "Waste not, want not." "Haste makes waste." During the Great Depression, we were very careful to husband what we had and not be wasteful with what we spent. We learned to live cautiously, to fear debt, and to limit our ambitions and the chances we were willing to take. Most of us still want to be sure we don't give away too much, so we always parcel out a little at a time, making sure we hold back more than we might need.

As a consequence, we often underestimate the gifts we have from God: life, talent, ability, knowledge, freedom, influence, and plenty of opportunities to do something extraordinary. We have to remember that our lives will become shrunken if we act only from a cautious sense of duty. It is the reaching, the inspiration, the extra commitment that provide the foundation for a full and gratifying life.

After we satisfy all our personal needs and desires, then what? It is not through gratifying physical needs that we find our purpose in life. We shouldn't carry around what we are in a closed jar and use a medicine dropper to expend it. The "little dash" can be a glorious experience.

As I go through my years of existence, whether thirty,

fifty, or seventy, what things most occupy my thoughts? What preoccupies me when I'm in my most self-analytical mood?

Is my life meaningful, or at least interesting and gratifying? How do I relate to my spouse, my children, and my grandchildren? Am I happy or at least content with the decisions I am making? Am I taking care of my health? How well do I interact with the people I know? Do I live by the Golden Rule? What kind of reputation or influence will I leave behind? Am I ready for the future, both in this life and after death? Am I helping my community and my nation live up to their ideals?

It's not easy to match these sorts of global thoughts with the mundane experiences of the moment. But there are simple ways to make each day more meaningful. We can't transform the world, but when we are in a grocery line with two or three other people, we can remember our faith or moral values and at least exchange a kind word. As Eloy Cruz said, we can "love God, and the person in front of us."

One common goal in life is happiness, or joy, and it is the keeping of God's commandments that provides us with a real opportunity to experience this joy. The Scriptures say, "If you keep my commandments, you shall abide in my love. . . . These things have I spoken unto you, that my joy might remain in you, and that your joy might be full" (John 15:10, 11).

When was the last time we felt almost totally at ease within ourselves? Through religious faith we are also promised peace, even when we are worried or filled with fear: "My peace I give unto you. . . . Let not your heart be troubled, neither let it be afraid" (John 14:27). And we are promised "The peace of God, which passes all understanding" in our hearts and minds (Philippians 4:7). We are offered these blessings through faith.

For The Carter Center, Rosalynn and I still maintain a full schedule of travel and activities, and we visit regularly with destitute and suffering people in places like Haiti, Ethiopia, Rwanda, Bangladesh, and the ghetto areas of America's cities. It is not often that we spend time with people in an affluent society who seem to be completely at peace *without* television, electricity, automobiles, telephones, and other "necessities."

Recently, though, we went to Indiana and visited with an Amish bishop. Although his farm and home were comfortable and beautiful, the family attempted to continue a special kind of set-aside life, as had their ancestors as far back as the sixteenth century. We were met at the door by two small girls, about four or five years old. We soon learned that they didn't speak English; their language would be restricted to Pennsylvania Dutch until they began their formal school education at the age of six. There were no telephone or electrical lines entering the home, the fields were cultivated by hand and with plows pulled by horses, and black buggies were used for transportation. The large family gathered around us and seemed to be intrigued by our stream of questions.

The Amish religion is based on the New Testament, with an emphasis on Jesus' Sermon on the Mount, and the

Amish do not accept any intermediary between the individual and God. All their religious services are held in private homes, and when a congregation grows too large to meet comfortably in a house, they split into two groups. A pastor is chosen by lot from among the men. The bishop places a marker in one of a group of hymnbooks, and then each man selects a book. The one who draws the marker is assumed to have been ordained by God as the new leader. Bishops, who usually serve from two to four congregations, are chosen in the same manner from among the pastors. They are considered to be servants; they help resolve any disputes or issues that arise but have very little actual authority over others.

For each worship service, a big black wagon full of benches is driven to the designated home, and the worshipers gather. No one knows in advance who will preach the morning sermon; again, this leader for the day is chosen by lot or by last-minute consensus. I asked the bishop how people could prepare for a sermon if they didn't know when they would be called, and he replied, with a genuinely modest attitude, "We always have to be prepared." For Rosalynn and me, it was an interesting and inspirational visit.

A few months later, there was a story in my Sunday school lesson text about a group of Christian laymen involved in missionary work who descended on a small village near an Amish settlement. As is often the habit of eager amateurs seeking a possible convert, they confronted an Amish farmer and asked him, "Brother, are you a Christian?" The farmer thought for a moment and then said,

"Wait just a few minutes." He wrote down a list of names on a tablet and handed it to the lay evangelist. "Here is a list of people who know me best. Please ask *them* if I am a Christian."

I can understand why a number of our Mennonite friends left the Amish faith because of their desire for higher education and in order to use their talents in our technological society. However, both the Amish and the Mennonites offer significant examples of Christian living for me because of their apparently successful attempt to live out, within their close-knit families and communities, the principles of peace, humility, and service above the grasping for modern luxuries.

In addition to a life of joy and peace, we want a life that is focused in a meaningful way.

When I was in school, my classmates and I used to sprinkle iron filings on a piece of cardboard or paper and then put a magnet underneath to see the filings concentrate and make interesting designs. As the magnet moves, so do the filings, but they are always focused on a certain point.

What things in life cause our interests to be concentrated or brought into a proper perspective? Or are our interests like a pile of iron filings without a magnet? Many things can serve as worthwhile focal points for our lives. For some people, it may be enough just to take care of their families, the people they love. This can be beautiful and gratifying.

When I was a child, I would visit my grandmother Gordy, who was almost exactly the opposite of my flamboyant grandfather. He was hyperactive, often impatient with others, and always searching for a new project to undertake. The last thing he wanted to do was stay around the house, even during his brief periods without a real job. Grandma was calm, sedentary, and perfectly satisfied with her home-centered way of life. She would concentrate on preparing breakfast for a big family, getting the children off to school, cleaning the house, and working in the garden.

She also had to cook a big noon meal, wash and iron the family's clothes, and then prepare supper. By the time it was dark, we'd go to bed. On Sundays, everyone went to Sunday school and church, so Grandma had to prepare the large dinner in advance, perhaps just cooking the biscuits and fried chicken after the services were over. For one afternoon a week, she joined some other ladies in a quilting bee, sewing while they discussed the affairs of their families and the community.

Although her family more or less took her for granted, I can see now that hers was a complete life of service and dedication, focused on other members of her family.

For most of us, a life of such peaceful service seems foreign or inappropriate, especially in the competitive, high-pressure world of today. Many people wonder how to reconcile belief in a loving God with the uncertainty, anxiety, and fear we all feel from time to time over the dangers and difficulties of life.

The twentieth-century theologian Paul Tillich maintained that *anxiety* grows out of the awareness of our own
fragility, uncertainty, and impending death. By contrast,
fear is of a specific, identifiable threat or object that can be
faced or endured with courage. Tillich said that we should
strive to change overwhelming anxiety into fear, with
which we may deal more effectively.

Fear, then, seems to be transient and justified; anxiety
seems to be more permanent and about things imagined or
unknown. Fear and anxiety are two of the most troubling
human emotions. But we can greatly reduce our feelings of
worry and despair if we have faith in ourselves. First having
faith in God is the best avenue to this goal.

We have to realize that much of our suffering is the
result of our own actions. If we commit crimes and have to
serve time or pay a fine, that's not God's punishment. If we
lead a selfish or egocentric life and end up with few friends,
our loneliness is not God's punishment. If someone jumps
off the top of a building, we can't expect God to suspend
the laws of gravity. Extensive studies at The Carter Center
have shown that two-thirds of our physical ailments and
premature deaths are caused by our own choice of
lifestyle—smoking, improper diet, lack of exercise, sexual
promiscuity, carelessness with firearms, and driving while
intoxicated. With God's help, these semisuicidal habits can
be changed.

There is a general realization that alcoholism and drug
addiction are diseases, but by a combination of self-will,
faith in God, and support from others, it is possible to correct or cure them. I have seen personal evidence of this in

the experiences of my brother, Billy, who became an apparently hopeless alcoholic while I was president. But ten years before his death Billy decided on his own, encouraged by his wife, Sybil, to combat his addiction. He never drank again, was reconciled with his family, and lived a full life. During these years, he and Sybil worked with thousands of others who were struggling to break their dependence on alcohol and drugs.

Of course, we must confront head-on the small but troubling problems that cause us worry and tend to lure us away from the important commitments of our lives. The New Testament tells us to go ahead and struggle with these challenges but to keep clearly before us the simple, pure, comprehensible reassurance that we can draw from the life and teachings of Jesus. In this we have a great reservoir of strength and power to guide us through both the troubling and disappointing times and the exuberant and successful times.

The Bible message is that each of us is blessed with God's love and grace, overcoming fear:

> For God has not given us a spirit of fear, but a spirit of power, of love, and of self-confidence. (2 Timothy 1:7)
>
> So we say with confidence, "The Lord is my helper; I will not fear what man can do to me." (Hebrews 13:6)
>
> There is no fear in love, but perfect love casts out fear; for fear has to do with punishment, and whoever fears has not reached perfection in love. (1 John 4:18)
>
> Do not let your hearts be troubled. Believe in God, believe also in me. (John 14:1)

As I grow older, I have a greater daily awareness that death will one day claim me. Sometimes when I watch a beautiful sunset or have a delightful experience with Rosalynn or my grandchildren, I wonder how many more of these I will see. It is sobering to realize that our inevitable fate is physical death, apparent proof of the relative insignificance of our earthly lives. To people who can't accept this fact with equanimity, death becomes an overwhelming tragedy and a source of constant distress.

However, the realization of our mortality and its correlation with our daily lives is one of the challenges that can be met most effectively by our faith. Except for giving us incentive to live a fuller life, knowledge of our coming death should not affect our spiritual or secular attitudes. My own religious faith is strengthened when I seek God's help in facing the inevitability of death and other uncontrollable or unpredictable events.

Ultimately, we have to find the ability to face the uncertainties of life with equanimity, and a commitment to a higher calling is often the best source of strength. Everyone who serves in the military in times of combat must accept the potential danger. As a young submariner, I realized the inherent risks and was willing to face them.

There was even a strange sense of liberation when we left port for a few weeks, with our responsibilities limited to those within the confines of the submarine hull. Monthly reports concerning personnel and equipment were minimal, and even the cherished duties of a husband and father were left behind. I would be with seventy-one other men for a fairly certain time, putting in to a few ports as scheduled. The duties were onerous but—with the exception of unforeseen crises in operation—routine and predictable. The simplicity of this life was surprisingly satisfying. I dealt with potential concerns, even the possibility of tragedy, by focusing on my duties, realizing that all results could not be within my own control, and honoring my task as worthy of the danger involved.

On ship, we all knew that a few dozen men shared a bond, each depending on all the others. I had faith in the abilities and steadfastness of my fellow crewmen. Still, on at least three occasions, I thought that I would likely die. One example is especially memorable.

Our old fleet-type submarine could operate submerged for only a short time, by drawing a limited supply of electric power from batteries, so we spent most of the time on the surface of the sea. Even then, our ship was almost submerged, with only a very low, flat deck along the pressure hull just above the surface. The bridge was about eight feet higher. Once I was on the bridge at night in a storm, as we proceeded slowly with our bow held carefully facing the large waves. Quite frequently, a swell would rise under me, the water washing around my ankles.

Then suddenly an enormous wave lifted me off my feet, tearing my hands loose from the safety rail. For fifteen or twenty seconds, I swam freely in the sea, not knowing where I was. Then the wave receded, planting me on the low deck behind where I had been standing. I was not injured, and I scrambled frantically back up on the bridge before another wave came along. Had the ship been moving at the slightest angle to the surging sea, I would have come down in the water and been lost in the dark.

Although all of us studied, planned, and practiced to minimize danger, we had made a commitment to serve our country, and we accepted the risks with a feeling of inevitability. We felt that our cause was worthy, we wanted our lives to be significant, and we had faith in one another, our ship, and America. There are somewhat similar concepts in my religious beliefs.

If we are people of faith, we should remember the things that are important in the eyes of God, the surpassing concepts that should influence us. Whether we like it or not, longevity is not one of them. If we have faith in God's promises, we face life beyond our earthly years with equanimity, if not anticipation. Jesus has promised to prepare a place for us.

At any time, we can empty ourselves of anxiety and turn to God. But doing so requires a deliberate effort, or at least a willingness to change our focus from transient things to something that will never be lost. This can be found through Christ and his promise: "And I give unto them eternal life; and they shall never perish, neither shall any man pluck them out of my hand" (John 10:28).

Jesus used a simple verse to emphasize that this opportunity for an intimate relationship with him is always available, but we have to respond: "Behold, I stand at the door and knock. If anyone will hear my voice and open the door, I will come in and have supper with him" (Revelation 3:20). For Christians, this intimacy is what shapes our spiritual life. It is a powerful force, a source of joy, or as I mentioned earlier, the "peace that passes understanding" (Philippians 4:7).

I remember how stricken I felt when I learned that my father had a terminal illness. I was far away, in the navy, and though a grown man, I lay across the bed and wept. Later I witnessed the deaths of my mother, both my sisters, and my only brother. In all these cases, we knew that they had terminal cancer and that death was imminent. The finest medical care was available to them, but all four chose to spend their last days without artificial life-support systems.

With a few family members and friends around them, they died peacefully and within an environment of mutual love and support. Each person seemed to retain his or her lifelong character. My sister Ruth remained deeply religious in her final days; my father tried not to show that he was weak or suffering; my mother urged all of us not to worry about her; my sister Gloria discussed the features of Harley-Davidsons with her biker friends; and my brother, Billy, retained his sense of humor. Even during the last hours of his life, he caused all of us to roar with laughter with a final practical joke or two.

We can face death with fear, anguish, self-torment, and unnecessary distress among those around us. Or, through faith in the promises of God, we can confront the inevitable with courage, equanimity, good humor, and peace. Our last few days or months can be spent in a challenging and exhilarating way, seeking to repair relationships and to leave a good or even noble legacy, in an atmosphere of harmony and love.

Despite religious reassurances, there are times when I miss my family very much and wish they could have shared some of my recent experiences. But my memories of them are pleasant, not filled with anguish or pain.

We would all like to have full and abundant lives. For me, there is a direct response to this desire in something Jesus said: "I am come that they might have life, and they might have it more abundantly" (John 10:10). This full life does not depend on natural talent, IQ, social standing, bank account, or on influence. A full life can be based on seemingly trivial things, simple interrelationships.

Sometimes it seems that there are two parts of our lives. One is when we're rushing to get somewhere on time, or can't decide how to deal with a family crisis, or are hard at work on our jobs. Maybe we are even trying to finish a Habitat house by Friday at noon so we can move folks into their new home. At moments like these, it seems that we can't quite get everything done.

But how do we spend our time when we are not striving, pushing and impatient, with too much to do? We tend to ignore this part of our lives as if it were just the gap between important things. But that nondemanding time is when the fullness of life needs to be nurtured. Who decides what is the quality time? We do.

In 1 Corinthians 13, perhaps the most beautiful chapter in the Bible, Paul emphasizes how relatively insignificant are all kinds of human achievements, even the gifts of prophecy, faith, and generosity, when compared with the gentle and humble act of love. That's a lovely thought, much better than having to do something frantic, ambitious, or competitive. What we are offered in God's love is a new life, but one that is described in such simple terms that we usually pass it by.

The grand things we often spend our days striving to achieve fade into relative insignificance in the little dash, the scope of life from birth to death. It's the simple things, the way we spend our waiting time, that can matter most. So while we are waiting for a profound life experience, or retirement, or death, we are using up the days of our lives. In his letter to the Romans, Paul tells them to be diligent but to act with generosity and joy: "He that gives, let him do it with simplicity, he that shows mercy, with cheerfulness, let love be without dissimulation . . . be kindly affectioned one to another . . . rejoicing in hope, patient in tribulation . . . given to hospitality" (Romans 12:8–13). These words are not telling us to waste time but to act beneficially and joyfully, without pride or criticism of others.

We can follow Paul's advice today. We can take a few minutes on a relaxed day and walk down the street to visit one of our neighbors who is not feeling well or is lonesome and say, "I had some cake left over, and I was thinking about you and I brought you some. I wonder if maybe we could have a cup of coffee together?" It would take less than an hour, but it might be the most enjoyable experience of the entire week. That's the kind of simple thing that won't be on the front page of a newspaper or on television. But we have to be somewhat innovative; it's a shame if we can't think of *anything* to do.

In one of Jesus' parables, the master said, "Well done, good servant! Because you have been trustworthy in a very small thing, take charge of ten cities" (Luke 19:17). He also said, "If you then be not able to do that thing which is least, why take thought for the rest?" (Luke 12:26) and "He that is faithful in that which is least is faithful also in much" (Luke 16:10).

In one of my poems about the people of our town of Plains I refer to their "modest, tempered dreams." Most often, our grandiose dreams are transient in nature, so for all practical purposes we live permanently with our modest, tempered ones. This is not necessarily bad.

Sometimes the simplest things in life can become all-important. Recently Rosalynn and I visited a number of formerly homeless men who had just moved into tiny compartments of their own that had been walled off in old railroad boxcars. They acted as though they owned castles! One of them said, "This will be the first time in many years that I've slept where I could take off my shoes and not tie them to my wrist. Now I can wake up in the morning and know that my shoes will not be gone."

After leaving the White House, I wrote my presidential memoir, *Keeping Faith*, which required careful research into the details of my four years in office. As I examined the 6,000 pages of personal diary notes I had written and the voluminous official documents prepared at the time, I was surprised at how faulty a memory I had. I could hardly recall some truly historic events.

But recently my ten-year-old grandson Joshua and I were out on a little two-person fishing boat with an electric motor, and he wanted to be captain of the ship. He was in the front seat with two buttons that are pushed with your foot to make the boat go right and left. Despite our erratic course, every now and then we caught a nice bass. Just me and my grandson. After a long period of silence, Josh looked at me and said, "Papa, this is the life." It won't appear in any history books, but that was a moment I'll never forget.

A few months later, I had an equally important experience. Our smallest grandchildren were with us, Maggie, Jeremy, and Jamie. They all had an opportunity to go to the movie *The Lion King*. But I had mentioned to the children earlier that we would be raising the water level of our pond over the top of the old pier, so we needed to tear it down. When we tried to get the children to see the movie, they didn't want to go. They insisted on helping Rosalynn and me dismantle the old pier. So we went out and waded around in muck about knee-deep all afternoon, laboriously tearing off the boards, one by one, with crowbars and hammers. We all cheered when the job was finished.

The next morning I had a large backhoe coming in that could have squeezed twice, picked up that whole dock, and dropped it on the bank, crumpled into firewood, so we didn't achieve very much in a practical sense. But what I had instead was another unforgettable experience, just spending an entire afternoon with my wife and grandchildren, sweating and bogging down in the mud.

I like two lessons from Jesus' life that encourage us to

see how small acts of sharing can help us reach beyond normal expectations, routine ambitions, and even the usual standards of religion. One was when Jesus sat down in the temple and watched wealthy people throw sizable offerings into the collection plate. Then he saw a poor widow, who gave two coins, worth less than a penny. He called his disciples to him and said, "Truly I tell you, this poor widow has put in more than all those who are contributing to the treasury. For all of them have contributed out of their abundance; but she out of her poverty has put in everything she had, all she had to live on" (Mark 12:43).

The other event, described in chapter 12 of the Gospel of John, was more strange and dramatic. It concerns a visit with Jesus' friends Mary, Martha, and Lazarus just before he went to Jerusalem to face his accusers and his crucifixion. These three seem to have been Jesus' closest personal friends. It may be that, above and beyond the affection between Jesus and any of his disciples, there was a special closeness between Jesus and Mary. We don't know how much he shared with her about what was going to happen to him, the purpose of his life on earth, and his relationship to God. But we do know there were long periods of time when the two sat together, perhaps in front of her little house, and Jesus explained to Mary the nature of his ministry and perhaps the coming tragic events in Jerusalem. Jesus had told his disciples that he was going to die, but they refused to believe it. Apparently, however, Mary knew and believed. She may have been the only one who did.

This family knew that Jesus liked to have a good time. Some of his parables include memorable and funny events, and Jesus enjoyed outwitting those who were hostile to his teaching. He gave answers to questioners that destroyed their arguments, embarrassed his tormentors, and amused and enlightened the spectators. As far as give-and-take is concerned, he could have taken over easily from David Letterman or Jay Leno. He liked to go to parties and have a good time with strange people who invited him into their homes, including disreputable people like tax collectors and infamous sinners. Many of these happy times in Jesus' life were shared with this family.

It's interesting to conjecture that, after Jesus had raised Lazarus from the grave, his three friends pooled their wealth and considered what they could do to repay him for this miracle. Maybe they were waiting for an appropriate time to entertain him and his disciples. In any case, on this particular night, they threw a party for him. During supper, the Bible says, "Martha served, and Lazarus was one of those reclining at the table with him." Then Mary took a pint of perfume, its value equal to a full year's income for the average worker. She poured it on Jesus' feet and wiped them with her hair.

That's a troubling scene to me. It was an abnormal event 2,000 years ago; it would be even more strange today. The setting is intriguing, the waste of money seemingly inappropriate, the intimacy between the woman and the honored guest disturbing. It was an act far beyond the expected—a transcendent act that described Mary's feelings toward Jesus. Her love for him went beyond boundaries.

Is this just a bizarre ancient story about someone who loved Christ so much that she did what she could to honor him? How does this apply to me and my life?

If I had been there, and I had known that this was the Son of God, who was going to die in six days as a sacrifice for me, I hope that, like Mary, I would have done something dramatic to show him my love and gratitude, without considering whether it might be gauche, excessive, or embarrassing.

The Bible describes Mary's act as a "good" one. The Greek word for "good" is usually *agathos*, but the word here is *kalos*, which is best translated "good and lovely." To me, "good and lovely" brings Mary's act down to a human, intimate level. All of us need to look at ourselves, our circumstances, the environment in which we live, and ask: Within my own talent and realm of possibilities, what can I find to do that would be good and lovely? If we are somewhat embarrassed when considering such acts, perhaps ours is a small world.

God's world is very large, a world we should always explore, to comprehend the problems of troubled people who may be hungry for what we could offer. It's like eating peanuts—if we can decide to be adventurous and generous once, it may be hard to stop! And if we are afraid we'll give away all we have, remember Mary, who had a lot left after the ointment was gone. She had the riches of life and the love of her savior, who, at least symbolically, she had anointed for burial. As we expand our lives and do things that are challenging, innovative, and unpredictable, we can know what it means to be filled with joy and the peace that passes understanding.

A few times in life, a "good and lovely" adventure wouldn't hurt.

Acknowledgments

My original concept of this book was a collection of some of the more interesting Sunday school lessons I have taught, perhaps fifty-two of them to cover a year of weeks. However, after discussions with my publisher, Peter Osnos, it became clear that it would be better to describe how these Bible texts have helped to shape my Christian faith and how these religious beliefs have affected my life.

Adding these personal elements to the text has been a great challenge, made possible with the help of my wife, Rosalynn, and my two editors, Karl Weber and Nessa Rapoport. With probing questions and suggestions, they have also encouraged me to relate my interpretation of Scriptures to some of the most interesting and controversial issues of modern society. The Rev. Dr. James Bell provided helpful editorial comments on Scripture and theology.

I am grateful to these advisers, and to those people mentioned in this book whose actions, based on faith, have been an inspiration to me.

Index

Chad, 177
charismatic life, 206, 207
children
    freedom for, 82
    immunization of, 173, 174
Christ Jesus
    accepting, 19–22
    as bridge to God, 233
    and building relationships in
        marriage, 77–78
    Carter's commitment to,
        78
    crucifixion of, 232
    and fears in life, 247–48
    happy times for, 253–55
    historical, 223–25
    and Last Supper, 233
    miracles of, 228, 229–31
    as model of human existence,
        235
    and Nicodemus, 230–32
    personal relationship with, 234,
        247–48
    as personal savior, 230
    resurrection of, 223
    temptations of, 226–29
    visualizing, 226
    See also New Testament; specific
        verse
Christian Coalition, 34
Christian Right, 34, 186–87
Christianity/Christians
    as commitment, 234
    defending against charge of
        being, 208–9
    definition of, 234
    divisiveness among, 33–38,
        189, 195–99
    and faith as unifying force,
        36–38
    and prejudice, 189, 195–99

church and state relations, 9,
    125–27, 129–30, 131–34,
    186, 198
churches
    attendance at, 210
    and Carter's childhood/youth,
        11
    as center of Carters' lives,
        62–63, 70
    as center of social life, 11, 18–19
    as community, 38
    financial responsibility for, 131
    and gender discrimination,
        191, 192–93
    and justice, 107–11, 112
    membership in, 208–9, 210–11
    in Plains, Georgia, 71, 195
    and race issues, 67–68, 112,
        118–20
    women in, 194–95
    See also specific church
citizenship, 107–11, 209
civil disobedience, 117, 118
civil rights, 117, 118–21, 185
Clark, Jack and Rachel, 188
Clinton, Bill, 152, 153, 154
Cohen, Leonard, 33
Coleman, Julia, 134
commitment, 27, 46, 78, 92, 107,
    109, 178–79, 234
communication
    among Carter family, 76–77,
        81–82
    with God, 222
    in marriage, 76–77
    and search for peace, 142–47
communism, 68–69
community, 12, 23–24, 38, 41,
    44–45
compassion, 206, 207
confession, 85

SOURCES of STRENGTH

SOURCES of STRENGTH

Meditations on Scripture
for a Living Faith

Jimmy Carter

Preface

Sources of Strength is a companion to *Living Faith*.* In fact, when I began writing the earlier book, I intended it to be like this one, a collection of some of the favorite Bible lessons I have taught. As the text evolved during the spring of 1996, however, it became increasingly obvious that the overall impact of my personal faith on my life and thinking needed first to be explained. The resulting book—part spiritual autobiography, part Christian teaching—was *Living Faith*.

Now, a year later, I have returned to my original plan. Although I began teaching Sunday School classes when I was eighteen years old, I've retained written outlines and transcripts of entire texts only during the past twenty years. I asked Karl Weber, a fine editor, to help me choose some of the more interesting ones. Together, we abbreviated each of the forty-five-minute talks down to a few pages, and I added some more recent personal anecdotes to help illustrate key points.

Nine of the Bible lessons I've included here came from

---

* New York: Times Books, 1996.

when I taught adult Sunday School at First Baptist Church in Washington, the church our family attended while I was president. Like other Christians, our family needed spiritual fellowship, not special recognition or honors, so as much as possible we were treated the same as any other members of the church. There was never any advance announcement when I was to teach, and I didn't even know that the lessons had been recorded until after I left the White House.

Nowadays, I teach about two-thirds of the Sundays at Maranatha Baptist Church in our hometown of Plains, Georgia. We have only about thirty families as active members, and most of them are teaching other classes, keeping the nursery, and managing church affairs while I teach. However, there are usually several hundred visitors who come to hear my lessons. I'm sure that they have many motivations, including the desire to meet a former president, to hear what a politician has to say about the Scriptures, to explore or debate ideas expressed in my previous books, to seek a new religious experience, or just to enjoy an unusual Sunday morning outing. Some have never before attended a religious service, and others are pastors, scholars, or well-known authors of religious books. About a fifth are Southern Baptists, but most are members of other Christian traditions, Protestant, Catholic, and Orthodox. We also welcome Jews, Muslims, and adherents of different faiths— and some who have no faith but perhaps are searching for one.

For me, and for many of those in the classes, there is a surprising element of interest and even excitement in exploring Scripture together. I have chosen the texts in this book from those that stimulated the more intriguing discussions in class. I have arranged the meditations to provide some aspects of both continuity and diversity of ideas, but each really stands on its own. Since I have almost a completely new group each Sunday, I do repeat some favorite themes. There are, therefore, a few repetitions of both ideas and texts in this book, but the basic thrust of each lesson is meant to be distinct. Some of them should be comprehensible on first reading, while others will require some contemplation.

There are fifty-two meditations in this book, one for each week of the year. But don't feel constrained to pace yourself accordingly. Since the Scripture selections and comments are so brief, my hope is that you will supplement what I have presented with further study of the Bible and associated commentaries. The book includes passages from both the Hebrew and Greek texts of Scripture. I refer to the two portions of the Bible as the Old Testament and New Testament, the traditional designations I have always used in my classes.

I have thoroughly enjoyed recapitulating the lessons I've taught over the years; for me, the ancient texts always come alive when I explore them with a searching heart. I hope they will be for you, as they have been for me, sources of strength.

Jimmy Carter
Plains, Georgia
June 1997

Contents

TO KNOW AND WORSHIP   139

GOD'S RICHES AT CHRIST'S EXPENSE   159

WHEN THE ROAD IS ROUGH   183

GOD'S CALL   207

Why Should We Read the Bible?

All scripture is inspired by God, and profitable for teaching, for reproof, for correction, for training in righteousness; that the man of God may be adequate, equipped for every good work.

2 TIMOTHY 3:16–17

In December 1996, I was on *The Tonight Show* discussing my book *Living Faith*. The host, Jay Leno, showed a videotape of some extemporaneous interviews with people he met on the streets of Los Angeles in which he asked them questions about the Bible. The answers were both hilarious and disturbing. For example, there were some who thought that the first commandment was "freedom of speech," that Eve was created from an apple, and that Noah's ark landed on Mount Everest. I played the tape for my Sunday School class, and subsequently someone sent me a news article containing funny comments by students about the Bible, including these:

"Noah's wife was called Joan of Ark."

"Lot's wife was a pillar of salt by day and a ball of fire by night."

"Seventh commandment: Thou shalt not admit adultery."

"Epistles were wives of the apostles."

"A Christian has only one wife. This is called monotony."

One middle-aged woman interviewed by Leno responded proudly that she had a Bible in her house. When he asked her to name the last time she had opened it, she said she thought it was when she had used it in a college course. If we're honest, many of us might have to say the same. But if we'd bought a new automobile for which we had saved for several years, there is little doubt that we would study the manual until we mastered it and would refer back to the text whenever we had a problem. I have several thick books on how to use my computer and printer, a CD-ROM encyclopedia, and other books on how to explore the Internet. The authors of *Word for Dummies, Windows 95 for Dummies,* and other similar texts have gotten rich. Yet the operating manual for life on earth is sadly neglected. We don't really need a *Bible for Dummies,* since the meaning of the inspired word of God is clear enough to meet our needs. The Scriptures are full of interesting, shocking, helpful, and inspiring stories—but, unfortunately, they go unexplored by many of us.

The theologian Paul Tillich says that religion is the search for the truth about ourselves, and how we relate to God and to other people. Since this is the essence of life, it is obviously valuable for us to understand these relationships. One way is through the study of the Holy Word of God—the Bible.

Another theologian, Karl Barth, said that our relationship to the Bible is like being inside a house and gazing out at a group of people on the street. They are all looking toward the sky with faces expressing delight, wonder, pain, hope, guilt, or joy. They are obviously intrigued by something remarkable, perhaps miraculous or mysterious, but out of our view. For thousands of years, these have been the reactions of hundreds of millions of people who read Genesis, Isaiah, Micah, Luke, the letters of Paul, or Revelation. Shouldn't we be curious about what those millions have seen?

Paul's letter to the young Timothy, quoted at the beginning of this introduction, was probably written before any of the four Gospels. These two verses are the most succinct biblical description of the value of the Scriptures. "The inspired word of God" doesn't mean that every translation or interpretation of Scripture is literally accurate. We can select an isolated verse here and another there and use them to justify almost any of our personal prejudices. In fact, the earliest and most constant conflict between Jesus Christ and certain religious leaders of his time occurred because they were inclined to focus on the individual verses, or their interpretation of them, instead of on the essence of God's message. They were so concerned about exactly what one could do on the

Sabbath, what was acceptable to eat or to wear, and the detailed procedures for worshiping and making religious donations that they forgot that God was a creator filled with love, grace, and forgiveness.

Let's look at some other words in Paul's advice about reading Scripture. "Reproof" means constructive criticism or self-analysis, and "correction" means improvement of our behavior or our priorities in life. "Training in righteousness" means learning to do God's will, or becoming more like Christ. The meaning of the other words is clear, but "equipped for every good work" warrants a few more thoughts.

All of us can try to live an average life—nothing special, but good enough to get along and to make us feel self-satisfied. But an important reason to study the Scriptures is to help each of us define and strive for a transcendent life—a life that reaches above and beyond what is normally expected of us. From Scripture, we can learn how Jesus Christ lived and what he set forth as proper priorities for human existence. We are aware of this opportunity in moments of exaltation or inspiration, when we are embarrassed by our own inadequacies, or perhaps when we are in total despair. The Bible offers concrete guidance for overcoming our weaknesses and striving toward the transcendent life for which we were created.

It's almost always helpful to share our studies or questions with someone else in whom we have confidence. For the last twenty years, Rosalynn and I have read a portion of the Bible each night. When we're together, we alternate reading aloud, and when we're apart we enjoy knowing that we are contemplating the same text. We have been through the entire Bible several times in Spanish, to practice our foreign language as we nurture ourselves spiritually.

After a personal witnessing experience with Eloy Cruz, an admirable Cuban pastor who had surprising rapport with very poor immigrants from Puerto Rico, I asked him for the secret of his success. He was modest and embarrassed, but he finally said, "Señor Jimmy, we only need to have two loves in our lives: for God, and for the person who happens to be in front of us at any time." That simple yet profound theology has been a great help to me in understanding the Scriptures. In essence, the whole Bible is an explanation of those two loves.

The Word
Became Flesh

CHAPTER ONE

What It Takes to Be a Christian

The jailer asked, "What must I do to be saved?"

Paul answered, "Believe in the Lord Jesus, and you will be saved—you and your household."

ACTS 16:30–31

Many people have asked the question the jailer does here, and Paul's simple response is the answer that has been accepted by almost two billion Christians living around the world today.

As a young man, I joined other members of our church in carrying this same message about Jesus Christ to the families in our rural community who were not Christians. This was very difficult for me, because I was always doubtful about the reception we would receive. I usually knew the families well, so I was somewhat embarrassed about implying that I was superior in some way, having knowledge or a privileged position that they didn't.

However, the company of another man always strengthened me. We were well versed in the rudimentary tenets of what we called "The Plan of Salvation," which was the basis for our brief presentation.

Later, beginning in the mid-1960s, I traveled to more distant places for a week or so as a volunteer lay missionary, joining others in Pennsylvania, Massachusetts, and in the suburbs of Atlanta to visit homes and share our faith in Christ. We approached each family with sincere prayers, and learned to rely on the presence of the Holy Spirit to overcome our timidity and uncertainties. In other words, we just did our best and had faith enough to relax and leave the results to God.

The Plan of Salvation is still an integral part of my weekly Bible lessons. I often outline it briefly when I receive a question about the nature of Christian faith from a visitor or when the lesson text has an evangelical meaning—as most of them do. In this first meditation, I want to share the Plan of Salvation with you, relying more on a few passages of Scripture than on my own words.

1.   *God loves all of us.* "For God so loved the world that he gave his only Son, so that everyone who believes in him may not perish, but may have everlasting life" (John 3:16). "For God, who is rich in mercy, out of the great love with which he loved us even when we were dead through our trespasses, made us alive together

with Christ—by grace you have been saved" (Ephesians 2:4–5).

2. *All of us are sinners.* Some of us may be satisfied with the way we are, feeling that we don't need God's mercy, but the Holy Scriptures are clear: "All we like sheep have gone astray; we have turned every one to his own way" (Isaiah 53:6). "There is no one who is righteous, not even one" (Romans 3:10). And "All have sinned, and fall short of the glory of God" (Romans 3:23).

3. *Sin separates us from God.* What are the consequences of our violating God's moral code? There is a clear and disturbing answer: "For the wages of sin is death" (Romans 6:23).

4. *We cannot save ourselves.* Only God can save us, through our faith. Even the Hebrew patriarch Abraham did not earn his righteousness before God; it came because of his belief, or faith: "For if Abraham was justified by works, he has something to boast about, but not before God. For the scripture says, 'Abraham believed God, and it was reckoned to him as righteousness' " (Romans 4:2–3 and Genesis 15:6).

"For by grace are you saved through faith, and this is not your own doing; it is the gift of God—not the result of works, so that no one may boast" (Ephesians 2:8–9).

5. *Jesus came to remove the barrier of sin.* "But God proves his love for us in that while we still were sinners Christ died for us" (Romans 5:8). "He himself bore our sins in his body on the cross, so that, free from sins, we

might live for righteousness; by his wounds you have been healed" (1 Peter 2:24).

6. *It is through our faith in Christ that we receive these blessings.* "If you confess with your lips that Jesus is Lord and believe in your heart that God raised him from the dead, you will be saved. For one believes with the heart and so is justified, and one confesses with the mouth and so is saved" (Romans 10:9–10).

These are the premises that all Christians have accepted. Some people may think this path to salvation is too simple and easy—that something else must be required for us to receive God's mercy and everlasting life. After all, most of the achievements in life—education, a good family, a successful career—require hard work, persistence, and sacrifice. Yet God's forgiveness and blessings are given to us freely, by pure grace.

This mistaken attitude reminds me of the reaction of the Syrian general Naaman, who went to the prophet Elisha to be cured of leprosy. Without leaving his tent, Elisha sent word that Naaman needed only to bathe in the little Jordan River seven times to be cured. The powerful man stormed away, furious at the simplicity of the prescription. But his servants said, "If the prophet had commanded you to do something difficult, would you not have done it? How much more, when all he said to you was, 'Wash, and be clean'? So he went down and immersed himself seven times in the Jordan, according to the word of the man of God; his flesh was restored like the flesh of a young boy, and he was clean" (2 Kings 5:13–14).

The simple but profound fact is that our lives can be changed—beginning now—by professing our faith in Jesus Christ. The rest of this book will explore the fascinating, exciting, and remarkable ramifications of this basic, life-giving truth.

CHAPTER TWO

A Humble Servant

All we like sheep have gone astray; we have turned every one to his own way; and the Lord hath laid on him the iniquity of us all. He was oppressed, and he was afflicted, yet he opened not his mouth: he is brought as a lamb to the slaughter, and as a sheep before her shearers is dumb, so he openeth not his mouth.

ISAIAH 53:6–7

Christians are, by definition, "little Christs." As such, we ought to know as much about Jesus as possible and to emulate him as fully as we can. As we know, even the disciples who were with him every day did not really understand what aspects of his life they were supposed to adopt. It is interesting now to go back into the Old Testament, to correlate the prophecies with what we know from the Gospels about Jesus as a human being, and then try to apply this awareness to our own lives.

Although we Christians believe that a number of ancient prophets depicted the coming Messiah, the most fascinating descriptions come from the Book of Isaiah. Biblical scholars disagree about the authorship and meaning of the verses, but I believe that these were the words of the great prophet and that he was referring to Jesus as Messiah. One reason for this assessment is that Jesus, in his hometown synagogue, quoted directly from Isaiah and applied the prophecy to himself.

When invited to read from the Scripture, Jesus picked up the scroll and turned to this passage: " 'The spirit of the Lord is upon me because he has anointed me to bring good news to the poor; he has sent me to heal the brokenhearted, to preach deliverance to the captives, recovery of sight to the blind, to let the oppressed go free, to proclaim the year of the Lord.' Then he rolled up the scroll and said, 'Today this scripture has been fulfilled in your hearing' " (Luke 4:18–21).

The quoted words come from Isaiah 61:1–2. They lead us to examine other prophetic texts about Christ—how he lived, looked, and acted. We are inclined to think of our Lord as being tall, slender, and handsome. He was, we assume, an eloquent and convincing speaker, who attracted and retained loyal disciples and adoring crowds. In fact, almost all these images are incorrect, as an unbiased reading of the Gospels reveals.

There is a remarkably descriptive passage from Isaiah: "For he grew up before him like a tender shoot, like a root out of parched ground; he had no stately form or majesty that we should look at him, nor appearance that we should be attracted to him. He was despised and forsaken of men, a man of sorrows, and acquainted with grief; and like one from whom men hide their face, he was despised, and we did not esteem him. Surely our griefs he himself bore, and our sorrows he carried; . . . He was pierced through for our transgressions, he was crushed for our iniquities, . . . and by his scourging we are healed" (53:2–5).

Remember that Jesus came from a lowly family that could afford only two doves for an offering in the temple. Although he was charismatic, we can only imagine his physical appearance, which is never described in the New Testament. And what about the effectiveness of his preaching? At the end of his perfect life and three years of preaching, primarily to his apostles, they were not fully convinced. Confused and disillusioned by his trial and execution, which he had frequently predicted in clear language, they abandoned him when he needed them most.

It was only later, with Jesus' resurrection and the coming of the Holy Spirit, that his followers were personally transformed and remembered the events of his life as transcendent and inspirational. Now, in retrospect, we have the same perspective. We are able to correlate omnipotence, majesty, and judgment with humility, mercy, forgiveness, and love.

As Christians, we are servants of God. But does this mean that we are superior to others, self-sufficient, or naturally blessed with material riches? This question was answered repeatedly in the history of the Israelites. Although they were God's chosen people, they always failed when they became arrogant, decided they didn't need God, or defined success by

selfish human standards. We Christians face the same temptations—and, like those ancient Jews, we frequently succumb.

Jesus came to explain these truths in human terms, so that
we might comprehend them and apply them in our own lives.
The most succinct description of Christ is as a suffering servant, and he tried to give his followers the proper definition of
greatness: "But he that is greatest among you shall be your
servant" (Matthew 23:11).

Looked at objectively, it is extraordinary that the symbol of
Christianity is the cross—something like an electric chair, a
hangman's noose, or a lethal hypodermic needle. How could
the instrument of the most savage human executions be so
greatly exalted? It is a vivid reminder of the humanity of Jesus,
who sacrificed his own perfect life that we might know the
blessing of God's mercy, forgiveness, and love.

CHAPTER THREE

Full of Grace and Truth

The Word became flesh and lived among us. We have seen his glory, the glory of the one and only Son, who came from the Father, full of grace and truth.

. . . No one has ever seen God, but God the only Son, who is at the Father's side, has made him known.

JOHN 1:14, 18

This is one of the most beautiful passages in the Bible. The description it offers of Christ is profound: mysterious yet comprehensible, simple yet filled with meaning. The longer we meditate on these words, the more they mean to us.

The verses quoted begin by saying that the Word—

meaning both Greek *logos*, standing for truth or wisdom, and the word of God, as given to the Jews through Moses—became "flesh." What more common yet descriptive word could we choose? Flesh—the very living stuff of which our bodies are made, the substance that makes up a pounding heart, or a working brain, or a grasping hand. The inexhaustible paradox of God as human is captured in that phrase. The Word became a fleshly person, like one of us, walking the dusty roads of Palestine; sleeping in the open with a stone or a rolled-up cloak for a pillow; eating, drinking, laughing with friends: the Word became flesh.

Yet this was no ordinary human but an extraordinary being, full of grace and truth. Here we have another word, *grace*, that conveys so much meaning in such a small space. Grace is unmerited favor, the undeserved gift of God's love and forgiveness, bestowed on us freely, unlimited and inexhaustible. Jesus Christ, in his teaching, his miracles, his life, death, and resurrection, embodies God's generosity to us: full of grace, indeed.

Isn't it remarkable to see God coming to earth in this form? Not as a triumphant ruler, riding a white horse and wearing a crown, leading an army to expel the hated Romans and fulfilling human desires or ambitions, but rather as one who epitomizes unlimited forgiveness, compassion, service, peace, and love. A man, yet God, who was there when the universe was created, knowing everything, totally powerful.

No one has ever seen God, John goes on to say, and of course this is true. People in all times and places have struggled to visualize God, and artists have depicted God in accordance with the customs of their societies. Michelangelo, for example, created my first physical image of God: white hair, a long, flowing beard, a white robe. This is the God I pictured when I was a child, sitting on a throne in heaven and keeping tabs on me, writing down in a book the good things and the bad things I did.

Yet we know that God is neither male nor female; only sexist assumptions make God into an old white-haired man. And our assumptions about God as judge need to be qualified and corrected as well. As John assures us: "But if we love each other, God lives in us and his love is made complete in us" (1 John 4:12). He makes the point this way: "Whoever does not love does not know God, because God is love" (4:8).

God is love: this is the first Bible verse many children learn by memory and the most succinct description in Scripture. Christ will indeed be our judge at the end of days, as he tells in the beautiful passage about separating the sheep and the goats (Matthew 25:31–46). But God's basic nature is not judgmental. God is love: *agape* love, forgiving love, love for those who are unattractive, those who don't deserve to be loved, those who don't love us back. God is love in its purest, most exalted, and most exciting, challenging, and difficult meaning. This is what Jesus came to earth to teach us, and this is why John describes him as full of grace.

But remember, too, the word John places in juxtaposition to grace: *truth.* Grace is gentle, grace is nice, but truth can be difficult to face. What is the truth about my life, or yours—judged not by human standards but by the standards of Jesus Christ? Have I lived in a way that is truly compatible with the teachings of the humble, human, yet all-loving and all-knowing God I have pledged to follow? This truth can be troubling, even humiliating—though *humbling* may be a better word.

But, fortunately, in John's Gospel, and in the life of Christ, grace and truth go together. If it weren't for the assurance of grace, how could we acknowledge the full truth about ourselves? We can depend upon the love and forgiveness of Jesus to correct and cleanse us. This, too, is part of John's beautiful and reassuring message.

CHAPTER FOUR

The Laughing Jesus

The chief priests and the elders came to him as he was teaching, and said, "By what authority do you these things?" . . . And Jesus answered, "I also will ask you one thing, which if you tell me, I will tell you by what authority I do these things. The baptism of John, whence was it? From heaven or of men?" And they reasoned together, saying, "If we shall say, 'From heaven,' he will say unto us, 'Why did you not then believe him?' But if we shall say, 'Of men,' we fear the people, for all hold John as a prophet." And they answered Jesus, and said, "We cannot tell." And he said unto them, "Neither will I tell you by what authority I do these things."

MATTHEW 21:23–27

I received several angry letters from readers of my book *Living Faith* because I commented there that Jesus could easily have substituted for Jay Leno or David Letterman on the late-night talk shows. My correspondents seemed to believe it was sacrilegious to think that Jesus Christ had a sense of humor. One person, however, sent me a copy of "The Laughing Jesus," a delightful painting that could very well have represented him and the bystanders after a witty exchange like the one just quoted.

It's a shame that so many people believe that Jesus was always solemn, and that therefore the proper demeanor for his followers is to be grim, stern, even haughty toward others. In fact, Jesus had a good time, and he encouraged his disciples to join him in enjoying life. There are numerous accounts of his going to parties and associating with a broad range of apparently carousing acquaintances. Jesus and his friends were chastised by the scribes and Pharisees: "Why do you eat and drink with publicans and sinners?" and later, "Why do the disciples of John fast often, and make prayers, and likewise the disciples of the Pharisees; but yours eat and drink?"

Jesus replied, in effect, that it was important for him to be a friend to sinners, who needed him, and that he and his disciples wanted to enjoy each other's company while they had a chance, because he would not always be with them.

I never knew anyone who had more close friends than my brother, Billy—probably ten for every one that I have. He had a great sense of humor, which sometimes got him into trouble. During the summer of 1976, after I had been nominated as the Democratic candidate for president, our hometown of Plains was filled with reporters, many of whom spent a lot of time around Billy's service station. They enjoyed and wrote down the idle and sometimes ribald statements they heard and, unfortunately, later used them as serious quotations to make Billy look foolish.

Earlier that year, before our family members were well known, a new reporter in town asked Billy if he didn't agree that he was somewhat peculiar. He replied, "My mother went into the Peace Corps when she was sixty-eight years old; my youngest sister is a holy-roly preacher; my other sister is eight years older than I am and spends half her time on a Harley-Davidson motorcycle; and my brother thinks he's going to be President of the United States! I'm the only one in the family who is normal!"

My mother was a lot like Billy. The following year, in January, I had just been inaugurated, walked down Pennsylvania Avenue, reviewed the parade with my family, and then begun to walk with my family, for the first time, toward the White House. Eager news reporters with cameras surrounded us, and my press secretary said, "Don't anyone stop to answer questions." Typically, Mama ignored him and stopped to talk to the press. The first question was "Miss Lillian, aren't you proud of your son?" Mama replied, "Which one?"

Billy and Mama enjoyed life and even on their deathbeds retained their equanimity and their sense of humor. As did Jesus', Billy's and Mama's joy and humor helped draw people together, assuaged sorrow, and, when necessary, deflated pride in a positive way.

It is good for us personally and as Christian witnesses to remember that, in spite of trials and tribulations, we should also enjoy life—more like Jesus and not like the scribes and Pharisees, solemn, proud, and inclined to judge others. Did Jesus laugh? Yes, he did—often, and with a full heart.

CHAPTER FIVE

The Special Message of Jesus

You have heard that it has been said, "You shall love your neighbor, and hate your enemy!" But I say to you, "Love your enemies, bless them that curse you, do good to them that hate you, and pray for them which despitefully use you and persecute you."

MATTHEW 5:43–44

On my bookshelf I have an interesting book that was published in 1978 called *The 100*, by Michael Hart. It is a ranking of the most influential persons in history. I disagree with a lot of Hart's opinions. For instance, he ranks Jesus third, behind Muhammad and Isaac Newton (Buddha,

Confucius, and St. Paul come next). Despite this, it is an intriguing text, with some thought-provoking analyses. For example, Hart explains that he ranks Muhammad first because he was the sole founder of Islam, while Jesus and Paul share the responsibility for Christianity. Muhammad was also a great secular leader, while Jesus Christ refused to accept any worldly authority.

What is most pertinent is the author's description of the unique message of Christ. Almost all religions adopt some form of the Golden Rule as a premise, but Jesus was alone in commanding that we forgive enemies, turn the other cheek, or walk a second mile. Hart then quotes the text for this lesson and says that if these words and others from the Sermon on the Mount "were widely followed, I would have no hesitation in placing Jesus first in this book."

There is no legal demand that a human being should love an enemy. In fact, it is difficult for us to love anyone unless we have the security of being loved. Except in a case of sexual infatuation, it's just not logical to expect us to love anyone who doesn't reciprocate our love.

It is even more difficult for us to forgive others if we don't have the assurance of being forgiven. We feel we have to wait, until we are sure that the other person will also forgive us. All of us have probably fallen uncontrollably in love with a potential sweetheart who rejects us. But we don't fall uncontrollably into forgiveness, especially of an enemy! Also, we can love people and not forgive them—a fact proven by the high rate of divorce in our society.

Peter heard the troubling command of Jesus and wanted to ingratiate himself with the Lord—but he also wanted to be sure he didn't go too far. Knowing that some rabbis advocated forgiveness three times, he came to Jesus and asked, "Lord, how often shall my brother sin against me, and I forgive him? until seven times?" Jesus said to him, "I say not to you, 'until seven times,' but 'until seventy times seven'" (Matthew 18:21–22).

Many of us have computed that this is 490 times, but the command is not for me to count patiently if my wife burns toast 490 mornings and then on the 491st time I can finally condemn her! The point of Jesus' teaching is to make forgiveness a permanent attitude, a way of life.

He immediately explained this to Peter with one of his most interesting parables. A servant owed the king 10,000 talents (the modern equivalent is more than $25,000 per talent)—an almost immeasurable debt. The king forgave him, and immediately the servant cast one of his subordinates into prison because he failed to repay a debt of about $15. The other servants reported this to the king, who severely punished the unforgiving one (verses 23–34).

It is somewhat shocking that Jesus says, "Forgive and even love your enemies." Does he mean that we should do this even if we aren't sure that we will be forgiven and loved? Strangely, the answer is no, because forgiveness and love are available to all of us—through Christ. Jesus draws a parallel with us when he adds, "So likewise shall my heavenly Father do unto you, if you from your hearts forgive not every one of his brothers their trespasses" (verse 35).

We have already agreed that it is difficult to love without being loved, and almost impossible to forgive without being forgiven. The teachings of Jesus are predicated on the fact that we receive the unbounded love of God and absolute forgiveness of all our trespasses. Like the king in the parable, God forgives our great debts and expects us to forgive the relatively insignificant grievances we may have against others.

His Healing Touch

CHAPTER SIX

Jonah and the Big Fish

Now the word of the Lord came to Jonah the son of Amittai, saying, "Arise, go to Nineveh, that great city, and cry against it; for their wickedness has come to me."

But Jonah rose up to flee to Tarshish from the presence of the Lord, and went down to Joppa; and he found a ship going to Tarshish, to go with them to Tarshish from the presence of the Lord.

JONAH 1:1–3

As is the case with "Doubting Thomas" and many other Bible characters, most of us know one thing about Jonah—that a whale (the Bible actually says "big fish") swallowed him. One of the challenges of Bible study is to delve more deeply into a dramatic story and to see how its message might possibly apply to us. Let's take a closer look at this intriguing event.

Nineveh was a city established by Nimrod, son of Cush, son of Ham, son of Noah. It was the massive capital of Assyria, which the prophet Nahum described as "cruel and evil." In the time of Jonah, Nineveh was the ultimate enemy of the Israelites, inhabited by despised Gentiles. It was considered a city condemned by God, with leaders whose equivalents in our day would be a Mu'ammar al-Gadhafi or a Saddam Hussein.

Jonah grew up as a rich kid, welcome even in the royal palace. He was an archconservative, jingoistic supporter of Israelite leaders who were prejudiced against anyone who was not Jewish or might oppose the unrestricted expansion of Judaism. In some commentaries, he has been described in modern language as a klutz or a jerk—one of the most foolish and stubborn biblical characters.

Now let's take another look at this text. God wanted to give the people of Nineveh a chance to repent and be forgiven. How could Jonah betray his own people by traveling to this hated place and delivering such a message? Understandably, this command was abhorrent to Jonah, who wanted the people of Nineveh to be condemned to hell.

Jonah had three options: to obey God, to stay where he was and ignore the command, or to run away and hide. As we know, he chose the third option. Tarshish was at the southern tip of Spain, which was then at the farthest edge of the known world; some people thought that anyone who went farther would fall off the edge and vanish into oblivion. The ships and sailors of Tarshish were known as the finest on the seas.

The ship Jonah was on ran into a great storm and began to founder on the way to its destination, and the crew somehow knew that this was a special tempest sent to punish someone. The sailors cast lots and identified Jonah as the guilty person onboard. They found him asleep in his cabin, and he confessed that he was trying to escape from God. So far as we know, he was the only one on the ship who wasn't praying; he just identified himself as a Hebrew who worshiped "the God of Heaven who made the sea and the dry land."

It's typical of Jonah that he acknowledged the power and omnipresence of God but still refused to pray, repent, or obey. Instead, he finally chose to commit suicide by telling the crew, "Pick me up and throw me into the sea." This they did, the sea was calmed, and Jonah was saved by being taken into a big fish.

Later, Jonah was vomited up on dry land and finally agreed to go to Nineveh. And we note that, despite their sinfulness and rebellion, forgiveness was available both to the people of Nineveh and to Jonah. "So the people of Nineveh believed God, and proclaimed a fast. . . . And God saw their works, that they turned from their evil way; and God repented of the evil that he had said that he would do unto them; and he did it not" (Jonah 3:5, 10). When Jonah saw this, he went into a rage because of God's benevolence, and the story ends, with the fate of the resentful prophet unknown.

The primary lesson of the Book of Jonah is that the Gospel message and the grace and love of God are for all people, not just a few fortunate chosen ones. God is eager to have all people repent and be forgiven. Our own arrogance or prejudice toward others is mistaken and condemned. There are other lessons in this book that compare the all-encompassing mercy

and concern we are given by God with the relatively insignificant grievances for which we should be forgiving to our
neighbors and loved ones.

For Christians, the words and actions of Jesus provide clear
commandments. We should be receptive to them, and we are
sadly mistaken if, like Jonah, we think we can escape from the
presence of God or the Holy Spirit. This belief separates us
from the joy and peace we have been promised.

CHAPTER SEVEN

No More Hiding

When she heard about Jesus, she came up behind him in the crowd and touched his cloak, because she thought, "If I just touch his clothes, I will be healed." Immediately her bleeding stopped and she felt in her body that she was freed from her suffering. . . . [And Jesus] said to her, "Daughter, your faith has healed you. Go in peace and be freed from your suffering."

MARK 5:27–29, 34

There are many healing miracles in the New Testament, but this story from Mark is the only instance I know in which Christ healed someone without taking the initiative or responding deliberately. Frequently, people would come to Jesus—the traveling teacher about whom so many were talking—and say, "I am sick; can you heal me?" But in this case, Jesus did not even know that the healing was taking place until after it had happened, when he realized that power had gone out from him.

By the way, we sometimes assume that Jesus, being God, knew everything; yet in this story, after Jesus becomes aware of the healing, he asks his disciples, "Who touched my clothes?" (verse 30). Clearly Jesus was human enough to have to wonder who touched him when he was jostled in the crowd. It reminds us that he was, in that sense, a person like you or me.

Why did the woman in the story feel the need to sneak up on Jesus rather than ask him directly to heal her? Under the circumstances, it was probably a natural inclination. Remember, first of all, that women were severely oppressed, beginning at birth. When a baby girl was born, neighbors would sometimes wonder, What did those parents do wrong, that they should be given a girl instead of a boy? Economics played a role: a boy was viewed as the future breadwinner of the family, a kind of social security for the future, whereas a girl was considered a burden, someone who couldn't even be married off successfully unless an expensive dowry could be provided. And throughout the life of a girl or a woman, custom would hold her down, restricting her freedom.

So for this suffering woman to come out alone in public was, in itself, probably a difficult thing to do. Furthermore, this woman had a disease that was considered embarrassing or shameful in the Jewish culture of her day. Mark says that she had been subject to bleeding for twelve years. We know that a woman having her monthly period was considered unclean for religious purposes: she could not participate in any sort of religious ceremony or enter the Temple, even its outer porches, and anyone who touched her was considered unclean as well. Imagine the deprivation and loneliness this woman had suffered: for twelve years she had been shunned by other people, forbidden even to go to worship. No wonder she would have been ashamed to make herself known openly. So we can understand the feelings of the suffering woman and her desire to conceal her affliction, even from Jesus.

Many of us have a tendency to conceal our weaknesses, our failures, and our needs. We prefer to demonstrate that we are strong and self-sufficient. This tendency comes out in many ways. In men, it may appear as a macho attitude: "I can stand on my own feet and deal with my own problems. I don't need help, so don't try to help me!" In a business meeting, we may be afraid to admit that we don't know the answer to a question; in a prayer group or Bible study class, we may be embarrassed to confess that we don't understand a passage of Scripture. And when we have a deep personal or spiritual trouble, we may hesitate to seek help from pastors, counselors, or friends, fearing that they will respect us less for admitting we need their guidance.

As a result, we put on disguises—facades to make us appear better, stronger, more self-assured than we really are. And in so doing, we cut ourselves off from other people and from the healing power of God's love, which we can enjoy only if we have the courage to open ourselves to it. Finding that courage begins with facing the truth about ourselves.

A half hour of quiet, sincere contemplation and self-analysis might be the first step. Perhaps we'll want to take a notebook and write down the things we discover about ourselves. "This is what I am, my strengths and weaknesses, the

good and the bad in my life so far; and here are the opportunities—and needs—that can bring me closer to God in the future." It's difficult to do this, and to make the commitment to
change that it implies, but faith in Jesus and his forgiveness
can help.

God doesn't want us to hide our weaknesses and needs but
is eager to satisfy them. Remember the end of the story of the
bleeding woman: Jesus sought her out in the crowd, told her,
"Your faith has healed you," and urged her, "Go in peace." Because she'd found within herself the courage to reach out to
Jesus in her need, she was renewed and made whole, not only
in body but in spirit, forgiven and freed from her sins, her sub-
terfuge, and her shame.

Christ is ready to do the same for us.

CHAPTER EIGHT

She Forgot Her Bucket!

When a Samaritan woman came to draw water, Jesus said to her, "Will you give me a drink?" The Samaritan woman said to him, "You are a Jew and I am a Samaritan woman. How can you ask me for a drink?" (For Jews do not associate with Samaritans.)

Jesus answered her, "If you knew the gift of God and who it is that asks you for a drink, you would have asked him and he would have given you living water." . . .

The woman said to him, "I know the Messiah is coming (He who is called Christ); when that one comes, he will explain all things to us." Jesus said to her, "I who speak to you am he." . . . So the woman left her water pot, and went into the city. . . .

JOHN 4:7–10, 25–26, 28

The encounter between Jesus and the woman at the well is one of the most beloved stories of the New Testament. If you've been to the Middle East, you know that most places are very hot and dry. In Jesus' time, and still today in some places, the women had the job of fetching water from communal wells. It wasn't easy work. In the story John tells, Jesus arrives at the well around noon: about the sixth hour of daylight, as the Bible says. It was unusual to be going to the well at noontime. Most of the women would have drawn their supply of water hours earlier, before the heat of the day.

Why did this particular woman have to go at midday? We can figure out the reason from some of the other things we learn about her. The other women ostracized her because of her promiscuity. "I have no husband," she tells Jesus in verse 17, and he replies, with an insight that amazes her, "The fact is, you have had five husbands, and the man you now have is not your husband" (verse 18). So this was a despised woman, in effect a prostitute, rejected and unforgiven by the people around her.

Imagine the life of such a woman. In the morning, the other women of the neighborhood must have gathered at the well and talked together, shared a joke or two, passed along the latest village gossip, and maybe bragged about their children or grandchildren. Meanwhile, this much-married outcast would have sat in her house, perhaps looking out the window until the others returned home. Only when the road was empty, and she could be sure that she wouldn't be cursed or spat upon, did she dare to slip out of her house to fetch water.

This woman was someone the followers of Jesus would

have condemned and shunned. She was a Samaritan and a whore—both words that would have come like curses from the mouths of many Jews at the time. To ethnic and religious prejudice, we can add the sense of superiority most of us have toward someone we consider immoral.

How did Jesus demonstrate the breaking down of prejudice in his encounter with the Samaritan woman? First, he asked her for a cup of water. No doubt Jesus was thirsty, having been walking on the hot, dusty roads of Samaria all morning. But in asking her to share her water cup, he was very deliberately violating a powerful taboo. It's one that many Americans can understand. It embarrasses me to say it, but I remember well that, when I worked in the peanut fields with my daddy as a young boy, it would have been inconceivable for a white person to drink water from the same dipper as one of the black workers. This was true despite the fact that we were working side by side in the same field and that, on the weekend, I might easily play ball, go fishing, or even sleep with my black friends in their house if my parents were away. Still, the sense of taboo we felt and our prejudice against sharing a cup with a black person were strong and unquestioned.

Jesus shattered a similar prejudice with his matter-of-fact request: Will you give me a drink? It's a simple act, but in the context of his society it's a startling one. From this plain yet revolutionary beginning, the meeting between Jesus and the Samaritan woman goes on to become one of the most remarkable encounters in the Bible. Jesus treats the woman in a way she must have found strange and wonderful. Rather than revile, condemn, or lecture her, Jesus speaks to her with frankness, compassion, and respect. He tells her about his own mission on earth—to become a spring of water welling up to eternal life in the souls of those who believe in him (verse 14). And when the woman expresses her faith that one day a savior called Messiah will come, Jesus confesses, "I who speak to you am he" (verses 25–26).

Amazed and moved by Jesus' understanding of her and by the depth of conviction his words carry, she becomes a follower and a witness for him, and helps to convert many of her fellow Samaritans (verses 39–42). In effect, she takes her place alongside Mary Magdalene as one of the great female disciples of Jesus, who rose from a despised social position to become an inspired witness.

She learned about Jesus Christ, the Messiah, completely forgot her water jug, and ran to the village. Realizing that she was probably considered the most sinful person in the community, she didn't report that she had found the long-awaited Messiah. She only said, "Come and see a man who told me all the things I ever did." And she added a question, "Is not this the Christ?" Then the villagers went to the well to see for themselves, and the Bible says, "And many of the Samaritans of that city believed on him" (verses 29, 39).

She may have lost her bucket, but she gained instead the living water of God's love.

CHAPTER NINE

Where Are You, God?

Look down from heaven and see from your lofty throne, holy and glorious. Where are your zeal and your might? Your tenderness and compassion are withheld from us. . . . Why, O Lord, do you make us wander from your ways and harden our hearts so we do not revere you? Return for the sake of your servants, the tribes that are your inheritance.

ISAIAH 63:15, 17

Isaiah writes in the so-called postexilic period, when the Jews had returned to Jerusalem after sixty years of captivity under the Persian emperor Cyrus. It was a time much like ours: chaotic, hopeful, and perilous, filled with both opportunities and problems. The Jews were rebuilding the temple, the traditional heart of their faith, but the work was proceeding slowly, and even when it was completed the reconstructed temple would be a far cry from the magnificent edifice Solomon had built, which had been destroyed a generation earlier. Worse still, intermarriage among the Jews and the Canaanites was threatening the Jews' commitment to their faith, and there was a growing sense that the Israelites were a people adrift, lacking in the moral certainty and strength that had sustained them for centuries.

Many Christians today are filled with a similar sense of uneasiness. A number of things seem to be going well in our society: the economy is healthy, democratic principles are on the upswing around the world, and no major military enemy threatens us. Yet in some ways modern life seems increasingly destitute. Crime, violence, greed, drugs, and the dilution of traditional family values are weakening our society's foundations.

Just one statistic: Every day in the United States, seventeen children are killed by gunfire. That's about 6,000 children each year who are killed by guns, as compared, for example, with about 3,000 a year who died at the height of the polio epidemic of the 1950s. We rose up as a society to fight against polio. Why do we not act more forcefully to halt today's even greater scourge? And where is God in all this evil and suffering? These are the kinds of questions that Isaiah asked about his own troubled society more than 2,500 years ago. In the verses quoted here, Isaiah is crying out to God for answers: "Why do you let us abandon your ways? Why do you tolerate evil among us? God, do something!"

The honesty and passion of Isaiah's prayer impress me. It's a cry of anguish, of suffocation, of abandonment, of disappointment. He didn't do what many of us do, which is simply complain about our problems. He approached God directly. Nor did he pray in the superficial, rote manner we often adopt—reciting a few traditional words for perhaps sixty seconds a day. He leveled with God in an intensely personal way.

My sister Ruth had a habit of praying as though she was talking to a friend about the constantly evolving events of her life. She always seemed to be aware of the presence of the Holy Spirit and could communicate easily and with complete confidence. It was disconcerting that, despite our sincere attempts, she was never able to impart to me such a highly personal and intimate relationship with Christ. My prayers are usually more formal, as I speak somewhat cautiously to Almighty God.

Let's imagine that we've become alienated from our closest friend, someone we've known and loved and with whom we've shared life for many years. Maybe one of us has said or done something cruel or thoughtless to hurt the other; perhaps we've allowed the faithless act to make us grow apart, so that we haven't spoken for months. Yet all the while, we've longed to be reunited in the old love that meant so much to us both.

Now, imagine further that we have just a short time—ten minutes, say—to see our friend and be reconciled. What would the conversation be like? Would it be superficial, formal, and polite? No, it would more likely be a cry from the heart. That's what Isaiah's prayer to God is like. "God, where are you?" he cries. "Come back to me, let me see you! We are your children, the ones you chose to love. Open up the heavens and help us!"

It's rare for us to pray with such perfect frankness. Even in our most private thoughts, we like to conceal who we really are. We don't want God to see our selfishness, our inadequacy, our weakness. But Isaiah got to the heart of things. Seeing God's people floundering in sin and alienation from God, he expressed their anguish fully and freely.

And what is God's answer to Isaiah's painful questions? In the prophet's day and in our own the answer is the same, one that, perhaps, we know in our hearts. Though we cry out, "Where is God?" it's not God who is lost—it is we. As human beings have always done, we wander away from the presence of God and find ourselves suddenly alone. But we are the ones who have left the right road; God has not abandoned us.

Where is God? God is here, in you and me. In the Book of Revelation, Jesus says, "Here I am! I stand at the door and knock. If anyone hears my voice and opens the door, I will come in and eat with him, and he with me" (3:20). We are always in the presence of the Holy Spirit, as my sister Ruth seemed to know. Whether the door is open or closed is our decision.

CHAPTER TEN

The Cost of Grace

We then, as workers together with him, beseech you also that
ye receive not the grace of God in vain. . . .

For ye know the grace of our Lord Jesus Christ, that,
though he was rich, yet for your sakes he became poor, that ye
through his poverty might be rich.

2 CORINTHIANS 6:1, 8:9

As followers of Jesus Christ, we must realize that grace—the
free gift of God—is not free. Someone has spelled out *grace*
as God's Riches At Christ's Expense, and the phrase isn't just
beautiful but very apt. We have seen that the early disciples of
Jesus were eager to face severe deprivation or punishment as
they proudly exhibited their faith.

In our own era, one of the best examples of this lesson is the great German theologian Dietrich Bonhoeffer. He was a Protestant pastor during Hitler's Nazi regime, leading churches not only in Germany but in Spain and England as well. A good friend of Reinhold Niebuhr, Bonhoeffer was lecturing in America at Niebuhr's invitation when Hitler attained power in Germany.

Niebuhr urged Bonhoeffer to remain in America, for his own safety. Bonhoeffer refused. He felt he had to be among the other Christians who he knew were being persecuted in Germany. So he returned home, and for the rest of his life he played a role in the resistance to Hitler. He preached publicly against Nazism, racism, and anti-Semitism. And he kept secret the plot to assassinate Hitler, which one of Bonhoeffer's relatives helped to organize in 1944. Naturally, each of these acts put his life at risk.

Bonhoeffer was finally arrested and imprisoned, and in 1945, just a few days before the allied armies liberated Germany, he was executed on the orders of Heinrich Himmler. He died a disciple and a martyr. His life, we can see, was a modern parallel to the martyrdom suffered by many of the earliest Christians. One of Bonhoeffer's most famous books is titled *The Cost of Discipleship*. Although he wrote this book several years before his execution, the cost of Bonhoeffer's own faith is obvious: he paid the greatest earthly price, his life. Yet Bonhoeffer's message is that, for all of us, there is no such thing as cheap grace.

Personally, I find this message especially challenging: that it's never easy to follow Christ with a full commitment. The temptation—a powerful one—is always there to temper our acts, to modify our commitment, to equivocate or make excuses when we are called upon to do something challenging, painful, or sacrificial on behalf of Christ. We don't want to seem naïve or foolish. To live up to our faith in every moment of our lives is impossible for us as human beings.

For most of us it costs nothing to preach, to speak about our Christian beliefs, to attend church services, or to say, "I'm a Christian." But there's another element to our Christianity. We need to ask ourselves, "What have I actually done that proves my loyalty to Christ? How many times have I sacrificed my own well-being for that of others, in the name of Christ—this week, this month, or even during the last five years?"

Fortunately, the same Holy Spirit that energized and encouraged the first disciples, and that gave Dietrich Bonhoeffer the strength to stand up against Nazi tyranny, is available to us today, wherever and however we live. And if we ask for the help of that Spirit, we will receive it.

CHAPTER ELEVEN

The Good Shepherd

I am the good shepherd. The good shepherd lays down his life for the sheep. The hired hand is not the shepherd who owns the sheep. So when he sees the wolf coming, he abandons the sheep and runs away. Then the wolf attacks the flock and scatters it. The man runs away because he is a hired hand and cares nothing for the sheep.

JOHN 10:11–13

Rosalynn and I have visited China a number of times, and as a result I feel very close to the Chinese people. As president, I decided that the United States would normalize diplomatic relations with China, and when this was done in January 1979 the late premier Deng Xiaoping visited the White House. He explained to me the changes he planned for China. At that time the communal farms were all owned by the state and were worked together by the local farmers.

By 1981, when we made a return visit to China, Deng had permitted each farm family to have the crop from 15 percent of the land, and he'd also allowed each farmer—but no urban families—to start one small industry. They could make clay pots, repair bicycles, raise a few mink, and so on. This was the start of the capitalist-style industry now exploding throughout China. In explaining his plan, Deng made an interesting observation: that no Chinese farmer would stay up all night with a sick hog if it belonged to the state farm, but if it was his own animal, he'd tend it until morning to make sure it survived. That's human nature, he said, and he admitted that he'd probably act the same way.

It's also the image Jesus is drawing in these verses, to describe his love for us. He is the good shepherd, who lays down his life for the sheep, rather than the mere hired hand, who flees when danger comes near.

Of course, it's not very flattering for us to be compared to sheep! When I grew up, we always had a flock of sheep on our farm, and we considered them dumb and meek. They look big, but most of their size comes from their fluffy wool, and they appeared pitiful and even a little ugly after we sheared the wool. When attacked, sheep are utterly unable to defend themselves. Stray dogs were the main predators that concerned us. It seemed that once a dog killed sheep for food, he would later do so even when he wasn't hungry, almost as an addiction—because they were so vulnerable and helpless. Such a dog had to be destroyed.

So calling us sheep is not very flattering, but in using the imagery of sheep and shepherd to describe God's relationship to humans, Jesus was drawing on a wealth of biblical tradition. Maybe the most beloved chapter in the Bible is the Twenty-third Psalm, the beautiful poem that begins, "The Lord is my shepherd, I shall not want. He makes me lie down in green pastures." Pastors report that this is the Bible passage most requested by people who are seriously ill or overcome with grief. The presence of God as a guardian and comforter in our lives is something we desperately hunger to believe, and this psalm expresses that faith magnificently. We Americans, being especially proud of our independence, willpower, and self-sufficiency, may not like to think of ourselves as followers, but there's nothing wrong with being subservient if Christ is our leader.

The truth is, we're all vulnerable, not only to danger and misfortune but also to temptation, fear, doubt, and selfishness. We're vulnerable, like sheep, to being led astray; we're vulnerable to forces that can destroy our lives, turning us away from our families, friends, and neighbors. And the superficial trappings we hope will protect us—possessions, reputation, pride—do no more to make us secure than the sheep's fluffy wool. Just below the surface, we're helpless and in need of Christ's guidance and protection.

And when we think of sheep in a biblical context, we should also remember the special use of the image of a sheep in Isaiah's description of the suffering servant: "We all, like sheep, have gone astray, each of us has turned to his own way; and the Lord has laid on him the iniquity of us all. He was oppressed and afflicted, yet he did not open his mouth; he was led like a lamb to the slaughter, and as a sheep before her shearers is silent, so he did not open his mouth" (53:6–7).

Christians, of course, read Isaiah's description as a prophecy of Christ: the savior who took upon himself the iniquity of us all, suffering in silence on our behalf. How vividly the words evoke the last hours of Jesus and his willing, unprotesting death at the hands of his enemies!

The imagery seems paradoxical. Isaiah is describing the ruler of the universe, the Savior and Messiah, in the form of a sheep, vulnerable and helpless. But the nature of Christ is equally paradoxical: victim and redeemer, servant and ruler, man and God.

The vulnerability and foolishness of a sheep may not be characteristics we're eager to confess we have. We may prefer to imagine that we are strong and able to take care of ourselves. But that belief is an illusion, as the troubles and failures of our lives show us. Fortunately, in Jesus we have a shepherd whom we can trust with our weakness and helplessness. He took our vulnerability upon himself and laid down his life for us, only to rise again in triumph. Now he offers us hope, reassurance, and security as part of his wandering but ever-loved flock.

Who Is My Neighbor?

CHAPTER TWELVE

I Will Be with You

But now, this is what the Lord says: "Fear not, for I have redeemed you; I have called you by name; you are mine.

"When you pass through the waters, I will be with you."

ISAIAH 43:1–2

The presence of another person can be a transforming experience in our lives. At times, it can mean the difference between life and death. Something most parents know, which
physicians have now proven, is that a baby has an innate need,
a hunger, for the loving presence of an adult. If a baby is not
touched and held, it will not grow and mature properly.

At Grady Hospital in Atlanta, we see vividly what this
means. Many premature babies are born there, and some of

their mothers are addicted to crack cocaine. In fact, more than 15 percent of the babies are addicted to cocaine at birth. All too often, their mothers are incapable of caring for them properly. These babies would languish without proper nurturing; some would even die. Fortunately, there are a lot of volunteers who go to Grady and do nothing more than sit and hold them. It makes all the difference in the world to the babies; it makes them feel well and strong, and it teaches them to respond to other people. And the volunteers tell me it's one of the most gratifying times of their week.

Not only babies have this deep need for contact with other human beings. My mother, whom everyone called Miss Lillian, was a registered nurse who volunteered to go into the Peace Corps at the age of sixty-eight. She was sent to India, where she served in a small village near Bombay, working in a clinic. The people she cared for were terribly poor; many of them didn't have enough to eat, and they lacked access to proper health care, education, and good jobs. What made their plight worse was that some of them suffered from terrible diseases, including leprosy, which made others shun them.

We know from the Bible that the people of Jesus' time also shunned those suffering from leprosy. There was a common belief that God was punishing lepers for their sins, or perhaps the sins of their parents. So nobody would go near them, not only because of the risk of contagion but because lepers were considered inferior, even subhuman. (Think of how we sometimes treat people suffering from AIDS today. This helps us understand the significance of Jesus' example.)

Jesus Christ broke down this barrier, as he broke down so many others. He reached out to the lepers, curing many and comforting all, and teaching us a lesson in the importance of sharing our presence even with people who are despised or rejected by others.

During her time in India, my mother discovered the truth of that lesson. But she learned it the hard way, as described in one of my poems.

Miss Lillian Sees Leprosy for the First Time

When I nursed in a clinic near Bombay,
a small girl, shielding all her leprous sores,
crept inside the door. I moved away,
but then the doctor said, "You take this case!"
First I found a mask and put it on,
quickly gave the child a shot and then,
not well, I slipped away to be alone
and scrubbed my entire body red and raw.

I faced her treatment every week with dread
and loathing for the chore, not the child.
As time passed, I was less afraid,
and managed not to turn my face away.
Her spirit bloomed as sores began to fade.
She'd raise her anxious, searching eyes to mine,
to show she trusted me. We'd smile and say
a few Marathi words, then reach and hold
each other's hands. And then love grew between
us, so that when I kissed her lips
I didn't feel unclean.

After this, my mother spent much of her time with people suffering from leprosy and through her nursing skills was able to bring relief to some of them, helping to cure the sores on their bodies and restore their strength. Perhaps her patients had the same needs as the babies at Grady. And what Mama found was that she received from the experience as much as she gave. When she held the hand of a leprous girl, gave a poor villager some food delicacies we had sent her from home, or used the few dollars in pay she received from the Peace Corps to buy medicine for the clinic, she found her own life transformed in a wonderful way. After her return from India, Mama traveled around the country giving humorous but emotional lectures about her experiences and encouraging her audiences not to let advancing age or anything else prevent them from reaching out to others.

God's promise to the Israelites is a promise we all need to hear: "I love you, and I will be with you, no matter what happens." The presence of one who cares for us is a healing, nurturing gift. And when we give our presence to another person, especially one who is lonely, needy, or outcast, the blessing returns to us.

CHAPTER THIRTEEN

Knowing and Being Known

When Jesus saw Nathanael approaching, he said of him, "Here is a true Israelite, in whom there is nothing false." "How do you know me?" Nathanael asked.

Jesus answered, "I saw you while you were still under the fig tree before Philip called you."

Then Nathanael declared, "Rabbi, you are the Son of God; you are the King of Israel."

JOHN 1:47–49

The Gospel of John has a unique role in the New Testament. The other three Gospels, often called "synoptic," have much in common: they tell many of the same stories, often using the same words, and they follow similar outlines of Jesus' life. In fact, most biblical scholars believe that the synoptic Gospels are all based on the same source, which may be either the Gospel of Mark or some undiscovered document from which Matthew, Mark, and Luke all borrowed.

John's Gospel is quite different from the others in tone and style, as well as in many of the details of Jesus' life. One of the most significant differences is that, for John, the divine nature of Jesus is present and apparent from the very beginning of the story, whereas for the other evangelists, it becomes obvious only gradually. John's Gospel begins with the beautiful verses "In the beginning was the Word, and the Word was with God, and the Word was God. He was with God in the beginning. Through him all things were made; without him nothing was made that has been made" (1:1–3). The theological meaning of these verses is complex and profound, but their central message is that Jesus' divine nature not only predates his life on earth but predates the very beginning of time itself.

Most Christians are familiar with the biblical scene in which Peter responds to Jesus' question "Who do you say I am?" with the words "You are the Christ, the Son of the living God" (Matthew 16:16). We tend to think of this as the first time that any of Jesus' followers knew that he was the Son of God. We're inclined to forget that Nathanael, quite early in the earthly ministry of Jesus, says to him, "You are the Son of God." This exclamation reminds us that, for John, Jesus' divinity is clear from the beginning.

How did Nathanael perceive so quickly that Jesus was the Christ? Was he given some kind of revelation? We don't know. But John's account suggests that Nathanael knew because of the simple statement "I saw you while you were still under the fig tree before Philip called you."

It's a curious scene; perhaps if I had been Nathanael, I would have looked for some natural explanation for Jesus' words. Maybe, in the moments before Philip called Nathanael, Jesus had followed Philip and had seen Nathanael from afar, perhaps by standing on a hillside or behind a large stone. Yet Nathanael did not consider this possibility. He reacted to Jesus' words as if being seen under a fig tree had some special meaning for him.

This may be the case. The King James Bible refers to figs or fig trees forty-one times in thirty-nine different verses, several of which describe the fig tree as a place of worship. For the ancient Jews, it seems, the shade of a fig tree was a special location one might seek if one wanted to be secluded for a few moments of intense prayer. Maybe Nathanael was praying under the fig tree when Philip approached him; we don't know. This was a momentous event, almost miraculous: that Jesus and Nathanael knew each other intimately, and almost instantaneously.

In our lives, knowing others and being known are experiences of great psychological and spiritual significance. In fact, the two really go together. "Know thyself" was the motto of the Greek philosophers; but how do we get to know ourselves? Is it simply by looking inward? More often, I think, we come to know ourselves through our relationships with others. As we interact with the people around us, we find reflected back to us the characteristics we reveal to them. By the ways in which they respond to us, we can see how we appear and what sort of impression we make upon them. As we grow up, our self-images—and character—are largely shaped by our encounters with those around us.

Naturally, in most of our relationships we try hard to

control how we appear. We're usually eager to reveal only our better sides. Rather than show qualities like selfishness, pride, or weakness, we work at appearing generous, modest, and strong. This desire to impress people favorably is, in moderation, a good thing. We are better people because we are concerned about others' opinions of us.

But in our most intimate relationships—with a spouse, a close friend, or anyone with whom we feel really comfortable—we are more likely to reveal our true selves. In a perfect friendship, we can be truly intimate because we trust the other person to accept and forgive our flaws, failings, and weaknesses. And if we can do the same for the other, then a richly rewarding relationship of increasing mutual knowledge and self-improvement is possible. A person who is unwilling or unable to enter into such an intimate relationship loses one of the great opportunities in life.

As for Nathanael with Jesus, there is something special in any relationship where we feel known and understood from the very beginning, as if we've known each other for years. We marvel, because such a relationship is rare and precious; not everyone is lucky enough ever to experience it.

But for all of us, a friendship of this kind is available with Jesus Christ. Just as he knew Nathanael from the beginning, Jesus has always known us. His understanding and his love for us are perfect and absolute. We can share with him the truth about ourselves, both good and bad, in the certain knowledge that he will forgive—has forgiven—our every sin and flaw, and can guide us to a better life.

CHAPTER FOURTEEN

The Jealousy Trap

When the men were returning home after David had killed the Philistine, the women came out from all the towns of Israel to meet King Saul with singing and dancing, with joyful songs and with tambourines and lutes. As they danced, they sang: "Saul has slain his thousands, and David his tens of thousands."

Saul was very angry; this refrain galled him. "They have credited David with tens of thousands," he thought, "but me with only thousands. What more can he get but the kingdom?" And from that time on Saul kept a jealous eye on David.

1 SAMUEL 18:6–9

Saul, Israel's first king, ruled the nation at the time of their war against the Philistines. And although God had anointed

Saul as king, he had turned away from God's commandments, becoming proud, arrogant, and disobedient. By the
time David killed Goliath, the champion of the Philistines,
we are told that the Spirit of the Lord had departed from
Saul (1 Samuel 16:14), so, although he was still sovereign, his
self-confidence and his hold on power were increasingly
insecure.

Thus, we can understand all too well his reaction to the tri-
umphal greeting that David receives when he returns home
after killing Goliath. In David, Saul sees a potential rival,
someone whose popularity and heroism have won him the acclaim of the Israelites and may, Saul fears, win the throne as
well.

But notice the effect that Saul's jealousy has upon him.
First of all, it blinds him to David's true nature. David has
no ambition to replace Saul; he is interested simply in serving his king, his nation, and his God. Through all the rest
of Saul's life, as we learn from the later chapters of the first
book of Samuel, he will seek David's death, driven by his jealousy; yet David will remain loyal to Saul. This will still be true
even at the end of Saul's life, when the king meets his death at
the hands of his own armor bearer, whom Saul has begged to
kill him. David punishes the armor bearer with death, declaring that in striking down Saul he has killed the Lord's
anointed. David's behavior is one of the most remarkable
demonstrations of loyalty and humility anywhere in the Bible.
Yet Saul, driven nearly insane by jealousy, is unable to recognize it.

Notice, too, how Saul's jealousy destroys joy in his own accomplishments. Saul is the undisputed leader, and the victo-

ries of his army, including the deeds of David, are ultimately to Saul's credit. Yet Saul is unable to celebrate them. His triumphs bring him no pleasure because he perceives David's as greater.

Finally, Saul's jealousy gradually erodes the remnants of virtue in his character. In the latter portions of chapter 18, we see Saul engaging in ever-greater acts of treachery toward David. He promises each of his daughters in marriage, not intending to keep his word but hoping that David will be killed by the Philistines before the wedding can take place. When these plots fail, he simply orders his son Jonathan to murder David; this, too, fails. Throughout, Saul's jealousy and fear feed each other. When Saul realized that the Lord was with David, we are told, he became still more afraid of him (18:28–29).

What role does jealousy play in our lives? Our society is so largely based on competition—in business, in schools, in sports, in the arts, in politics—that jealousy is difficult to escape. Think about the situations that provoke feelings of envy in us. Maybe it's when we meet a high school or college classmate who has become very successful; perhaps it's when a competitor in our business or profession wins a big contract or makes a lot of money. Maybe it's when a person that we don't much like builds a house nearby that's nicer than ours, or raises a child—or even worse, a grandchild—who is more successful than ours! Our innermost hearts can tell us what pushes our personal jealousy buttons.

Almost all of us are prone to jealousy; I'm no exception. I'll admit, I'm inclined to envy the accomplishments of my successors in public office and to resent their sometimes blaming problems on me. "Nothing succeeds like successors," as some wit once said. But jealousy is a trait I struggle to overcome.

When jealousy is left unchecked, its effects on our character can be devastating. It makes us want to drag down others who've achieved something rather than celebrate their accomplishments. So we look for opportunities to talk about their small flaws, failings, or sins; we join the rumor mill and share negative gossip every chance we get. And the more we do this, the more mean and petty we become, and the more pleasure in our own good things is spoiled.

How can we escape the downward spiral of jealousy that helped to destroy Saul? One key is to reexamine our standards of success. Remember that as Christians we've pledged to pattern our lives after Jesus. The real measures of success are the things that he said were important—in the words of St. Paul, the things we cannot see, like truth, compassion, justice, service, and love.

Another key, perhaps more difficult, is to develop a genuine sense of friendship toward our neighbors, so that we can relish their achievements. This is the same feeling we would normally have, for instance, about our own children.

Rather than asking, "How can I increase my income to surpass that of my neighbor?" or "How can I get a better job than my classmate at college?" try asking, "What can I do to make my life more significant in the eyes of my Savior, Jesus Christ?" If we can reorient our lives to make this our focus, then we can be freed, little by little, from the burning desire to excel our neighbors in the realms of power, wealth, and prestige. Instead, we may find that we are able to admire and share the joys and achievements of those around us, to boost them up rather than tear them down. That's a liberation more gratifying, exciting, and permanent than any worldly success.

CHAPTER FIFTEEN

The Art of Forgiving

Do not judge, and you will not be judged. Do not condemn, and you will not be condemned. Forgive, and you will be forgiven.

LUKE 6:37

One of the most difficult challenges in life is truly to forgive someone who has injured us. In some cases, the passage of time can help. As the years go by, the pain we suffered grows less, and so does our resentment, until one day we discover that our anger and bitterness are almost or completely gone. We may not even remember the original dispute.

In other cases, however, the anger grows. This may be particularly likely in instances where our paths repeatedly cross those of the people who hurt us. It's easy to find ourselves selectively noticing everything hateful or despicable about the other people and ignoring all they do that is admirable or generous, so that our feeling of condemnation increases with the years. In the most extreme case, we can become obsessed with someone else whom we blame for blighting our life. The result can be an existence mired in bitterness and despair.

As Christians, we have a special responsibility to avoid letting resentment of others fester in us. Jesus specifically commands us to forgive our neighbors—and not just once or twice, or even seven times, but seventy times seven (Matthew 18:22). Furthermore, the Scriptures repeatedly state or imply that unless we are willing to forgive others, we ourselves will not be forgiven—not only by our fellow human beings but by God.

We're warned, then, that our resentment of others constitutes a barrier, not only between ourselves and them but between us and God. It's a danger that Christians need to take seriously. This was brought home to me years ago, during my 1966 campaign for governor of Georgia. While on a political tour of the Georgia coast, I made plans to attend Sunday morning services at an old Episcopal church on St. Simons Island with Philip Alston, a good friend. I was surprised when he called me at the last minute to explain that he couldn't receive holy communion that Sunday because he felt unable to forgive someone who had slighted him.

At first I thought he was foolish, but soon I realized that Philip's scruples were biblically based. In his Sermon on the Mount, Jesus warns us, "If you are offering your gift at the altar and there remember that your brother has something against you, leave your gift there in front of the altar. First go and be reconciled to your brother, then come and offer your gift" (Matthew 5:23).

To forgive and to be forgiven, then, are reciprocal acts. We can't have one without the other. But to forgive another who has seriously wronged us is not easy. Anger has a way of springing back to life inside us, even when we feel we have laid it aside for good. Perhaps Jesus' admonition to forgive our brother seventy times seven times refers to the fact that we may have to overcome our own inner anger in reaction to a single offense that many times! Sometimes the only way to put aside our resentment is deliberately to take an overt step toward reconciliation—difficult though it may be.

One of the most important events in my political life was the debate between then-governor Ronald Reagan and me during the 1980 presidential campaign. Sometime afterward we learned that a copy of my secret, personal briefing book for that debate had been stolen beforehand by a Reagan supporter who worked for me in the White House. Eventually, it became known that a noted columnist and author had used the purloined briefing book to help prepare my opponent for the debate. My positions on all the important issues, my analyses of Reagan's positions, my assessment of his vulnerabilities, my tactical plans for the debate, the words and phrases I hoped to use for verbal parries and responses—all of these were known and used against me by a respected journalist who professed fairness and objectivity.

Obviously, I think that what he did was very wrong. But, to my detriment, I retained the resentment for years after the event. Try as I might, I could not bring myself to forgive him until one day, as I was preparing a Sunday School lesson on this very topic of forgiveness, my own hypocrisy was too much to ignore. I decided to think of some concrete step I could take to break down the barrier of anger I'd allowed to grow between the columnist and myself. Casting about for something—anything—that he and I had in common, I finally thought of books we'd written.

My family and I have long been avid baseball fans, and I knew that he had written a book on the subject. I'd avoided reading it, but now I visited a used bookshop near The Carter Center in Atlanta and bought an old copy for a dollar.

I had to admit it was a good book. After reading it, I wrote the author a note, telling him how I had bought his book, expressing my appreciation for the insights he had given me into some of the intricacies of baseball, and offering reconciliation after our long feud. He responded in good humor, only regretting that I hadn't bought a new copy of his book at the full price! Now, much to my relief, I can read his column or see him offering his opinions on television with a much more positive reaction than before. At least partially, one of my resentments has been removed.

Is there a burden of anger, hurt, or resentment toward someone weighing upon us? We shouldn't ignore it any longer. With God's help, we can think of some gesture of forgiveness and reconciliation to offer, and have the courage to make the first move. Doing so can be an important step toward emotional and psychological healing and a new freedom in the grace of Christ's love.

CHAPTER SIXTEEN

The Least of These

Jesus said, "A certain man was going down from Jerusalem to Jericho; and he fell among robbers, and they stripped him and beat him, and went off leaving him half dead. And a certain priest was going down on that road, and when he saw him, he passed by on the other side. And a Levite also, when he came to the place and saw him, passed by on the other side. But a certain Samaritan, who was on a journey, came upon him, and when he saw him, he felt compassion. . . . Which of these three do you think proved to be a neighbor to the man who was robbed?"

LUKE 10:30–33, 36

And as Jesus entered a certain village, ten leprous men . . . said, "Jesus, Master, have mercy on us!" And . . . they were cleansed. Now one of them . . . fell on his face at His feet, giving thanks to Him. And he was a Samaritan. And Jesus said, "Was no one found who turned back to give glory to God, except this foreigner?"

LUKE 17:12–18

So he came to Sychar, a city of Samaria, and Jacob's well was there. Jesus therefore, being wearied from his journey, was sitting thus by the well. It was about the sixth hour. And there came a woman of Samaria to draw water. Jesus said to her, "Give me a drink."

JOHN 4:5–7

In 1976, I was invited to speak to the 17,000 delegates assembled for the Southern Baptist Convention. Later that year, I would be elected U.S. president, but I was asked to speak because I was an active member of the Brotherhood Commission, not because of my political status. Three of us were asked to represent Baptist men, and we were requested to limit our speeches to five minutes each.

I was very concerned when I looked at the program, because the first speaker was the eloquent and charismatic Billy Graham, and I had to follow him. And then I was somewhat relieved, because the person speaking after me was a truck driver. I was told that he was literate, but not well educated, and I thought to myself, "Well, I suppose that at least I'll sound good compared with him."

As we sat on the stage waiting to be introduced, the truck driver told me he had never made a speech in his life. "I don't think I can live through it," he said. "I just can't do it." He was drenched with sweat, and I was barely able to prevent his fleeing. Billy Graham gave one of his usual forceful and inspirational talks, and I did the best I could with my own remarks.

Then the truck driver got up, and for a long time he just stood there. Someone took him a glass of water, and he almost mumbled into the microphone, "I was always drunk, and didn't have any friends. The only people I knew were men like me who hung around the bars in the town where I lived." Then someone—he didn't remember who—told him about Christ, and he wanted to tell other people. He studied the Bible, and talked to some men in the local church where he became a member. The only places he felt at ease were barrooms, and he began to talk to customers there. The bartender told him he was ruining his business and should find some other place to make a nuisance of himself.

But he persisted, and eventually the folks in the bar looked forward to asking him questions. He said, "At first they treated me like a joke, but I kept up with the questions and when I couldn't answer one, I went and got the answer and came back with it. Fourteen of my friends became Christians." He stood there a few seconds, and then returned to his seat.

The truck driver's speech, of course, was the highlight of the convention. I don't believe anyone who was there will ever forget that five-minute fumbling statement—or remember what I or even Billy Graham had to say.

Shortly before I taught this lesson in Washington, Rosalynn and I had been to the play *Man of La Mancha*, in which the archidealist Don Quixote falls in love with a prostitute. He calls her Dulcinea, and she spits on him and makes fun of him. Later, as he lies on his deathbed, she reappears and we discover that her life has been transformed. This old, foolish man had had confidence in her—much more than she thought she deserved. He had exalted her out of her absolute sinfulness, and her life was changed.

Now let's look at the Samaritans. Rosalynn and I visited Israel in 1983 and went to Mount Gerazim, which is traditionally viewed as their holy place and center of worship, much as the Jews viewed the city of Jerusalem. We met some Samaritans there, among about 600 Samaritans still left at that time. I don't know how many there are now.

In New Testament times, the Samaritans were a half-Jewish group, related to yet separate from the mainstream Jewish community. Descended from Abraham, Isaac, and Jacob, the Samaritans worshiped God, although they accepted only the first five books of the Hebrew Scriptures—the Torah, or Pentateuch, as it is sometimes called—as authoritative. They'd settled in Samaria at the time that the Jews were permitted by the Assyrian Empire to return to Israel and, rejecting the preaching of Ezra, many Samaritans intermarried with members of other local tribes. In time they came to be regarded as half-breeds, Jews who had betrayed their people and their faith by intermarriage.

At the time of Jesus, the Samaritans were generally despised by mainstream Jews and were forbidden to worship in the Temple at Jerusalem (even if they'd wanted to). They were considered unclean, physically and spiritually. Even to set foot in Samaria was thought improper by many Jews.

The Scriptures quoted at the beginning of this lesson are the only three occasions when Jesus is known to have dealt with Samaritans. In every case, they turn out to be heroes.

The context for Jesus' stories about the Samaritans, then, is a highly prejudiced, sharply divided society—one not unlike our own. To understand the attitude, just think about how many Americans feel about the very poor, about people of color, about certain immigrant groups, or about people of different faiths. For Samaritan, substitute black, Muslim, AIDS victim, Haitian—or perhaps roll them all into one! For Jesus to speak with a Samaritan—and a Samaritan whore, to boot— was a bold blow against deeply ingrained prejudice. His acknowledging the gratitude of the healed leper and using a Samaritan's actions as epitomizing the Golden Rule are powerful lessons against prejudice.

Like those of the alcoholic truck driver and Dulcinea, the lives of the Samaritan woman and the leper were transformed when someone was interested in and cared for them. There are always barriers between us and people who are different, lonely, or in need, and it is natural and convenient for us to refrain from crossing those lines. One of the greatest fears is of being embarrassed—of being publicly scorned or rejected, or of getting ourselves out on a limb and having it chopped off. But who builds and maintains the barriers? We do.

We have the same mandate about witnessing to others that Jesus gave his disciples when they rejoined him at the Samaritan well: "Behold, I say unto you, 'Lift up your eyes, and look on the fields; for they are white already to harvest' " (verse 35). But some of us will live out the rest of our lives—ten, twenty, thirty years—and never attempt to break through the obstacles that separate us from those who may be eager to have a new friend, or to learn about Jesus Christ, our Savior.

The truth is that we are too comfortable with our prejudices. They become so deeply ingrained that we're scarcely aware of them. We can go on happily for a lifetime, barely aware of the thoughts, needs, and talents of others who look, sound, and behave differently from us. But that's not the way of life Jesus intends for us. By his own example, Jesus shows us how to overcome the barriers that separate us from other people, and the amazing ways our lives can be enriched when we dare to take the first step toward an "unattractive" person.

CHAPTER SEVENTEEN

Who Among Us Is Superior?

The other disciples therefore said to Thomas, "We have seen the Lord." But he said to them, "Unless I shall see in his hands the print of the nails, and put my finger into the print of the nails, and thrust my hand into his side, I will not believe."

JOHN 20:25

After Jesus was crucified, the disciples were afraid for their own lives, and there is little doubt that they were also blaming each other for the tragedy that had occurred. They hadn't even stayed awake when Jesus was in distress and praying in the Garden of Gethsemane, and no one had come forward to testify for him during his trial before the Sanhedrin. All were guilty of abandoning him, but they were undoubtedly arranging others in degrees of guilt, with Judas at the top, perhaps Peter second because he had denied Christ, all the way down the line. It was natural for each to seek some justification for his own actions.

There was a new scapegoat when Christ appeared, and Thomas, who was absent, later refused to believe that the Lord was risen. Down through the ages, Peter's name has become exalted, while his compatriot has been stigmatized by the epithet Doubting Thomas. We are inclined to ascribe an inferior status to Thomas because of his lack of faith.

It is human nature to arrange other people in some kind of order, based on our personal observations or prejudices. Somewhere on the list we insert ourselves, perhaps in a somewhat exalted position. Jesus warns us against doing this, in a stern manner: "Judge not, that you be not judged" (Matthew 7:1).

The habit of judging and ranking people applies across societies, nations, and ethnic groups. I hear ostensibly enlightened and humanitarian people deriding Africans as lacking ambition, intelligence, and ability—much as we used to hear during segregation days from racists about our black neighbors. We at The Carter Center have had the opportunity to know and work with countless Africans, and we see the reality behind the stereotypes. We have helped with an agricultural project that we call Global 2000, mostly financed by a Japanese foundation and guided by Nobel Laureate Norman Borlaug, a noted agronomist and the father of the "green revolution" in India and Pakistan during the late 1960s. After I conclude an agreement with the leader of each nation in the project, we provide the country with one scientist, who trains several hundred native extension workers. They ride bicycles from one small farm to another, teaching and supervising the planting, cultivating, and harvesting practices of the local farmers. The average farm size is only about two acres.

The program is amazingly successful throughout Africa— primarily because these "backward" families are intelligent, competent, and as eager to succeed as anyone we've ever known. In most cases, we are able to increase their production of corn, wheat, sorghum, and millet threefold, using primitive implements, the right varieties of seed, moderate applications of fertilizer, planting in contour rows, and harvesting at the right time. We now have about 600,000 families in twelve African nations participating in this program.

Our most notable success has been in Ethiopia, where abject starvation in 1986 precipitated the global Live Aid concert. When we began our Global 2000 program in 1993, Ethiopia was producing 5.5 million tons of grain for its 60 million people—still a starvation diet. In 1996, the nation's grain yield was 11.7 million tons! In January 1997, its leaders were proud to announce that they were exporting surplus corn to adjacent nations and would be self-sufficient in wheat in 1997. That's what Africans can do!

Now let's take another look at Thomas. When Jesus decided to go to Bethany to console Mary and Martha because their brother Lazarus had died, everyone knew that this was a time of extreme danger. Jesus had already warned his disciples about the cruel fate that awaited him. Listen to the courageous reaction of the same disciple we often disparage: "Then said Thomas, which is called Didymus, unto his fellow disciples, 'Let us also go, that we may die with him' " (John 11:16).

It's significant to see what happened eight days after Jesus' resurrection, when he appeared again to the disciples, this time with Thomas present. There was no cataclysmic event.

Jesus just said, "Peace be unto you," and to Thomas, "Reach here your finger, and behold my hands; and reach here your hand, and thrust it into my side: and be not faithless, but believing." And Thomas then said to him, "My Lord and my God!" (John 20:26–28).

It is surprising that Thomas is the only person in the Bible ever to call Jesus "God." The disciple we stigmatize as the "doubter" had an especially insightful faith. So Thomas is not all that bad, not any worse than the rest of the disciples—or us. All of us doubt; all of us sin; all of us sometimes forget how much Jesus loves us.

It's clear that everyone is different, we sometimes react in strange ways, and we can never fully understand one another. But we know that Christ understands us and forgives our mistakes, and his love is unshakable. He teaches us to do the same: "Judge not . . ."

What We Believe

CHAPTER EIGHTEEN

What Is Special About Christianity?

For God so loved the world that he gave his only begotten Son, that whosoever believes in him should not perish, but have everlasting life.

JOHN 3:16

Be kind one to another, tenderhearted, forgiving one another, even as God for Christ's sake has forgiven you.

EPHESIANS 4:32

Perhaps as well as any two verses, these two encapsulate the meaning of Christianity. Being blessed and forgiven by God through Christ, we have the motivation to apply his teaching and example in our own lives. There is little here about the broad scope of society, a philosophical dissertation, or international war or peace. The emphasis is on each individual human being, precious in God's sight, alienated because of sin; the acknowledgment of our mistakes; and, through Christ who died for us, total forgiveness and reconciliation.

It is necessary to comprehend the uniqueness of Jesus as a human who was not famous or revered when he grew up in Nazareth. But when he began preaching and healing, the crowds flocked to him, and he gathered fervent followers—then and now—perhaps because of his words, his miracles, and his popularity. His ministry was universal but focused on individuals. His parables were about the value of one sheep lost out of one hundred, or one coin out of ten—the precious single soul.

When Jesus became famous, he was envied and despised by religious leaders who emphasized strict and sterile rules that tried to define the criteria for our acceptance by God. The personal aspect of God's love was secondary to them. Jesus, expected by many to be like the Pharisees, Sadducees, and scribes, shocked and often alienated his potential supporters by his revolutionary ideas. He cared for the outcasts and despised, the afflicted, the poor, or the different.

While negotiating a peace agreement at Camp David, I once shared a Friday night meal with Prime Minister Begin and other Israelis. I was impressed by their special prayers and ceremony, which lent a deeply religious quality to their Jewish meal, and as a result I could better understand the negative reaction when Jesus invited himself to supper with Zacchaeus, a sinful tax collector, and his friends. They were probably "birds of a feather" who drank too much, told ribald stories, and rarely if ever went to a synagogue to worship. When severely criticized, probably even by his own followers, Jesus replied, in effect, "I came to seek and to save the lost. The righteous don't need me" (Luke 19:10).

Jesus changed people's perspectives. A crippled man, obviously loved by his friends, was lowered through a hole in the roof into Jesus' presence. Just wanting him to be able to walk, his friends were as shocked as the Pharisees when Jesus said to him, "Your sins are forgiven." Sins were supposed to be forgiven only by God, after appropriate sacrifices were offered through the priests. When accused of blasphemy, Jesus added, almost as an afterthought, "Oh, by the way, take up your stretcher and carry it home." When the man did so, the people were amazed, filled with reverential fear, and they glorified God.

The primary emphasis of Jesus' teaching was on a proper relationship with God, with the physical healing clearly resulting from faith—in this case among the man's friends. This is just one of the many lessons from this remarkable event: people can be healed because of the faith of someone else. Jesus raised Lazarus through the faith of Mary and Martha, and he healed the children of a centurion and a synagogue leader because their fathers believed.

Jesus was a leader and a teacher who taught in synagogues, in people's homes, on the streets, in the countryside, and from boats. He taught with his words, his actions, his suffering, his death, and his resurrection. Through him we are given the assurance of God's forgiveness toward those of us who acknowl-

edge our sins because we believe in Christ. We are reconciled
with God through Jesus' love.

The result, for Christians, is that we should emulate what
our Savior epitomized: kindness, tenderheartedness, forgiveness—and humility. When we assume an attitude of superiority, we depart from Christ, and forget his intense and
unwavering love for us as individuals.

CHAPTER NINETEEN

A Theology Primer

Therefore, since we are justified by faith, we have peace with God through our Lord Jesus Christ, through whom we have obtained access to this grace in which we stand; and we boast in our hope of sharing the glory of God. And not only that, but we also boast in our sufferings, knowing that suffering produces endurance, and endurance produces character, and character produces hope, and hope does not disappoint us, because God's love has been poured into our hearts through the Holy Spirit that has been given to us.

. . . Rarely will anyone die for a righteous person—though perhaps for a good person someone might actually dare to die. But God proves his love for us in that while we still were sinners Christ died for us. . . . So that, just as sin exercised dominion in death, so grace might also exercise dominion through justification leading to eternal life through Jesus Christ our Lord. Where sin abounded, grace did much more abound: that as sin has reigned unto death, even so might grace reign through righteousness unto eternal life by Jesus Christ our Lord.

ROMANS 5:1–5, 7–8, 20–21

Most of us are leery about the word *theology*, considering it a controversial and confusing subject best addressed by college professors and authors of thick and incomprehensible books. Simply speaking, "theology" means the study of the nature of God and religious truth. Perhaps all of us have intriguing questions to be answered: What is my relationship to the Creator? To Christ? To other humans? How do good works relate to faith in God? How can we have inner peace when we are often frustrated, fearful, discouraged, or in despair? Theology deals with these vital questions.

We could spend a lifetime in study, delving ever more deeply into the nuances of religious scriptures and how they might be interpreted and applied to human consciousness and actions. While we may not all want to become biblical scholars, no one can expect to understand deeper meanings of the Scriptures with just a cursory reading. It's always valuable to think more deeply, and to seek written and verbal explanations. In early June 1997, I had a wonderful discussion with Hans Küng, one of the great theologians of our time. Although I had found some of his writings quite difficult to understand, his words in conversation were clear and incisive. He outlined for me a "Universal Declaration of Human Responsibility." With his help, a group of national leaders will use this document to strengthen and supplement the Universal Declaration of Human Rights that was adopted by the United Nations in 1948, following the Second World War.

The most famous and respected Christian theologian, Paul of Tarsus, wrote the passage at the beginning of this lesson in a letter to one of the new and struggling churches after the death and resurrection of Jesus. In this brief passage, he covers most of the basic elements of the Christian faith but uses some words whose meanings we need to explore somewhat carefully.

Let's look first at the word *hope*. Its modern meaning is to wish with some expectation of fulfillment. I might hope that I will live to be a hundred years old, that my grandchildren will always make good grades in school, that Navy's football team will beat Army's next year, or that it won't rain the next time I go fishing. In both 1976 and 1980, I hoped to win the presidential election. The archaic definition of the word was much closer to Paul's meaning: "to have confidence; to trust." In the letter to the Romans, there is absolutely no doubt that hope will be fulfilled; it's almost the same as "assurance."

"Justified" means that we are brought into a proper relationship with God, even though we have not merited this blessing because of our own character or good works. This seeming miracle is made possible by our faith, or trusting commitment to Christ and to God. Without this faith, we cannot be reconciled with God. The peace to which Paul refers is a transcendent sense of well-being and fulfillment, brought about by being in the presence of the Holy Spirit, as promised by Jesus.

Paul intends for human "righteousness" to mean absolute faith in and commitment to God. It has the connotation of fulfilling a promise or a covenant. God grants undeserved salvation to us sinners by his love, through Jesus Christ. This act is grace—a word that has the connotation of a free gift of joy, peace, and pleasure. Paul says in another letter, "By grace are you saved through faith; and that not of yourselves: it is the gift of God; not of works, lest any man should boast" (Ephesians 2:8–9).

There are two other interesting points that Paul makes in these few verses. One describes the unique sacrifice of Christ for us sinners—far beyond anything normally to be expected even for righteous people. The other, also surprising, is that we should welcome suffering because it leads us to endurance, then to character, and hope—hope that will never disappoint us.

With some understanding of justification, peace, faith, grace, righteousness, and hope, isn't this a wonderful message? Although many volumes have been written to analyze and explain Christian doctrine, the simple theology of this passage is all we need to know to understand the richness of our faith. Read it again, thoughtfully.

CHAPTER TWENTY

Joy in the Desert

It is written in Isaiah the prophet:
"I will send my messenger ahead of you,
who will prepare your way, a voice of one calling in the desert,
'Prepare the way for the Lord,
make straight paths for him.' "

And so John came, baptizing in the desert region and preaching a baptism of repentance for the forgiveness of sins.

MARK 1:2–4

The wilderness has always had a kind of mystique about it. Moses and the people of Israel wandered in the wilderness for forty years, and some of their most profound religious experiences took place there. We think of the miraculous manna from heaven and the water from the rock, both sent to sustain the Israelites in need, and the giving to Moses of the Ten Commandments while the people of Israel were camped in the desert beneath Mount Sinai. President Anwar Sadat urged Rosalynn and me to visit this site, and we enjoyed climbing the rocky slope of the mountain and talking to the priests who serve in the isolated monastery; we were amused when they showed us a flowering shrub that they called the "burning bush." Elijah and others of the prophets came out of the wilderness, and in later times Christian mystics, hermits, monks, and saints all retreated to the desert to be alone with God.

So the appearance of John the Baptist in the wilderness with his message of baptism and repentance was a natural part of the tradition of desert encounters with the Lord. The three key words in this passage from Mark are *baptism*, *repentance*, and *forgiveness*. Let's consider all three words and the relationship among them, which John was the first to describe.

Baptism is a ritual most Christian churches employ. In some churches, infants are baptized as a symbol of being part of the family of God. Usually, the baby is sprinkled with just a few drops of water on the head, symbolically cleansing the infant of sin. In other denominations, including my own Southern Baptist church, young people are baptized by full immersion in water, but only when they've reached an age where they can independently choose to dedicate themselves to Christ and become full members of the church. I was baptized at the age of eleven after having publicly accepted Christ as Savior during our church's annual revival.

Baptism is a joyous occasion and a meaningful ritual, but

for us Baptists—and I believe for most Christians—it is not
necessary for salvation. Rather, it is a symbolic gesture that
follows repentance and makes our inner commitment outwardly visible, demonstrating to our family, friends, and other
church members our beginning a new life in Christ, as well as
implanting that decision more firmly in our own memories,
minds, and hearts. Jesus believed in the symbolic value of baptism and went himself to John to be baptized. Most Christians
today follow his example. But we should remember that in all
his teachings, Jesus emphasized the preeminence of inner
truths over outward symbols. We are not saved by fasting, by
offering sacrifices, by wearing sackcloth, by baptism, or even
by good deeds. Faith, repentance, and the forgiveness of our
sins through Christ are what saves us.

What is repentance, then, that precedes baptism and gives
it meaning? It begins with self-analysis—an honest examination of our hearts and minds and of our actions, both the
major commitments we make and the small, daily acts that determine the character of our lives. If we're honest, none of us
can emerge from such self-analysis unscathed. For the Jews of
Jesus' time, the standard against which they would measure
their thoughts and deeds was the Ten Commandments and
the Jewish laws as taught since the time of Moses. For Christians today, the standard is the life and teachings of Jesus. By
either standard, none of us is perfect.

It's the nature of human life that "all have sinned and come
short of the glory of God" (Romans 3:23). We may break one
of God's laws by shading or twisting the truth, by hurting
other people, by being insensitive to their needs, or by treating God's name with contempt. Or, more subtly, without ap-

parently violating the law, we may fail to center our lives on the values that Jesus and the prophets taught. Rather than focus our time and energy on living the virtues of justice, compassion, truth, and giving to others, we let our lives become complacent and self-satisfied. This, too, is a failing that calls for repentance.

Repentance describes the inner action of recognizing our own failures and making the decision to change—to commit ourselves to a new course of action and a new way of life, more closely attuned to the model provided by Jesus Christ. This may require giving up some of our favorite habits, which makes it difficult and uncomfortable to do.

Fortunately, the message of John does not stop with baptism and repentance. It isn't complete without the third, most joyous element, forgiveness. And in the teachings of Jesus, and in his life, death, and resurrection, the principle of forgiveness comes to complete fruition. It is important not to wallow in guilt or embarrassment but to wipe the slate clean, turn away from the past, and fully accept the good news of Christ's complete and total forgiveness. We couldn't confess without the assurance of forgiveness. If self-examination brings us the sorrow and shame of recognizing our sinfulness, then accepting God's mercy, promised to us by Christ, makes possible a new life of peace, joy, and adventure. No longer uneasy about our past failings, we can concentrate today and tomorrow on a closer walk with God and our fellow human beings.

When we wander from God's ways, repentance is a necessary step. From time to time, we all need to visit the wilderness—if not a literal wilderness, then the spiritual desert of sorrow and regret that honest self-examination brings. But we aren't meant to live out our lives in solitude. We're meant to do as Jesus did: return from the wilderness to rejoin our brothers and sisters in the world, rejoicing in the good news of God's forgiveness and enjoying the new life of freedom, creativity, and love that it makes possible.

CHAPTER TWENTY-ONE

Are the Ten Commandments Enough?

And Cain talked with Abel his brother: and it came to pass, when they were in the field, that Cain rose up against Abel his brother, and slew him.

And the Lord said unto Cain, "Where is Abel your brother?" And he said, "I know not: Am I my brother's keeper?"

GENESIS 4:8–9

Breach for breach, eye for eye, tooth for tooth: as he has caused a blemish in a man, so shall it be done to him again.

LEVITICUS 24:20

You have heard that it was said to the people long ago, "Do not murder, and anyone who murders will be subject to judgment." But I tell you that anyone who is angry with his brother will be subject to judgment. Again, anyone who says to his brother, "Raca," is answerable to the council. But anyone who says, "You fool!" will be in danger of the fire of hell.

MATTHEW 5:21–22

The verses about the biblical command "Thou shall not kill" illustrate the revolutionary nature of Jesus Christ's teaching. Of course, the Old Testament commands were familiar to any Jew. But in his sermon, Jesus dramatically redefines its meaning. After all, most of us can say, "I haven't killed anyone; therefore, I haven't broken this commandment, and I must be okay with God." Right? "Wrong!" Jesus says. If we have anger in our hearts toward someone, or if we use words to assault or condemn another, we are as guilty as if we'd taken a person's life.

To me, this reinterpretation of God's law offers a disturbing challenge. I almost wish it were possible to wipe away the Sermon on the Mount and return to the original Ten Commandments—they are hard enough to live by! Yet as a follower of Jesus, I know this isn't an option, so it's important to understand what he is saying here.

The truth is that we're all familiar with the destructive power of words. We experience it in families, when an angry, judgmental father criticizes his children so harshly that he shatters their self-esteem; we see it when kids taunt an unpopular classmate in school, or when motorists threaten and curse each other in traffic jams.

I've certainly witnessed the potential violence in words during my political career. There are still white people in the South who can't say "Negro," "Black," or "African-American," and seem to strain when they use the word "Colored," preferring a more vicious word. And we all know the damaging, even lethal effect of anti-Semitic slurs. There are many other kinds of racial slurs. For example, when I was negotiating peace agreements in the Middle East, some Israeli leaders habitually referred to all Palestinians as "terrorists," drawing no distinctions among them. Rosalynn and I have visited the West Bank and Gaza many times, and we've met with people there from many walks of life: orange growers, pharmacists, schoolteachers, lawyers, housewives, fishermen, and so on. Contrary to what many people assume, a good number are Christians. All of them are Palestinians, and only a tiny portion would commit acts of terrorism. To use derogatory words to describe, and dismiss, a whole people is a destructive, dehumanizing act—as it is to employ anti-Semitic slurs or racist language of any kind.

Furthermore, in a troubled setting like the Middle East— or in Northern Ireland, the war-torn Balkan states, or many other places—violent language can and does feed physical violence. We must hate people to justify killing them, as explained in one of my poems.

WITH WORDS WE LEARN TO HATE

We take lives in times of peace
for crimes we won't forgive,
claiming some have forfeited
the right to live.

We justify our nation's wars
each time with words to prove we kill
in a moral cause.
We've cursed the names of those we fought:
the "Japs" instead of Japanese,
German Nazis or the "Huns,"
and "Wops" when they were enemies.

Later, they became our friends,
but habits live in memories.
So now, when others disagree
we hate again, and with our might,
war by war, name by dirty name,
prove we're right.

In the end, there is no way to draw a firm distinction between words and deeds. So when Jesus tells us that hatred spewed out in verbal form is akin to murder, he isn't exaggerating; he is expressing a fundamental truth, though one we'd prefer to overlook.

Jesus' words are still revolutionary today because they challenge our human tendency to build our lives in an egocentric, self-satisfied way. The things I do, the decisions I make, are usually chosen to meet my own needs and to promote my own self-image. And when I examine myself, I'm usually pretty pleased with what I see. I do the best I can, I say to myself; I'm not perfect, but I'm better than a lot of folks I know. I don't violate the law, and I certainly try to follow the Ten Commandments. All in all, I think I measure up to the standards of the other members of my church.

But Christ challenges this complacent self-image. He

demands more of us. We can't just fulfill the letter of God's commandments (difficult though that is to do at times); we must also fulfill its spirit, in our words and thoughts as well as our deeds.

It's not only a revolutionary message but an expansive one. If we want to follow Christ, the Sermon on the Mount tells us how: it requires us to enlarge our understanding of words such as *forgiveness, honesty, justice, compassion,* and *love.* Is it easy to do? No! But it's the avenue—the only avenue—to personal peace and peace in our world.

CHAPTER TWENTY-TWO

The New Message of Jesus

> Think not that I am come to destroy the law, or the prophets: I
> am come not to destroy, but to fulfill. For verily I say unto you,
> Till heaven and earth pass, one jot or one tittle shall in no wise
> pass from the law, till all be fulfilled.
>
> MATTHEW 5:17–18

Jesus brought such a revolutionary message that he was
looked upon as a radical or, by some religious leaders, an anar-
chist. In the Sermon on the Mount, he reassured his listeners
with the well-known words just quoted.

Still, there are striking differences between the general
concepts of the Old Testament and the New Testament, re-
lating to the character of God, the results of violation of or

compliance with God's precepts, the identity of God's "chosen" people, and other issues of theological importance. Despite many efforts at reconciliation down through history, there are still sharp debates and even animosities created between some Christians and some Jews as we interpret the Scriptures.

One fact must be emphasized: It is a crime for any Christian to blame the Jewish people for the trial and crucifixion of Jesus. There is an inclination for some to forget that Jesus, Peter, Paul, and most of the earliest Christians were Jews, who shared their history, language, customs, and religious practices and faith with the Pharisees and Sadducees. Despite this, there was a continuing dispute between Jesus and many religious leaders of his day.

It is natural that, as in the time of the early church, there continues to be some disharmony today among Jews who await the coming of the Messiah and Christians who have faith that Jesus was and is the Messiah. In 1995, for instance, there were a series of confrontations in New York City between conservative rabbis and some Jews who had recently immigrated to the United States from Russia and had accepted Christ as Savior.

A major basis for contention is the interpretation of verses from the Book of Isaiah. Are the prophet's references to Jesus as the future Messiah, to the nation of Israel, to the contemporary Persian King Cyrus, or to some other leader? We can't resolve this argument, and there is no need for us to explore the differences in a judgmental way. But it is helpful for Christians to understand how our interpretations are different from those of non-Christians.

Let me take a few verses from Isaiah 49 as an example. We

Christians believe the prophet is referring to Jesus when he writes, "The Lord called me before I was born; while I was in my mother's womb He named me" (verse 1). And "It is too small a thing that you should be my servant to raise up the tribes of Jacob and to restore the preserved ones of Israel; I will also make you a light of the nations so that my salvation may reach to the end of the earth" (verse 6). Isaiah goes on to describe the Messiah as a suffering servant, and he and other prophets make it plain—at least to me—that the references are to Jesus. We know that Jesus himself declared that he was fulfilling the specific purpose that is described in the first two verses of Isaiah 61 (see chapter 2).

Jesus amazed his listeners with his interpretations of the Scriptures. In earlier times, "An eye for an eye and a tooth for a tooth" had been an enlightened commandment, limiting retribution for crime to an equal punishment; Jesus builds upon it by telling us to love our enemies, and to turn the other cheek if we are struck. "Thou shall not kill" is expanded to an admonition against hatred or cursing another person. Instead of animal sacrifices as a prerequisite for forgiveness, Jesus offered himself as the propitiation for our sins, and assured us of God's mercy and eagerness to forgive us as though we had not sinned at all.

Instead of a requirement that obeying laws or even doing good works serve as conditions for holiness, faith in God through Christ is sufficient for salvation. (It is interesting to note that, in the King James text, the word *faith* is used 245 times in the New Testament and only twice in the Old Testament.) Repeatedly, Jesus and his disciples violated the strict rules concerning the Sabbath, and he made the disturbing statement, "The Sabbath was made for man, and not man for

the Sabbath" (Mark 2:27). He condemned convenient interpretation of the Scriptures to accommodate selfish goals concerning the condoning of divorce and caring for parents. Jesus
reminded the religious leaders, "Moses said, 'Honor your father and your mother,' . . . but you say that if anyone tells father or mother, 'Whatever support you might have had from
me is an offering to God,' then you no longer have to do anything for a father or mother, thus making void the word of
God" (Mark 7:10–13).

One of the most significant and most condemned innova-
tions of Christ—predicted by Isaiah—was his extension of salvation to the Gentiles. In his own ministry and his final
command to the disciples, this was laid down as the foundation for the Christian church.

So there were a lot of differences in the prevailing interpretations of the Hebrew Scriptures and the Gospels, but
Jesus assures us that there are absolutely no incompatibilities.
Our Christian faith is best encapsulated in a few words he
spoke to Nicodemus, an influential Pharisee and a ruler of the
Jews: "For God so loved the world that He gave His only begotten son, that whosoever believes in him should not perish,
but have eternal life. For God sent not His son into the world
to judge the world, but that the world through him might be
saved" (John 3:16–17).

With these words, we can understand not only the compatibility between the Old and New Testaments but also the
transformations in our understanding of God and our personal relationship with our Creator that occurred with the
coming of Jesus as the Messiah.

CHAPTER TWENTY-THREE

Christianity's Open Door

And certain men who came down from Judea taught the brethren, and said, "Unless you are circumcised after the manner of Moses, you cannot be saved." Therefore Paul and Barnabas had no small disagreement and argument with them . . . and determined to go to Jerusalem to the apostles and elders about this question. . . .

And when there had been much disputing, Peter rose up and said unto them, . . . "Now therefore why tempt God, to put a yoke upon the neck of the disciples, which neither our fathers nor we were able to bear? But we believe that through the grace of the Lord Jesus Christ we shall be saved, even as they."

ACTS 15:1–2, 7, 10–11

Shortly before I taught a Sunday School lesson based on this Bible passage in the summer of 1979, Rosalynn and I went to South Korea. We were overwhelmed by the dynamic Christian spirit that was sweeping the country. Five hundred thousand converts a year were joining churches, and a million people had assembled at the Seoul airport to hear Billy Graham preach. Our visit was the same year that the Moral Majority made the so-called Christian Right famous, and the moderate-conservative split came to a head in the Southern Baptist Convention. These were modern reminders of the kinds of successes and divisions that were seen in the early Christian church.

The inspired witnessing of Paul, Barnabas, Apollos, and other apostles was building churches in many Asian communities, including Antioch. The church members were sharing the message of Christ with remarkable results. There were also thousands of Christian Jews, who composed a strong church in Jerusalem (Acts 21:20).

The church in Antioch was on fire with evangelical fervor, reaching out to tell people about Christ, who had lived, died, and been resurrected as Savior. The primary message was that God's grace is all-encompassing, and that through faith in Jesus their sins could be forgiven and salvation was theirs. When someone came forward and said, "I believe in Jesus Christ as my savior, and want my sins to be forgiven," the leaders in Antioch said, "Welcome, brother!" or "Welcome, sister!" It was simple: A Christian was any person who was saved by the grace of God through faith in Jesus Christ.

It was a time of success and celebration, but differences were arising among believers that were serious enough to threaten the survival of the still infant church. Whether because of jealousy or honest theological beliefs, a group in the Jerusalem church delivered this divisive message to Antioch: "In order to become a Christian, you must first comply with all the Jewish customs as prescribed for our forefathers by Moses."

It is sometimes difficult for us to accept that God can be so generous as to accept and love us without reservation—there must be something else required. It seems natural that there should be some reasonable standards of previous conduct for a convert to Christianity. It was difficult for Jews in Jerusalem to forget about the ancient rules so clearly stated in Deuteronomy and Leviticus, and the dozens of other customs and practices that had formed the basis for their worship down through the centuries. Suppose a Roman soldier who had been persecuting the people of Israel came forward and said, "I have faith in Jesus Christ!" How could he be accepted as an equal among devout people?

We can understand both sides in this momentous debate. All of us, including me, tend to want to define what a Christian is. Unfortunately, it is only natural for us to make the definition of a "real" Christian fairly close to a description of our friends and ourselves. "After all," we think, "if we're not careful, we may just drift and be too inclusive. How could God have standards low enough to include sinners like that drunk lying on the sidewalk alongside a wine bottle, or that unwed mother who may still be sleeping around, or that jailbird who was found guilty of pushing drugs? Look at my friends and me. We're not addicts, our children were born in wedlock, and we've avoided a criminal life. Surely *we* represent what Christianity is all about."

This is exactly the attitude found among the Jewish Christians who condemned the open-door policy that Paul and other apostles had adopted. "At least let them adopt Jewish customs first" was the demand. It is interesting to me that James, leader of the Jerusalem church, chose Peter to enunciate the reply. We tend to exalt Paul as the preeminent theologian and founder of the early church, but at this time he was just an associate to the pastor Barnabas! It was Peter who had first received the Holy Spirit and later, with some reluctance, had introduced faith in Christ to Cornelius, a Gentile.

Now in our text, Peter speaks with perfect clarity about the choice between salvation through simple grace or salvation through circumcision plus adherence to intricate laws. This was a turning point in the life of the Christian church, one resolved through God's influence on Paul, Barnabas, Peter, James, and other leaders. In such an important and hotly debated issue, their unity was truly impressive.

I particularly like the last three words of Peter as he states the decision: "even as they." I like to interpret this by stretching it a little: "Isn't it great that God would let us big-shot Jerusalem Christians be saved just the way he let those Antioch Gentiles be saved!"

Paul and other Christians throughout the known world continued their evangelistic efforts based on the same nonexclusive requirement: "For whosoever shall call upon the name of the Lord shall be saved" (Romans 10:13). And "For by grace are you saved through faith; and that not of yourselves: it is the gift of God" (Ephesians 2:8).

When we face difficult decisions, we can learn from this episode what resources we have: God's guidance through prayer, sustained faith, and a willingness to turn to others who share that faith—minimizing the narrow and exclusive human demands and requirements we're tempted to impose.

CHAPTER TWENTY-FOUR

A House with Many Builders

Now I beseech you, brethren, by the name of our Lord Jesus Christ, that you all speak the same thing, and that there be no divisions among you; but that you be perfectly joined together in the same mind and in the same judgment. For I have been told that there are contentions among you. Now this I say, that every one of you says, 'I am of Paul'; 'and I of Apollos'; 'and I of Peter'; and 'I of Christ.' Is Christ divided? Was Paul crucified for you? Or were you baptized in the name of Paul?

1 CORINTHIANS 1:10–13

Who then is Paul and who is Apollos? . . . I have laid the foundation, and another builds on it. But let everyone take heed
how he builds on it. For there is only one foundation, which is
Jesus Christ.

I CORINTHIANS 3:5, 10–11

Paul had spent at least eighteen months among these people
in Corinth, and he had been successful in establishing a strong
congregation there. Now, sometime later, he was obviously
concerned about divisions within the church, as members argued about conflicting loyalties to different preachers who
had visited them. As usual, Paul went to the heart of the issue,
emphasizing that there was only one foundation for their
faith: Jesus Christ as the Son of God and the promised Messiah. He went on to say, "Don't you know that you are the
temple of God?"

So Christ is the foundation, and we Christians are the edi-
fices built on it. But how were these early Christians erecting
the structure? Each group was beginning somewhere on the
foundation and building in its own way. As the walls rose, they
didn't match, and the roof was on sideways. Each group was
pursuing its own ideas, and then they wound up blaming each
other for the incompatibility.

What would Paul think about the modern Christian church?
Is there a separate Methodist or Presbyterian or Mennonite
foundation? Do Baptists have separate conservative and moderate foundations? Is there a Catholic or a Protestant foundation? Or should we all share the same foundation laid down by
Jesus Christ? There are unpleasant, bitter divisions, and even

wars, among those of us who compose the temple of God. Some want hardwood floors and others carpets; some like a hip roof and some prefer a more simple gable roof; there are strong preferences between wood and metal window frames; and how about the color of the front door? These are important issues, we insist, and we can't understand why anyone would disagree with us. Or perhaps it's best just to find a place on the foundation of Christ and build our own tiny houses out of straw or pasteboard, or plastic, and not even relate to others. After all, they are obviously wrong, and probably inferior!

We argue incessantly about separation of church and state, the priesthood of believers, ordination of women, prayer in schools, gay rights, predestination, inerrancy, public funds for church schools, and any number of other "crucial" issues. Perhaps worse than the Corinthians, we forget the solid, unquestionable, unifying foundation of our faith in the gentle Jesus, full of grace and truth. As Cecil Sherman, a leader of moderate Baptists, has said, "Too many churches are majoring in the minors."

We are given a foundation of excellence, truth, justice, service, sharing, and unselfish love. How should we build on this foundation? I can think of five ways, all admirable. One is good living, based on prayer and constant communication with God. A second is holiness, a life in which we are careful to avoid sin. A third is the spirit-filled, or charismatic life, exemplified by the disciples at Pentecost. Another is to be compassionate to the poor, perhaps building houses for them. And a final one is evangelism, telling people about Jesus Christ.

There is certainly nothing wrong with any of these. Do we need prayer, to be holy, to be filled with the Spirit, to minister to the needy, to witness for Christ? Certainly we do. The problem is when we Christians select one or two of these ways and say, "This is the religious foundation on which I build my life, and those who build in other ways are wrong." As Paul would advise, we need to meld them all into a beautiful and harmonious structure.

How can this be done? Harmony can be reached by referring to the most exalted goals of Christianity. It seems illogical, but these are the ones that require the most modest talents, intelligence, and influence. When we remember the pure teachings of Jesus, we realize that any human being can espouse truth, justice, humility, and compassion. This is where we find the common foundation for our Christian lives.

Christians in the World

CHAPTER TWENTY-FIVE

The Christian Citizen

Submit yourselves for the Lord's sake to every authority insti-
tuted among men: whether to the king, as the supreme authority, or to governors, who are sent by him to punish those
who do wrong and to commend those who do right. . . . Show
proper respect to everyone: love the brotherhood of believers,
fear God, honor the king.

1 PETER 2:13, 17

How startling this message of Peter's must have seemed in
his day! Consider that he wrote these words when the emperor of Rome, the supreme political authority throughout
most of the known world, was severely oppressing the Christian church, imprisoning and even killing the followers of

Jesus on account of their faith. For Peter to write a letter urging Christians to submit loyally to the government is, indeed, a curious act.

The same paradox has confronted Christians in many times and places. Revolution against British rulers gave birth to America. Germany under Hitler is another obvious example. Driven by a monstrous philosophy and supported by twisted distortions of Christian teaching, the Nazi regime carried out the greatest crime of modern history. How could Christians submit themselves for the Lord's sake to such an authority?

Occasionally, Rosalynn and I visit the African nation of Sudan, currently ruled by a fundamentalist Muslim government. Under their strict interpretation of Islamic law, known as Sharia, only Muslim men have full rights as citizens. Non-Muslim believers in God (other People of the Book, as they are sometimes called, including Christians and Jews) are second-class citizens; and nonbelievers are given few basic rights. What is the proper role of a Christian living under such a regime?

And there are examples closer to home. We all disagree with our own government at times. Fortunately, in a free society, there are peaceful ways to change the government with our choice of leaders. And between elections, we can use the power of our voices to influence laws and policies.

Nonetheless, even in a democracy there are times when submission to the government is not a sufficient response to injustice. When our sons were in college, movements for civil rights, the end of the Vietnam War, and environmental quality were examples of concerted public effort by millions of people, sometimes including acts that violated the law. It was the willingness of courageous protesters to break such laws and accept the punishment for breaking them that forced the nation to recognize the injustice of the laws and, ultimately, to change them.

Almost twenty years later, our daughter, Amy, was arrested four times, for demonstrating against apartheid in South Africa and against what she considered illegal activities of the CIA during the Contra war in Nicaragua. There was an extended trial on the latter charge, but she and her associates were declared innocent because the Massachusetts jury decided that their peaceful demonstration was a small crime intended to prevent a greater one.

Clearly, Peter is not saying that a particular government, with whatever laws and policies it currently enforces, is to be looked upon as sacred or unchangeable. If he'd believed that, he and his fellow Christians would not have faced prison and even death because they worshiped Christ and not the Roman gods.

By considering both Peter's teachings in this epistle and Paul's to the Romans (13:1–10), we can see their true meaning. In general, government is a necessary, often beneficent force, which preserves peace and order, punishes those who commit crimes against others, and to one degree or another gives citizens a voice in shaping the policies that affect their lives. To this extent, governments deserve our respect and support. As inhabitants of our world, Christians usually have a responsibility to play a positive role in supporting the social order for the good of all.

But when a government seeks to impose laws that are

unjust and contrary to God's commands, our responsibility changes. Under those circumstances, we should start by looking within ourselves: How do we understand God's will for us and for the world? What talents, abilities, and influence can we bring to bear on the situation? And in light of the answers to these questions, how can we work to moderate or modify government policies or, if necessary, dramatically change the government itself?

What each of us feels called upon to do as a Christian citizen may vary greatly. To vote our consciences, to express our beliefs in speaking and writing, to work on behalf of particular candidates or run for offices ourselves—all these are natural and important roles. In some circumstances, more dramatic steps may be needed, including forceful public protests or even civil disobedience. And sometimes the rejection of oppressive authority requires the willingness to accept punishment: prison, as in the case of Paul, or even death, as the life of Jesus illustrates.

To decide the right course of action in any given circumstances may not be easy. It requires thoughtful consideration, a spirit of openness, cooperation, and love, even toward those with whom we deeply disagree, and, of course, the seeking of God's guidance through prayer. The weak and oppressed are the ones most likely to turn to Christ. The essence of his teaching is to enhance justice, truth, freedom, service, and love. This must be our guiding light when we are considering how best to fulfill our role as Christians in society.

CHAPTER TWENTY-SIX

Do We Really Believe in Human Rights?

And Ahab said to Naboth, "Give me your vineyard, for a herb garden near my house. And I will give you a better vineyard, or, if you prefer, I will give you a fair price for it." But Naboth said to Ahab, "The Lord forbids that I sell my father's inheritance to you." And Ahab went into his house sad and displeased, and lay down upon his bed, and turned away his face, and would not eat. . . . And his wife Jezebel said, "I will give you the vineyard."

. . . And she put Naboth on a pedestal, and got two men to witness against him. And they carried him out and stoned him to death. . . . And Ahab got up and went to Naboth's vineyard, to take possession of it.

1 KINGS 21:2–4, 7, 12–13, 16

On April 25, 1979, Georgi Vins was in a cattle car in Siberia, being transported as an exile in his own country. Four days later, he was in a Sunday School class I was teaching at First Baptist Church in Washington. Perhaps not coincidentally, the title of the lesson was "A Cry for Justice."

As president, I had agreed with President Leonid Brezhnev to trade two convicted Soviet spies for the release of five men whom I considered human rights heroes, along with their families. Georgi Vins was a Baptist pastor who had been sent to Siberia because he insisted on professing his Christian faith despite orders from the Communist dictators to remain silent. He had no idea where he was being taken until he and the four others were placed on a commercial jet, destined for the United States. When he left Russia his head was shaven, he had a Bible in his hand, and I was told later that my photograph was hidden in his shoe.

A few days later, on Law Day, I spoke before the chief justice of the Supreme Court, the attorney general, and other leaders and referred to this lesson. Let me quote a few sentences from this speech:

> The highest goal that a government or societal structure can hope to achieve is justice. It's an end in itself; it's a means to an end; and it's a pursuit that is never completely realized. There are always challenges to it brought about by the fallibilities of human beings, the intense pressure of competition in a free society, the constraint of liberty where freedom does not exist. It's a responsibility on us, as it is on the leaders of every nation on earth.

The deprivation of justice is a serious matter. Those of us who don't suffer much from it can observe it, if we are sensitive. Quite often we benefit from an injustice, because those with power, wealth, or social prominence are very likely to profit when an advantage is meted out to our peers who, in gaining some advantages for themselves, cause those same benefits to accrue to us.

And if we stand silent and reap the benefits of injustice, then we ourselves are equally culpable with those who initiated the injustice.

The case of Ahab, Jezebel, and Naboth provides a good example of these premises. Ahab was a rich and powerful king who ruled Israel from 874 to 853 B.C. He professed to honor the laws of God and his nation, but he also worshiped idols and violated the basic principles of justice. He had married Jezebel, a Phoenician princess, who was worse than her husband and an evil influence on him.

In refusing to give up his small garden plot, Naboth was complying with Hebrew law expressed in Leviticus against the sale of land and also honoring the memory of his ancestors. Ahab's lying in bed, pouting, and refusing to eat was a strange reaction for a monarch, and we don't really know how much of it was designed to bring about the subsequent actions of Jezebel. But there is never any indication that Ahab questioned what she did.

There were religious laws in Israel designed to ensure justice and protect human rights. A king could not forcefully take property from any citizen, and no one could be convicted of a crime without two witnesses agreeing on evidence. Jezebel exalted Naboth to arouse public jealousy against him, bribed two false witnesses to swear he had blasphemed God and the king, and had him executed. Her fellow conspirators and many other citizens knew what she was doing, but they all looked the other way because they were rewarded, feared the king or wanted to ingratiate themselves with him, were jealous of Naboth, or just didn't want to be involved.

The lesson for us is that injustice can be perpetrated in a society only with the complicity or acquiescence of others who benefit or avoid responsibility while denying knowledge. As Christians, do we have a responsibility for those in our own communities or in other nations who are suffering, from either deprivation or persecution? Four well-known questions help to give us the answer. One was when God searched for Adam in the Garden of Eden: "Where are you?" Another was to Cain: "Where is your brother?" And the response: "Am I my brother's keeper?" One more was to Jesus: "Who is my neighbor?"

I wrote a poem a few years ago about this theme:

HOLLOW EYES, BELLIES, HEARTS

We chosen people, rich and blessed,
rarely come to ask ourselves
if we should share our voice or power,
or a portion of our wealth.

We deal with problems of our own,
and claim we have no prejudice
against the people, different, strange,
whose images we would dismiss:

Hollow eyes in tiny faces,
hollow bellies, gaunt limbs, there
so far away. Why grieve here
for such vague, remote despair?

Human debris tries to reach
a friendly port, however far.
We can't pay them mind forever,
wretched dregs from an ugly war.

With apartheid's constant shame
Black miners slave for gems and gold.
The wealth and freedom are not theirs;
White masters always keep control.

Bulldozed houses, olive trees axed;
terrorist bombs, funeral wails;
no courts or trials, prison still.
The land is holy, hate prevails.

One alone in a Chinese square
confronted tanks, while others fled.
He stood for freedom for us all,
but few care now if he's jailed or dead.

Visits in the dark of night
by lawful thugs—indrawn breaths
of fear, and then the last farewells.
The death squads won't admit the deaths.

Torture, murder . . . bitter loss
of liberty and life. But they
are friendly tyrants! What would all
our cautious questioning convey?

Why think of slaves, nameless deaths?
Best be still, as in other days.
Response was bland to Hitler's deeds.
Should we condemn our fathers' ways?

We chosen few are truly blessed.
It's clear God does not want us pained
by those who suffer far away.
Are we to doubt what He ordained?

If I am my brother's keeper, it's not enough for me to learn
about or even pray about his troubles. I'm called upon to act
on his behalf, even when that requires fighting injustice and
tyranny.

CHAPTER TWENTY-SEVEN

Woman and Man, Equal Before God

Wives, be submissive to your husbands so that, if any of them do not believe the word, they may be won over without talk by the behavior of their wives, when they see the purity and reverence of your lives. . . . Husbands, in the same way be considerate as you live with your wives, and treat them with respect as the weaker partner and as heirs with you of the gracious gift of life, so that nothing will hinder your prayers.

1 PETER 3:1–2, 7

There are passages in the Bible that are very difficult for people today to accept, and this is certainly an example. To one degree or another, almost all of us believe in the liberation of women and the equality of the sexes, and this makes Peter's words "be submissive" quite troubling to us. Paul makes a few comments that are very similar, and some religious leaders distort these verses to discriminate against women. This creates enough of a problem so that some Christians, including our daughter, Amy, have withdrawn from the church. And those of us who remain loyal churchgoers are nonetheless made uneasy by the misinterpretation of these verses.

How do we deal with this uneasiness? It's tempting to try to ignore these troublesome biblical passages, saying, "Oh, that was written 2,000 years ago—it doesn't apply to me now." But that's a dangerous path to take. We need to believe—and as Christians, most of us do believe—that the total wisdom of the Bible does apply to us today. If we begin eliminating verses that we consider outdated, we may find ourselves choosing just those verses that happen to suit our own temperaments, habits, or foibles. The Bible should help correct our personal tastes, not just reinforce them.

At the same time, it's true that the Bible, though inspired by God, was written by fallible human beings who shared the knowledge and beliefs of their times. The science and astronomy of the Bible are inaccurate by modern standards (speaking of the earth's "four corners," for example), and biblical writers in New Testament times still wrote as if slavery were a legitimate social institution that should not be questioned. So it is appropriate to consider the times in which the Bible was written when interpreting the meaning of Scripture and its message for us today.

In the Mediterranean world of the first century, when Jesus, Peter, and Paul all lived, women were forbidden to play any leading role in society. A single woman was the property of her father, and a married woman was the property of her husband. Women did not speak for themselves in the houses of worship, in the public squares, or in other forums. Both literally and figuratively, the woman walked several paces behind her husband.

As we see in the Gospels, Jesus challenged this prevailing suppression of women. Many of his most faithful and prominent followers were women, and throughout Jesus' travels he lived and spoke with women in terms of virtual equality. After his death, women were the first witnesses of the resurrection, and they were the ones who proclaimed the good news of his rising.

If we examine this lesson's text objectively, we see a strong element of equality, perhaps very startling to early Christians and nonbelievers. Also, Paul, who made some comments about women's not speaking in religious services, directly contravened this concept in the sixteenth chapter of Romans. He lists twenty-seven people who played a prominent role in the early church; ten of them were women. Phoebe was a minister or deacon, Junia was "outstanding among the apostles," and Priscilla was a pastor who worked with Paul and corrected the beliefs of Apollos, a great preacher.

To me, all of this is clear evidence that Christ intended women to play a major—even equal—role in his church. An increasing number of Christians believe, as I do, that no position, including deacon, pastor, or priest, should be withheld from women. Shortly after I left the White House, I served on a committee to draft a new constitution for our church. I proposed that both men and women should be permitted to serve as deacons. At the time, the proposal received only four votes at the church conference, but more recently our members voted to authorize women deacons.

One of the most pertinent verses of Scripture comes from Paul's letter to the Galatians, when he reminds them, "For as many of you as have been baptized into Christ have put on Christ. There is neither Jew nor Greek, there is neither bond nor free, there is neither male nor female: for ye are all one in Christ Jesus" (3:27–28).

An overall premise is that all of us, as equals, should accept the social order of the time and place where God has placed us and do our best to live loyally and faithfully as Christians, while questioning or challenging societal norms when they violate the equality of God's love and grace.

CHAPTER TWENTY-EIGHT

Leadership and Reformation

Then, at the evening sacrifice, I rose from my self-abasement, with my tunic and cloak torn, and fell on my knees with my hands spread out to the Lord my God and prayed: "O my God, I am too ashamed and disgraced to lift up my face to you, because our sins are higher than our heads and our guilt has reached to the heavens. . . . But now, for a brief moment, the Lord our God has been gracious in leaving us a remnant and giving us a firm place in his sanctuary, and so our God gives light to our eyes and a little relief in our bondage."

EZRA 9:5–6, 8

Ezra played an important part in the history of the Israelites during the time of the Babylonian captivity some 2,500 years ago, when the Jewish people were ruled by the Persian Empire. Born and raised in a Jewish community in Babylon, Ezra was among the Jews who returned to Jerusalem under the decree of King Cyrus with a mandate to rebuild the Temple, their traditional center of worship. And Ezra, a scholar and teacher of the Law, brought with him to Jerusalem his own copy of the Hebrew Scriptures, which became the basis for a revival and renewal of the faith. So important was Ezra's role that some scholars call him the father of Judaism.

When Ezra returned to the Holy City, he was appalled to observe the fragmented state of the Hebrew faith. He decided that much of the problem had been caused by intermarriage between the Jews and the neighboring tribes. Marriage between people of different races and ethnic backgrounds is a natural thing; it will happen whenever groups live closely together. And during the period when the Jews were in Babylon, they had continued to worship their own God, even in the midst of pagan worship and beliefs. In many ways they had become part of Babylonian society; many had become landowners, some had grown wealthy. In this relatively comfortable situation, it's understandable that some of the Jews would have married people from among the neighboring tribes.

But for Ezra, this was a serious mistake and a sin. The ancient law arose from a concern that, if the Jews married pagan men and women, the Jewish faith would inevitably be diluted and weakened. Ezra was called by God to speak out against this danger, and he does so in the ninth chapter of the book that bears his name.

Notice some significant things about how Ezra conveys this message that may be helpful to us. First, he begins by speaking openly to God about their sins. When we have gone astray in our lives, the first, essential step in returning to the right path is confession, difficult and painful though it may be. Second, look at the words Ezra uses to describe the Israelites' misdeeds: *our* sins, *our* guilt. Ezra had not married a Canaanite woman or strayed from the prescribed teachings and worship of God, but as the spiritual leader of the Jews, he felt and spoke as if he were equally guilty. Ezra didn't fall into the trap many of us do today, distancing himself from the wrongdoing of others, as if proud of his superiority. It's easy to fool ourselves this way. Sin is a common human condition. Ezra didn't preach down to his fellow Jews. Rather, he said, "I am in the same boat, morally and spiritually, with all of our people, and we pledge ourselves to do something about it together."

Based on this attitude of realism and humility, and on his willingness to confess sins and ask God for forgiveness, Ezra was able to lead a religious reformation that helped saved Judaism. The Israelites rededicated themselves to teaching and practicing their traditional faith, and vowed to marry among themselves.

What does the word *reformation* imply? Literally, to reform, to change in a way that is dramatic and total, closer to revolution than to evolution. When a pine tree grows to maturity, that is a gradual change. But if we chop down a tree and burn it, or cut boards from the wood and use them to build a house, that is a reformation. For a number of years, my brother, Billy, was a hopeless alcoholic, often embarrassing to his friends and alienated from his family. But with the unwavering love and support of his wife, Sybil, he overcame this affliction and spent the last decade of his life without alcohol. In fact, after this reformation Billy and Sybil became national leaders in ministering to other alcoholics, many of whom said, "If Billy can do it, so can I."

Reformation is an essential aspect of life. But I know from personal experience that moral and spiritual reformation of a society or of one human heart is not easy to bring about. It often takes both a crisis and the inspiration of another person, like Ezra or Sybil, to show a society or an individual the need for change and the path that must be followed to achieve it.

Ezra had several qualities that made him an effective voice for reformation. The Israelites felt that he was one of them, sharing their weaknesses and their sin and striving with them to repent, atone, and begin anew. And he was a man of prayer, opening his heart and speaking freely and honestly to God about the rights and wrongs of his people. In return, he understood the will of God and had the ability and strength to lead the Israelites. At the same time, Ezra knew that true power arises from the guidance of God, not from human talents or pride.

What are the areas of life in which today's society is desperately in need of reformation? We accept now without question the violation of God's laws. Reaction to the recent discharge from the Air Force of a female bomber pilot showed that the general public is inclined to criticize the military for enforcing rules that forbid adultery, lying, or disobeying orders. It's easy to think of other examples of the need for reform: society's acceptance of the plight of the hungry and the homeless, the suffering of innocents in needless wars, the gradual destruction of our natural environment, the evils of racial, ethnic, and religious hatred.

Fortunately, God's power to bring about dramatic change

in the human heart, beginning with confession and repentance, is available to us today just as it was to the Israelites in the days of Ezra. As Christians, all of us are capable of and trained for leadership. We can help at least one other person. All that's missing is our willingness to pray, to obey, and to act as he did.

CHAPTER TWENTY-NINE

What Can One Person Do?

And Jesus came and spoke to his disciples, saying, "All power is given unto me in heaven and in earth. Go therefore, and teach all nations, baptizing them in the name of the Father and of the Son, and of the Holy Ghost: Teaching them to observe all things whatsoever I have commanded you; and lo, I am with you always, even unto the end of the world."

MATTHEW 28:18–20

In 1976, two unprecedented things happened in the small congregation of the Baptist Church in the village of Plains, Georgia. One family was chosen to go to the White House, and another family was assigned to be missionaries in West Africa. One has become famous, but the other is, justifiably, more honored in our church. For as long as I can remember, our most exalted heroes have been missionaries who go to foreign lands to serve Christ.

Jerome Ethridge was an agronomist at the Southwest Georgia Experiment Station, located about a mile east of Plains. He was not a preacher, knew no foreign language, and had no religious education except as a member and deacon in our church. He and his wife, Joann, were given rudimentary training as missionary recruits, sent to France to learn the language, and then assigned to Sokodé, Togo. They ran a Christian library and taught languages to the young people who came by for books. Hundreds learned to read and write, but there was little chance for Jerome to use his agricultural skills or to be an effective witness for Christ.

When the opportunity arose, they were able to go to a much smaller and more isolated village named Moretan, in East Mono, a region of Togo. There, among people who mostly worshiped nature or crafted idols, the Ethridges assessed how they might meet urgent human needs. The greatest need was for drinking water, which was plentiful only during the rainy season. At other times, the women had to walk as far as sixteen miles each day to get water. With diesel well-drilling equipment furnished by some North Carolina Baptists and the help of local villagers, Jerome drilled 167 wells, 130 of them successful and capped with hand pumps. Over a period of eight years, every village within eighty miles of Moretan received a working well.

Next, with a leased bulldozer, Jerome constructed twenty-one deep ponds that hold the seasonal rainwater throughout the year. He stocked the ponds with tilapia, a fast-growing fish that provides a much-needed source of protein for the villagers. During these years, he also used his agronomy skills to help the people increase greatly their production of food crops, forage for livestock, and trees that provide wood for cooking and home construction. Joann works with families on health and education projects, helped build a pharmacy, and provides transportation to a distant hospital for those too ill to be treated locally.

Finally, Jerome was ready to undertake a long-postponed task, to correct a problem that had always afflicted all of East Mono. For four months of each year, rain changed the Mono River into an impassable barrier, isolating the area from the rest of Togo. Using cement furnished by his North Carolina friends, he and local volunteers built a bridge. When Rosalynn and I visited the Ethridges, we were amazed to see the 230-foot concrete span across the stream.

Much like Moses, Jerome Ethridge has modest skills as an orator, and he doesn't claim to be an expert on religious or theological subjects. He and his wife have just tried to serve the needy people around them, all without publicity or fanfare, and always in the name of Christ.

In addition to providing a better life for many people, what have the Ethridges accomplished in a religious sense? There are now 5,000 active members in eighty-one Christian congregations in East Mono, each served by a local pastor. This is vivid proof of what just two people can do, inspired by faith in Christ and willing, like their Savior, to be humble servants.

To Know and Worship

A Message in Creation

That which is known about God is evident within them; for God made it evident to them. For since the creation of the world, His invisible attributes, His eternal power and divine nature have been clearly seen, being understood through what has been made, so that they are without excuse.

ROMANS 1:19–20

My university degree is in engineering, and my postgraduate studies were in physics and nuclear technology. Since my college days, I have encountered a number of notable scientists, a few of them willing to discuss theological issues with me. My family and I spent one unforgettable evening with the late Carl Sagan, one of the most famous astronomers.

We drove from the White House to meet him at the vice president's home, where we enjoyed a slide lecture and then went over to the Naval Observatory, which is almost in the front yard. While everyone took turns looking through the large telescope, I asked Sagan about astronomical theories. He explained that either the universe is expanding indefinitely from a tiny point or "singularity" (the Big Bang theory) or, depending upon the amount of dark matter in the heavens, the entire world would expand further and then collapse on itself. He denied believing in a Supreme Being but didn't want to talk—at least to me—about what alternative might exist for the creation of it all.

St. Paul didn't know anything about cosmological theories, nebulae, or even telescopes, but he had a vivid concept of the grandeur of creation. He made it clear in the letter to the Romans that even if we have never read a Bible, listened to a sermon, or heard the name of Jesus, Moses, or Isaiah, we should still know God through the awareness of what has been created and the apparent miracles that surround us.

We resent the suffering, injustice, and violence in our society, and observe that the unrighteous often seem to prosper while the finest people we know seem to suffer unfairly. Even people who call themselves Christians may have occasional doubts about God, but we often feel that if we could only see miracles like those recorded in the Bible, then we would believe.

Paul responds to these kinds of doubts. He makes it clear that the rejection of our Creator despite all the clear evidence around us is foolish. What is that clear evidence? Do we have modern-day miracles on which to predicate our faith?

About 400 years before Paul wrote his letter, the Greek philosopher Aristotle had pronounced that everything had to be perfect, which implied for him that everything in the heavens had to be spherical and nothing new could ever be discovered about them. For centuries, religious leaders predicated their teaching of Paul's text on the centrality of the earth, with the sun, moon, and stars revolving around it. It was not until 1610 that Galileo used his new telescope to ascertain that the earth revolves around the sun, and announced that the Vatican should not base its religious tenets on scientific theories that would always be changing with increasing knowledge. He was condemned by philosophers and the church, and was excommunicated and imprisoned. (It's interesting to note that Pope John Paul II announced in 1992 that the Vatican had been wrong.)

This historic event illustrates that human interpretation of Bible texts cannot limit God's revelations through science about the universe. Evidence increases that a Supreme Being must have orchestrated the astounding things that we can now observe with improved instruments and shared knowledge. We know now that our sun is just one star of average size, that there are billions of stars in our Milky Way galaxy, and then billions of other galaxies. All of this is expanding at an enormous rate, as Carl Sagan explained to my family that night.

We've also learned incredible things about such wonders as the evolution of an infant in the womb and the complexity of the eye, and we now know that a human brain contains more connecting points than there are stars in the universe!

Some years ago a professor at Emory University, where I now lecture, declared, "God is dead!" Although his premises were widely misinterpreted, he was instantly famous, and theological debates raged. Many believers chortled over the response "God can't be dead. I talked to Him this morning." Innate faith and our own knowledge and experiences as Christians are adequate for most of us. But when we have doubts or feel our faith weaken, reassurance comes from the vastness, complexity, order, and beauty of God's creation.

CHAPTER THIRTY-ONE

The Mystery of Resurrection

But someone may ask, How are the dead raised? With what
kind of body will they come? How foolish! What we sow does
not come to life unless it dies. When we sow, we do not plant
the body that will be, but just a seed, perhaps of wheat or of
something else.... So it will be with the resurrection of the
dead.

1 CORINTHIANS 15:35–37, 42

How can we believe in life after death? How can we con-
ceive of such mysteries? These have always been profound
questions for most of the world's religions. This was the main
issue that divided the Pharisees and Sadducees, who claimed
that there was no life after death. In the early Christian

church, doctrinal questions like these also led to bitter arguments and even permanent, hostile separations between church groups. In his first letter to the Corinthians, Paul addresses these questions in an effort to explain the mystery and to heal one such schism.

How does Paul explain life after death? He tries to focus our attention on the most basic, inarguable facts. Paul begins with a commonly recognized earthly truth, something familiar to everyone in a farming community: When we plant a seed, what later appears is completely different from the seed, totally transformed in its character. A stalk of corn or a peanut vine doesn't resemble the seed kernel that is planted.

The same is true of every living thing. Take a caterpillar. It makes a little cocoon that may look like a piece of dead leaf, out of which miraculously comes a lovely creature. There is nothing in the appearance of a homely, crawling caterpillar that would let us predict, "That's going to become a beautiful butterfly!" The transformation is mysterious, even seemingly miraculous.

Paul uses this kind of analogy to say that our present physical bodies may have little relationship to our appearance after the resurrection. His message is simple: Don't even try to guess what we may become after death and resurrection. To argue over such things is foolish.

Paul goes on to say, "The body that is sown is perishable, it is raised imperishable . . . it is sown a natural body, it is raised a spiritual body" (verses 42, 44). This is a beautiful yet still mysterious explanation. The concept of a heavenly life remains elusive. It's hard for us to envision things that we can't put directly into human terms. We fall back on childlike concepts of heaven: pearly gates, golden streets, angels with wings sitting on clouds. Though we know these images are inadequate and inaccurate, they may be the best we can do.

Mary Magdalene and the other women had met the resurrected Jesus and told the rest of the disciples about it. Peter and John had seen the empty tomb with their own eyes. And later, Jesus appeared to all the apostles, to two grieving followers on the road to Emmaus, and to as many as 500 others assembled together. Most of them, Paul said, were still alive at the time the biblical accounts were written. The last dramatic appearance of Christ was to Paul himself. The resurrection of Jesus Christ is a truth on which all Christians agree, and it's enough for us to face death—and a future life.

Fortunately, it's not important for us to understand the concept of heaven or the life of the resurrected body. As Paul reminds us, we don't need to know the details of what awaits us. What we need to know is that Christ died for us and lived again, and that, through faith in him, we, too, can enjoy a resurrected life—whatever it may be like.

CHAPTER THIRTY-TWO

Ready to Worship

Lord, who may dwell in your sanctuary?
Who may live on your holy hill?
He whose walk is blameless and who does what is righteous.

PSALM 15:1–2

This Psalm excerpt challenges us to consider how we can be worthy to enter the presence of God. The sanctuary and the holy hill both describe the Temple in Jerusalem, the center of worship in ancient Israel. The psalmist is asking, "How can we prepare ourselves to spend time with God in a holy place?"

When I was a child of four or five, the offering envelopes that we used in our Sunday School class had accomplishments with points listed on the back. We got 20 points for being at church, 20 points for being on time, 30 points for studying our lesson, 20 points for bringing our Bible, another 10 points for giving an offering in the envelope. Every week, we'd fill out the envelopes and hand them in with our scores marked. A few kids would earn all 100 points. If we got 100 four Sundays in a row, we'd get a special treat, like an extra cookie. We had a clear idea in those days what it meant to be worthy, at least in the eyes of our Sunday School teacher—and what the reward would be!

Many of us have gotten away from preparing ourselves for worship. Instead, we assess church services almost as if they were shows put on to entertain us. When someone asks us, "How was church today?" we might answer, "Well, the choir did their best, but they obviously need more practice." Or we might say, "The sermon was too long. The pastor went on until five minutes after twelve and could easily have been finished ten minutes sooner." But this is not the way to think about a worship service. When we speak like this, we're putting the responsibility for worship on other people. What makes a successful worship service is not the beauty of the music or the eloquence of the preacher or even the friendliness of the greeting we receive. Instead, it's the presence of God in our hearts, and that depends on our attitude and what we are seeking.

We need to be prepared, mentally and spiritually, to participate fully in worship. This is something to consider as we make our way to church on Sunday morning, or whenever we worship. We must ask ourselves, "What is the state of my mind and heart as I go to church or approach God in prayer?"

Am I worshiping in a spirit of pride and complacency, or with a searching and humble heart, ready to receive whatever good thing God has in store for me? Is my mind closed to new ideas and to a challenging or surprising message, or have I tried to acknowledge my shortcomings and am I searching for the presence of the Holy Spirit—even if it may disturb me? I confess that it is a challenge for me even to concentrate on what the words mean and not let my mind wander when I join in reciting the Lord's Prayer.

Perhaps when the psalmist says that we must be righteous to dwell in God's sanctuary, this is part of what he has in mind: that we should go to public worship not to be entertained but to seek new and exciting possibilities for our lives as children of God. And I doubt that the only sanctuary of God is inside a church or synagogue. No matter where we are, we can always find the presence of God.

CHAPTER THIRTY-THREE

Pray Without Ceasing

I have posted watchmen on your walls, O Jerusalem; they will never be silent day or night. You who call on the Lord, give yourselves no rest, and give him no rest till he establishes Jerusalem and makes her the praise of the earth.

ISAIAH 62:6–7

We all experience rejection. When I was a child, the big boys would choose up baseball teams at recess, and I would often be the last one chosen, because I was small and not a very good athlete. I would have given half my savings from selling boiled peanuts if they would have chosen me as one of the early ones! But being left out, abandoned, or rejected happens to all of us at times. This passage describes the prophet

Isaiah's sense that God has forsaken the people of Israel. (Many of the earlier chapters of the Book of Isaiah describe the sins of the Israelites, and the desolation, despair, and suffering they had undergone as a result.) Isaiah's response in this time of tribulation is, perhaps, surprising. He calls on sentinels—watchmen—to sit on the walls of Jerusalem, God's holy city, and offer incessant, constant, repetitive prayer, until the wishes of the Jewish people for reconciliation with God are granted. It reminds me of the apostle Paul's admonition to the early Christians, hundreds of years later: "Pray without ceasing" (1 Thessalonians 5:17).

The message to us is this: Never give up on God, who always answers our prayers. Sometimes the answer is "Wait" or "No," or perhaps, as our pastor, Dan Ariail, says, "You've got to be kidding!" Then we must reassess what we are seeking. Continuing to pray hopefully in the face of profound disappointment seems contrary to human nature. Why should we do it? Because invariably we can learn and grow in the process.

One of the most humorous stories of Jesus was about the woman who irritated an unjust judge so persistently, even at his home at night, that he finally made a proper ruling (Luke 18:1–7). In another story, immediately following the Lord's Prayer, Jesus told of a man who had an unexpected guest and went to a neighbor's house to borrow some bread. The neighbor shouted, "Do not bother me: the door is locked and my children are with me in bed; I cannot get up and give you anything." The man persisted, and got the bread (Luke 11:5–8).

We often find that our prayers bring about change, at least in ourselves, as God opens our eyes to a better future than we could have envisioned for ourselves. The Bible assures us that, with patience and courage, problems, failures, even tragedies can be turned into great blessings. In fact, James tells us, "Consider it pure joy, my brothers, whenever you face trials of many kinds. . . . Blessed are those who persevere under trial, because when they have stood the test, they will receive the crown of life that God has promised to those who love him" (James 1:2, 12).

As we pray continually, even during times when God seems distant and prayer feels fruitless, we immerse ourselves in the benevolence, grace, forgiveness, and love of God. Our attitudes toward life are modified accordingly. This doesn't mean that we become passive or weak. Living in harmony with the omnipotent God makes us stronger, just as seeing the world through the eyes of the omniscient God makes us wiser. And with this new strength comes an increased ability to apply in our lives the blessings given us by God, even in times of rejection, failure, or sorrow. Like Isaiah, we need to maintain our confidence in God's steadfastness, even in times of loneliness and apparent rejection, and constant prayer is one of the best ways to both express and nurture this confidence.

Communicating our questions, hopes, and fears in prayer makes them—even to ourselves—more open and clear; and the stronger the ties that bind us to God, the more likely we are to live, react, and behave in harmony with exalted standards—and with greater joy, peace, and happiness.

CHAPTER THIRTY-FOUR

Letting In the Lord

When he was at the table with them, he took bread, gave thanks, broke it and began to give it to them. Then their eyes were opened and they recognized him, and he disappeared from their sight. They asked each other, "Were not our hearts burning within us while he talked with us on the road and opened the Scriptures to us?"

LUKE 24:30–32

These verses are from the memorable stories about the appearances of Jesus to his disciples after the resurrection. They concern two followers of Jesus, Cleopas and his brother, who met a stranger on the road from Jerusalem to Emmaus on the day of Jesus' resurrection. The disciples spoke with the stranger about the sad events they'd witnessed, and they were amazed at his ability to explain everything in terms of the scriptural prophecies about the Messiah. They did not recognize that the stranger was Christ himself until the moment described in these verses.

In human terms, why do we suppose these followers didn't recognize Jesus? After all, this was a man they knew personally; they had lived with him, talked with him, and perhaps shared many a meal with their beloved teacher during the three years of his ministry. And in their overwhelming sorrow following his death, surely the image of his face and the sound of his voice were frequently in their minds.

We can imagine many explanations. They were traveling toward the end of the day, near sunset (that's why they invited the stranger to join them for supper); maybe the light wasn't good. They were sad and probably distracted by their grief; Luke says, "They stood still, their faces downcast" (24:17); maybe they didn't pay much attention to the stranger, who was just one of many pilgrims walking the same road. And it seems from other verses that Jesus looked somewhat different after experiencing death, burial, and resurrection.

Most significant, it seems that they were not ready to recognize Jesus. Luke says, "They were kept from recognizing him" (24:16). After all, this was a man whom they may recently have watched being buried. How could they be prepared emotionally to recognize the risen Christ and to experience the presence of God Almighty in the person of our Savior? Perhaps their blindness is understandable.

Is there any parallel between the experience of the followers on the road to Emmaus and our own lives? Yes, there are times when each of us fails to recognize the presence of Christ or the Holy Spirit. Remember that the Scriptures promise us that Christ is with us—at least potentially—not just as an occasional, miraculous event but at all times. In Revelation 3:20, he tells us, "Here I am! I stand at the door and knock. If anyone hears my voice and opens the door, I will come in and eat with him, and he with me." So an experience like that of the disciples, who recognized Jesus in the breaking of the bread, is always available to all of us.

Yet as we go through our daily lives, we often tend to keep the door closed to the presence of Christ. Perhaps we wait until a time of crisis, when we are sorrowful or afraid. Maybe we've had the experience of being ill and having a doctor tell us, "I'll call you when I have the test results," or "We'll soon know whether the cyst is benign or malignant." I've had such moments of anxiety, and I know it's human nature to remember God then; our prayers become especially intense!

We remember to acknowledge the presence of Christ in moments that are special. But how about when we are just traveling along the road, as the disciples were—driving home from work, on a shopping trip, or going on vacation? So often, we are like Cleopas and his brother. We don't open our hearts, our minds, and our imaginations to the powerful truth of our risen Lord.

Convinced as we are that the miracle of Christ's resurrection really happened some 2,000 years ago, we must consider this the most important event in the history of the universe. For us, it means that Christ still lives, that his spirit is still with us, and that we can build our lives around him as our Savior. If all this is true, then why do we so rarely acknowledge the presence of Christ? Perhaps it's because of our human tendency to select from our faith the things that are most convenient, most comfortable for us.

I want to be identified as a good, religious man, of course. If I'm an insurance salesman or a store owner, for example, and I live in a predominantly Christian community, I want to be known as a good church member. So I'll go to church, teach Sunday School sometimes, maybe serve as a deacon. Activities like this are relatively easy, and they make me feel good. But reaching out to the kinds of people Jesus chose—lepers, the mentally ill, prostitutes, thieves, blind people, the homeless—that's outside the purview of our normal Christian environment. It might put a burden on me, a burden of responsibility for someone else. And that's not nearly so convenient or comfortable.

So it's easy, even for dedicated Christians, to put off opening the door to Jesus. We want to be good Christians, but when it's more convenient, at least not today. "Just wait," we say, "until we reach retirement age—or our kids get out of college—or we make the last house payment. Then we'll try to put into our lives the kinds of things we would want to do if Christ were here."

But Christ *is* here, right now. And when we open our hearts to other people, particularly those who are different from us, we are opening the door to him. This is a practical way that Christians can take a major step toward realizing the constant presence of our Savior. He says so specifically: "As ye have done it unto one of the least of these, my brethren, ye have done it unto me" (Matthew 25:40).

When we take such a step, our eyes are opened, as were those of the disciples; we expand our lives, escape from the cages we build around ourselves, and enter a new environment of surprises, adventure, and real gratification. This is some of what Cleopas and his brother learned on the way to Emmaus. Imagine their elation and excitement! I wonder how long it took them to get back to Jerusalem, to share what they'd seen and heard with their friends? They might have set a 10,000-meter speed record!

We are thankful that the miracle they experienced isn't a mystery or a secret any longer. It's a truth all of us can share. Our Savior lives, and if we let it happen—if we accept his presence—our lives will be changed forever.

God's Riches at
Christ's Expense

CHAPTER THIRTY-FIVE

The Source of Courage

The apostles left the Sanhedrin, rejoicing because they had been counted worthy of suffering disgrace for the Name. Day after day, in the temple courts and from house to house, they never stopped teaching and proclaiming the good news that Jesus is the Christ.

ACTS 5:41–42

Remember that these earliest Christians had no legal or civil authority: all political and military power rested with the ruling power of Rome, enforced by a governor and legions of Roman soldiers stationed in Israel. And closely associated with the Romans were the Jewish authorities, who had control over religious matters, led by the Sanhedrin, a kind of central committee of the faithful. And these civil and religious officials had ordered the disciples: "Do not preach anymore in the name of Jesus." Nonetheless, the preaching continued, even when the apostles were called before the Sanhedrin, threatened with death, and actually flogged for their disobedience.

Think of how the disciples reacted after the death of Jesus. It was a terribly painful and disillusioning event for them. Naturally, they were deeply hurt by the loss of their friend and teacher. But they were also very disappointed because of the apparent failure of Jesus' mission. Some of the apostles had believed they were following a man who was soon to become the ruler of the world. They could see themselves sitting by the side of the Messiah in an earthly kingdom, helping him rule nations: collecting taxes, running the government, giving orders to the army, even handing out welfare checks!

The death of Jesus shattered that fantasy. The powerful teacher whom they had revered proved to be fallible and vulnerable. The duality of his identity—both divine and human—suddenly shifted heavily toward the human side; he appeared not even as a strong and successful man but as a total failure, one who had been destroyed by the powers of the day. And with this apparent failure, the disciples saw their own future in jeopardy. Just having been associated with Jesus could put them in danger of losing their lives, or at least their freedom. Perhaps during this dark time after Jesus' death, Peter, who had been filled with remorse over denying Christ three times on the day of his death, thought, "I'm sure glad I didn't admit that I was one of his disciples."

Yet when we turn to this passage from the Acts of the Apostles, we find the disciples completely transformed. Oh, their names and appearances were the same, but they were new people, filled with hope and courage, eager to proclaim their faith in Jesus Christ in spite of the consequences. What caused this amazing change?

Two things had happened. One, of course, was the resurrection of Jesus. The effect of this event—the unprecedented conquest of death—on those who witnessed it cannot be overstated. And the disciples had shared multiple experiences of this miracle. It seemed clear, then, that his enemies had not conquered Jesus after all. Even death couldn't destroy him.

The second transforming experience the disciples shared was the coming of the Holy Spirit at Pentecost. This had been promised: "I will ask the Father, and he will give you another Counselor to be with you forever—the Spirit of truth" (John 14:16–17). In effect, Jesus had told his followers, "I can't be with everybody, everywhere, but the Holy Spirit can be with all of you at all times." And on the day of Pentecost, the Holy Spirit, symbolized by a violent wind, came upon all of the disciples, giving them renewed strength and a deeper, living sense of the presence of God. It was these two experiences—witnessing the resurrection and receiving the Holy Spirit—that gave the disciples the power to proclaim their belief in Jesus, even in a profoundly hostile environment.

It still takes courage to proclaim our complete faith in Christ. Most of us will never be called upon to make the kind of dramatic, life-or-death choice that the disciples had to make. So martyrdom is not a fate that many of us will face.

But always, Jesus set the example for us. When he reached out to people who were despised, different, lonely, or unattractive, and offered them his companionship, he was showing us the kinds of humble yet significant acts we can take in our daily lives that may require a great deal of personal courage. If we profess faith in Jesus, we should show it in our acts as well as our words.

The fact is that we have available what the disciples possessed: knowledge of the resurrection and the presence of the Holy Spirit. I'm still disturbed by a sermon preached in our church forty years ago. I don't remember anything except the title: "If you were arrested for being a Christian, would there be enough evidence to convict you?"

CHAPTER THIRTY-SIX

Remembering to Be Thankful

Praise the Lord, O my soul;
all my inmost being, praise his holy name.
Praise the Lord, O my soul,
and forget not all his benefits.
He forgives all my sins
and heals all my diseases;
he redeems my life from the pit
and crowns me with love and compassion.
He satisfies my desires with good things,
so that my youth is renewed like the eagle's.

PSALM 103:1–5

Psalm 103 is a beautiful solo, a song of praise and thanks to God. The entire psalm is worth reading, but even the first five verses contain much food for spiritual thought, just a bit below the surface.

Giving blessings to God may not be as habitual for most of us as it should be. Maybe we say a prayer of thanks when we sit down for a meal. It's a good feeling when our small grandchildren argue about who can lead the family in saying, "God is great, God is good . . ." That's a fine way to begin. Memorizing and reciting a little phrase of thanksgiving is all right, but do we think about what it means? Are we thanking God for giving us the good things we enjoy, or are we asking God to bless our food? The two meanings are interrelated and quite compatible.

When the psalmist says, "Praise the Lord, O my soul," he intends that we should give thanks to God continually, not just on rare occasions. And the word *soul* carries more profound connotations than we may realize. For the ancient Israelites, "soul" meant the totality of a person's being, character, and life, including what we might call the heart and the mind. The psalmist is calling forth a blessing that arises from the depths of all that he is: "With all my heart and soul and mind," we might say, "Lord, I bless you."

The psalmist goes on to praise God for the benefits God has given him, and much of the rest of the psalm delineates those blessings. Consider, for example, verse 3: "He forgives all my sins and heals all my diseases." It's not easy for us to admit that we are sinners. When we do—when we ask God for forgiveness, as when we recite the Lord's Prayer—we may tend to do it superficially. We may say, "Lord, forgive our sins," and overlook the words "as [provided] we forgive those who trespass against us."

It's certainly easier to skip over our inadequacies than it is to acknowledge them specifically. We don't want to think about the times we are selfish or gossip about our neighbors. We don't care to recall the ways we're self-centered or callous toward people in need. But God remembers and (if we do) is ready to forgive all these sins and more. It is spiritually healthy to thank God for freeing us from them as the psalmist does.

It may seem strange, at first, that the same verse speaks about God's healing our diseases. But remember that in biblical times disease was often considered a form of punishment for sin. Job's suffering was blamed on sinfulness, as was leprosy in Jesus' time. So a leper was to be avoided, not just as a carrier of an infectious disease but as a person being punished by God for sins, presumably serious ones.

Most of us have, at one time or another, faced the possibility of death, either from disease or from other causes. At the age of three or four, I had colitis—often a fatal disease back then—and the doctor thought I was going to die. And when I was a submariner, there were three occasions when I could have died had my luck been just a little different. God has saved my life to this point. But I rarely stop to say, "God, thank you for the gift of life." Perhaps, like our sinfulness, our mortal frailty is something we don't often want to ponder.

Both of these gifts from God—the forgiveness of sins and the healing of diseases—relate to the renewal and refreshment of our lives. This idea is beautifully embodied in the image in verse 5: "He satisfies my desires with good things, so that my youth is renewed like the eagle's." Why like the eagle's? For us, the eagle is an especially powerful, handsome bird, which we use as a national symbol as well as an emblem of strength and beauty. However, the eagle had an additional meaning for the ancient Hebrews. Because it molts (sheds and regrows) all its feathers annually, they viewed the eagle as having a new life each year. For them, the eagle was something like the phoenix for us—a symbol of new life emerging from old.

How can we enjoy the gift of renewed life that the eagle symbolizes? No matter how old we may be, we can have a youthful exuberance about life, as did my mother even after she passed the age of eighty. Our sense of wonder at the beauties of nature need never diminish. Every day we can ask, "What can I learn about God's world that I don't yet know? What are some of the wonders of creation that I don't yet understand?" If we have inquisitive minds, we can continually grow in our appreciation of God's handiwork, no matter how many years we've lived.

The gift of renewed life can be enjoyed in the feeling of hope we have because of God's presence with us. We have surely known disappointment, sorrow, or failure, and the pain may have seemed unbearable. We may even have said, "I can't go on." Yet for most people, the passage of time heals those wounds, thanks to the sustaining love and grace of God. The ability to emerge with hope for a better day is another aspect of the renewed life God continually gives us. This, too, is a gift for which we should thank and bless the Lord.

Almost every day is filled with opportunities to be grateful. When we wake up in the morning, when we meet a friend, when someone lends us a hand, when one of our children or grandchildren expresses love, when we go to a job that is gratifying, when an unanticipated opportunity arises, when we see a beautiful sky, or when we have any kind of exciting experience—all of these are opportunities to give God the credit and acknowledge God's greatness. It's a good habit to develop.

CHAPTER THIRTY-SEVEN

Unseen and Eternal

Therefore we do not lose heart. Though outwardly we are wasting away, yet inwardly we are being renewed day by day. For our light and momentary troubles are achieving for us an eternal glory that far outweighs them all. So we fix our eyes not on what is seen, but on what is unseen. For what is seen is temporary, but what is unseen is eternal.

2 CORINTHIANS 4:16–18

When we're children, the things around us seem permanent. Maybe it's because time passes more slowly for a child. I remember when a single afternoon of school seemed to last for days, and certainly the month before Christmas seemed to take forever.

I also remember good aspects of my life that I imagined would never—could never—change. One of these was the stability and strength of our family. The home that Mama and Daddy made for us children was the center of our lives, the place we returned to every evening, a haven whenever anything unpleasant or troubling happened. It was comforting to be able to return home to my parents when I got into a fight with another boy and had a bloody nose, or when I got a bad grade at school. (Well, I take that back. When I got a bad grade in school, I didn't want to go home to my parents!) Our family wasn't unique in those days. For most children growing up in Plains, the family was an unshakable foundation. When I left home to go to college, I had never heard of a divorced couple in our community. Divorce simply wasn't accepted; the assumption was that a binding oath had been made to God: a marriage was for life. We heard about people being divorced in Hollywood or New York, maybe, but never in Plains.

Today, of course, that has changed. Family instability and broken homes have come to Plains, just as they've come to small towns, cities, and the countryside everywhere in America. Is this change all bad? Not necessarily. Sometimes separation is the only option in a family where infidelity, abuse, or violence is an insoluble problem. But the lack of a solid home for children growing up today is a troubling thing.

When I was a boy, a trip to Americus, the nearest big town, was an adventure. The ten-mile round trip was generally an all-day affair, and we could count on getting at least one flat tire on the way. As for Atlanta, we'd go there every few years at most—a truly momentous event, perhaps to visit the enormous regional Sears, Roebuck store or to see the Atlanta Crackers play baseball. Travel was intimidating and difficult, but it also carried a degree of romance. The railroad engineer was an admired and envied figure. As a child, living two and a half miles out from town, I was excited to observe closely the six trains that went by our house each day, carrying freight and passengers to wonderful places all over the South. I'd often go out to stand near the track when the train was due and wave furiously at the engineer, and he'd wave back and maybe even toot his whistle for me. I'd have given anything to trade places with him!

Outwardly, our town hasn't changed much in the last century. We have about 700 people living in Plains, just as we have had for decades, and most of us make our living growing peanuts, pecans, pine trees, and cotton, or selling goods to the folks who do, just as we have for generations. But beneath the surface, life has changed in startling ways in southwest Georgia, just as it has all over America and the world. The descendants of people who in past generations might have lived in the same town for their whole lives now move from city to city every few years, pursuing work or school opportunities or simply seeking a better climate or a different lifestyle. Our children have lived in various parts of the country, and we frequently visit them, and also travel around the United States, Asia, Africa, Latin America, and other continents in my work on behalf of The Carter Center. It's a way of life that would have been unthinkable in my earlier days.

In my childhood, the radio was our only direct link to the larger world. When we got our first radio, we had no electricity in the house. We would hook up the big radio console to the battery from the car and gather around and look at the radio when our favorite programs came on. (I don't know why we looked at the radio, but somehow we felt we couldn't take our eyes from the dial and knobs.) Being able to listen to *Fibber McGee and Molly, Little Orphan Annie,* or *The Lone Ranger* as we sat in the living room of our farmhouse was a technological wonder for us. Now, even when we stay at home, our connections to other regions are vivid and instantaneous.

Greatly increased mobility and instant communications, throwaway marriages and broken families: these are just a few of the changes, good and bad, that we've seen in our lifetimes. In such a world, it's easy to lose the anchor of our lives, to become confused and uncertain about what really matters, or so obsessed with the rapidity of change that we lose sight of the changeless values that give our lives meaning.

I'm fond of quoting the wise words of Miss Julia Coleman, who was my high school teacher—words that I quoted in my inaugural address as president: "We must adjust to changing times, but still hold to unchanging principles."

In his second letter to the Corinthians, Paul addresses the same issue. He knew nothing about jet planes or the Internet, but he, too, lived in a world that seemed filled with complexities, troubles, and changes that were often unwelcome. His advice is not unlike Miss Julia's. He says we should fix our eyes not on what is seen but on what is unseen. For what is seen is temporary, but what is unseen is eternal.

What is seen is an ever-changing, confusing world, in which the only thing certain is that more changes will be coming tomorrow. But there remain unseen things that are truly permanent—more permanent even than the loving childhood home, built around my daddy and mama, that I never thought I would lose. The unseen, eternal things Paul had in mind are the values of which Jesus spoke: humility, compassion, justice, truth, friendship, and sacrificial love. When the world we live in today has passed away, the glory of these gifts will remain, unchanged and as precious as ever.

CHAPTER THIRTY-EIGHT

Facing Up to Sin

Blessed is he whose transgressions are forgiven,
whose sins are covered.
Blessed is the man whose sin the Lord does not count
against him
and in whose spirit is no deceit.
When I kept silent, my bones wasted away
through my groaning all day long.
For day and night your hand was heavy upon me;
my strength was sapped as in the heat of summer.
Then I acknowledged my sin to you
and did not cover up my iniquity.
I said, "I will confess my transgressions to the Lord"
and you forgave the guilt of my sin.

PSALM 32:1–5

Confession, I've found, is a topic that makes us uneasy. We may ask ourselves why we should want to get involved in something so unpleasant. After all, I've been profoundly blessed in my life. I have a nice family, a decent home, plenty to eat, a degree of comfort and security. If I'm so blessed, isn't it likely that there's a good reason for it? Maybe I've done enough to deserve it! And if I deserve all these blessings, what on earth could I possibly have to confess?

Well, we are blessed, it's true. We Americans, in particular, are a very fortunate people, with a high standard of living, a land abounding in natural beauty, and a degree of freedom rare in the world. But where do we get these wonderful gifts? Are they all our doing, or did our Creator have something to do with them?

Of course, we respond, our blessings come from God. And naturally we should be grateful. That's why we say a few words to thank God before meals—at least on holidays—and maybe give a few dollars to charity or to our church from time to time: to express our gratitude to God. But what does this have to do with confession?

The problem is that we can't be truly thankful unless we are willing to acknowledge our need for God. After all, if the good things we enjoy are our own doing—if we deserve them simply because of how hardworking, how decent, how special we are—then we really don't owe God anything. We can claim to be complete, needing no one and nothing outside of ourselves.

But we know, deep inside, that the reality is quite different. We realize that we're far from perfect, and we're willing to

admit as much: Sure, sometimes I act and think in ways that
don't make me proud. I focus too much on my own needs, and
not enough on the needs of others. Sometimes, I admit, I'm
not filled with compassion or love for those around me. If it's
company policy, I'll bend the truth to make a big sale. And I
even bear grudges against a few people. Yes, I'll admit all this.
But confession? That's for sinners, isn't it?

The truth is, the standard set forth in the life and teachings
of Jesus Christ is nothing less than perfection. Most of us have
a great many blessings. Yet most of us would agree that our
material possessions, and even our emotional and psychological blessings, like family and friends, are not enough to bring
us complete peace and happiness. Think about it. Have we
achieved the serenity and joy that comes from knowing we've
fulfilled all the potential God has given us? Have we embodied
in all our thoughts and actions the selfless love Jesus told his
followers to share?

If the honest answer is no—as it probably is—then the gap
between our lives and the model given us by Jesus is the
source of that dissatisfaction, that uncertainty, that lack of
fulfillment that makes us feel ever so slightly incomplete.
And this resulting state is sin, which can only be fully healed
through confession and forgiveness.

Fortunately, God's willingness to hear our confession and
forgive us completely is inexhaustible. The Psalms, traditionally attributed to King David, express beautifully the human
need for confession and the joy of forgiveness. Remember that
David, one of the great heroes of the Bible, was very much a
flawed, fallible human being. Whatever transgressions we may
have committed in life, the chances are good that David did
something even more wicked, from lying and adultery all the

way to murder. How could this man, who violated almost every one of God's commandments, become a mighty leader of the Israelites? Through confession. Again and again, he repented and turned to God, freely admitting his wrongdoing and seeking forgiveness and new life. And each time, God granted him that gift. Without confession, our failings and transgressions become a heavy emotional and spiritual weight.

David describes this burden vividly: "My strength was sapped as in the heat of summer." We all know the feeling of uneasiness or even depression when we know we've done something wrong, yet cannot or will not acknowledge it. David understood this absence of joy and expressed it precisely.

But he understood, too, the relief that grows out of confession, and the new life that forgiveness makes possible: "Blessed is the man whose sin the Lord does not count against him and in whose spirit is no deceit." Notice the subtle shift between the first and second halves of this verse. The first part speaks of the joy of forgiveness: God no longer blames us for our sins, which are wiped away as completely as if they'd never happened. But the second half ("and in whose spirit is no deceit") places a continuing burden on the forgiven one. Perhaps we are reluctant to enumerate our sins. Maybe we're concerned that if we actually list them we'll remind God of some sins that have been overlooked in heaven! It's not enough to say, "Lord, I confess my sins," and then go right back to a life of selfishness, lying, gossip, and animosity, expecting to be forgiven again in the future. True forgiveness cannot exist without our most earnest effort to continue in that state of reconciliation with God, with a spirit devoid of deceit.

Will we fail again to live up to God's moral standard of perfection? We will, just as David did. Yet reconciliation and a new start are always possible, always available, if we are willing to acknowledge our transgressions and ask for God's help. The crucial first step—the most difficult one—is to admit our inadequacy and our need. It requires honesty and courage to do this. But if we can take that first step, God has promised total forgiveness.

CHAPTER THIRTY-NINE

Forgiving Ourselves

For I was alive without the law, but when the commandment came, sin revived, and I died. . . . For we know that the law is spiritual, but I am carnal, sold under sin. . . . In my flesh is no good thing, . . . for the good that I would I do not, but the evil which I would not, that I do. . . . O wretched man that I am! Who shall deliver me from the body of this death?

ROMANS 7:9, 14, 18–19, 24

There is therefore now no condemnation to them which are in Christ Jesus. For the law of the Spirit of life in Christ Jesus has made me free from the law of sin and death.

ROMANS 8:1–2

These are some of the most troublesome and beautiful verses in the Bible. Paul has been struggling in this letter to the Romans with the most basic concerns of a person's relationship with God. In my own Christian witnessing, I have used the verses "For all have sinned and come short of the glory of God" (Romans 3:23) and "For the wages of sin is death" (Romans 6:23). Romans 7 continues with the anguished cry of Paul, who struggles with a fruitless effort to resist the temptations that confront him as a fallible human.

Under a strict interpretation of the law, there is only condemnation, and no forgiveness. It is agonizing for devout people to contemplate the consequences of sin as we face a righteous God who cannot abide anything other than perfection. Before Christ, many devout believers made earnest but frustrated efforts to comply fully with literally hundreds of religious rules and regulations, in a futile effort to fulfill God's requirements.

Then, in Romans 8, came the glorious declaration: There is no condemnation to those of us in Christ Jesus! Let's think for a moment about the meaning of the word *in*. It has the connotation of being within a single body, a more intimate relationship even than that between a husband and wife. If I have a serious ear infection, for instance, I might be cured with an antibiotic injection. But it wouldn't help if the injection were given to my wife. Yet as Christians we are in Christ, and he in us. There is an extraordinary commonality that results from accepting Christ as Savior—living in Christ, with the Holy Spirit within us.

Baptism is a symbolic expression of being buried in Christ and raised to salvation. If we acknowledge our lack of self-reliance and reach out to God through faith in Christ, then God forgives us, completely cleanses us, and accepts us through grace. But grace is not a license to sin. We realize that, on the cross, Jesus assumed the punishment for our sinfulness or failures. With this realization comes an obligation, which we are often inclined to forget or minimize.

Suppose, for instance, I knew that the responsibility and punishment for all my selfishness, gossiping, animosity, jealousy, lack of compassion, or other sins would be borne by my daughter, Amy. Imagine the feelings of any parents, knowing that their sins would mean suffering and torment for their children. There is no doubt that they would be striving constantly to live better lives. Do we love Christ less than we love our Amys?

We have within us the strength to reject temptation. We are not dormant supplicants, but, as Paul tells us in Romans 8:37, "we are more than conquerors through him that loved us." The last two verses of this chapter are a powerful guarantee: "For I am persuaded that neither death, nor life, nor angels, nor principalities, nor powers, nor things present, nor things to come, nor height, nor depth, nor any other creature shall be able to separate us from the love of God, which is in Christ Jesus our Lord."

There could not be any more total assurance of God's total forgiveness. Then why can't we, like Paul, find a way to forgive others—and ourselves?

When the Road Is Rough

CHAPTER FORTY

Rejected Yet Loving

O Jerusalem, Jerusalem, you who kill the prophets and stone those sent to us, how often I have longed to gather your children together, as a hen gathers her chicks under her wings, but you were not willing.

LUKE 13:34

The note of longing in the voice of Jesus here makes his feelings toward the people of Jerusalem very clear. Having been rejected and persecuted by them, especially by their religious leaders, he was deeply saddened, yet the overwhelming sense of the passage is the deep, abiding love of Jesus for his people, even for those who had turned against him. It's an amazing combination of emotions, especially when we think back to the experiences of rejection in our own lives.

Virtually every person must live through crises of this kind. As a candidate for governor and president, I deliberately exposed myself to public rejection, but politicians who must face the voters are not the only ones. Think back, for example, to our earlier years. As little children, we are usually encapsulated in the aura of protection created by our parents' benevolent care. As teenagers, we begin to break away from parental control or influence, and there is a torn element in our lives. Part of us clings to the protection of our parents' love, while another part reaches out for new sources of approval. This can be a traumatic time for both generations. Teenagers may reject their parents completely, making them feel guilty and inadequate, even as the parents question their children's newfound values and strange tastes in music or clothes or friends. Perhaps a sustaining love can help to heal the breach in time, but these years when a young person struggles toward independence are often painful for all concerned.

And teenagers' groping for a new life will usually bring with it new experiences of rejection and hurt. Remember when we first fell in love? When I was twelve years old, I had my first sweetheart. Her name was Eloise, though we all called her Teeny. I'd take her out in my daddy's pickup truck—this was in the days before drivers' licenses were required—and we would have a good time together. That is, until a new boy, who had his own automobile, came to our school in Plains. His name was Lonnie. To my dismay, Teeny abandoned me and began going with Lonnie. Smarting from the hurt to my pride, and not willing to relate it to my own failure as a suitor, I always said it was because of the automobile.

When I was twenty-one and in my last year at Annapolis, I fell in love with Rosalynn on our first date. Six months later, I asked her to marry me, totally expecting her to accept. But she said, "No!" I was in abject despair until months later, when she mercifully changed her mind.

All of us, then, go through times of rejection. How do we cope with them? It's very difficult for us to absorb the realization that we have been rejected, either as individuals or for the ideas or beliefs we have, and still feel love and acceptance toward those who have turned away from us. The pain and embarrassment of being cast aside are usually just too great to bear, especially at first.

So it is remarkable to see, in both the Old and New Testaments, how steadfast is the love of God toward us, despite our unfaithfulness. The Hebrew Scriptures repeatedly tell of the Israelites' rejection of the mandates of God. Not only did the Jewish people ignore or reject the teachings of the prophets, but they even turned at times to the worship of other gods or idols of their own making. Through it all, God's love for the Israelites and faithfulness to the covenants remained strong. Jesus was referring to this history in these verses from Luke's Gospel. Like the prophets before him, Jesus had been rejected by the people of Jerusalem, incited, in his case, by the powerful high priest and other members of the Sanhedrin, who were concerned about maintaining their own power and authority in the nation.

Despite this, and in full knowledge of the painful destiny he would soon face, Christ spoke these words of longing when he was going toward Jerusalem and facing trial, rejection, and death. He was motivated by his love for the people there and by the hope that, in the fullness of time, they would be saved and retained in the fellowship of believers.

What does this mean for us today? The lesson is twofold, I think. First, when we feel rejected, perhaps unfairly, we should strive to follow the example of Jesus in being persistent in generous love, even for those who may be rejecting and unloving toward us. This is never easy, but our Savior lived through the worst of it, and his spirit will strengthen us if we ask for that help in prayer.

And second, we should always remember that, when we are the rejecting ones who turn away faithlessly from our Creator, God's love, faithfulness, and desire to forgive our sins and shortcomings remain unchanged. The whole history of God's relationship with humankind shows that we will never be abandoned. Our faith in Jesus Christ as Savior is the guarantee of this promise.

CHAPTER FORTY-ONE

Facing the Future

The Lord said to Joshua ... "Be strong and courageous, because you will lead these people to inherit the land I swore to their forefathers to give them. Be strong and very courageous. Be careful to obey all the law my servant Moses gave you; do not turn from it to the right or to the left, that you may be successful wherever you go."

JOSHUA 1:1, 6–7

Remember Bert Lahr, the wonderful old comic actor who played the Cowardly Lion in *The Wizard of Oz*? He sang a funny song in that movie about the one quality he lacked—the one, he said, that could turn a slave into a king. That quality, of course, is courage. And courage of many kinds is a recurring theme in the Bible.

When we think of courage, we think first of physical bravery, thanks to movies about heroic crime fighters, soldiers, cowboys, and so on. King David, who fought Goliath, the powerful hero of the Philistines, exemplifies such courage.

Joseph is an example of moral courage. As a trusted slave in the house of Potiphar, an official of the pharaoh, he had the audacity to reject the sexual advances of Potiphar's wife. She was a beautiful woman who promised Joseph physical pleasure; political, social, and economic security; and personal advancement, if only he would betray his master. Yet he remained true to his principles and suffered imprisonment as a result.

Social courage is willingness to defy the standards or customs of our society in the name of a higher morality. Jesus is the supreme example of social courage. He gave his teaching, acceptance, and love to those generally considered least worthy of it: Gentiles, sinners, the sick, the outcast, and the despised. And he paid the ultimate price for his courage.

Joshua, who perhaps receives less appreciation than he deserves, gives us another example of courage. While Moses was relaying God's commandments to the Israelites, Joshua was fighting the battles. And unlike almost all the other Israelites, Joshua never deviated from his loyalty to God. So when Moses died, God chose Joshua to lead the Israelites into their promised land.

Think of how Joshua must have felt; imagine his trepidation, knowing that the fate of the Jewish people was now in his hands. The promised land, toward which they had journeyed for more than forty years, was still unknown, filled with unanticipated perils and enemy peoples. And the danger of rebellion or disobedience among the Israelites themselves was still strong. How could Joshua know whether he would be able to lead them in unity and faithfulness, when Moses himself had sometimes failed?

No wonder God, in these opening verses of the Book of Joshua, repeatedly admonishes him to have courage! But notice what else God says here. "Be careful to obey all the law my servant Moses gave you." The two instructions go hand in hand.

As we face changes and challenges, we need to hold on to the things that don't change, the foundations on which we can build our lives despite the uncertainty and danger of the future. God's law is the greatest of these foundations. Fear is a natural reaction to uncertainty; I myself don't like to face a challenge whose outcome can't be known. It sometimes seems that today's world forces us to cope with greater uncertainty than ever before. A sociologist recently found that average Americans now change jobs eight times in their lives. I've changed jobs at least that many times myself—from farmer to naval officer, nuclear engineer, farmer, businessman, governor, president, professor, author, and so forth. Each change of this kind requires courage; it forces us to take on new responsibilities, make new friends, and try things that may not succeed.

Long before we had tractors or even electrical power on our farm, I remember my father, a good and brave man, going outside at night and walking up and down in our yard, unable to sleep because he'd heard thunder in the distance. He knew that if it rained one more time, we'd probably lose the year's peanut and cotton crops. The destructive Bermuda grass, nut grass, and johnsongrass would take over, and the crop would be lost because we couldn't keep up with just mule-drawn plows. A religious man, my daddy prayed for some dry weather but also for strength and courage to deal with whatever came. Although the weather did not always suit him, the most important part of his prayers was answered.

The future is sometimes fearsome, and I haven't even spoken of the inevitable, devastating changes when friends and family are parted by death. Only the certainty of God's love can ultimately overcome the uncertainties of this earthly life.

When we are fearful about the future, Christ's message to us is the same one that God gave to Joshua: "I am with you, and the promises I have made shall certainly be fulfilled. But as you cross the river, be sure to follow my commandments, without swerving to the right or the left." If we do this, we can face the future with courage, no matter what unknown changes it may bring.

CHAPTER FORTY-TWO

We Underestimate Ourselves, and Others

Therefore, my beloved brethren whom I long to see, my joy and crown, stand fast in the Lord. . . . Rejoice in the Lord always; again I say, "Rejoice.". . . Be anxious for nothing, but in every thing by prayer and supplication with thanksgiving let your requests be made known to God. And the peace of God, which passes all understanding, shall keep your hearts and minds through Christ Jesus. . . .

I know how to get along with humble means, and I also know how to live in prosperity; in any and every circumstance I have learned the secret of being filled and going hungry, both of having abundance and suffering need. I can do all things through him who strengthens me.

PHILIPPIANS 4:1, 4, 6–7, 12–13

Paul was in prison, probably in Rome, when he wrote this letter to the small church at Philippi. He was hopeful of visiting the congregation again, but he was not to see them before his execution.

Paul expresses his hope in this letter that the church could overcome its difficulties and be united. He also says that he is concerned about other preachers who have made derogatory remarks about him but is still grateful that they are spreading the gospel.

The early Christians lived in turmoil, in a time of rapid change in the religious and philosophical world. It was only natural that there were serious divisions in the churches, as they struggled to survive and were bombarded by sometimes conflicting messages from Paul, Peter, Apollos, and other emissaries sent more directly from the church in Jerusalem. There was also intense competition and jealousy within the local congregations, particularly as Christianity became more acceptable and even popular.

Ours is a time of extremely rapid communication, and we are bombarded by conflicting voices on television and radio. In the Christian community—or communities—there are divisions, competition, and jealousy, and we face the kinds of personal challenges and fears about which Paul gives reassurance. Doubt about the future and particularly uncertainty about financial status is of concern to us all. We worry about whether we make $14,000 a year or $140,000 a year, when many people have to exist on $140 a year, or even less. Still, most of us are profoundly blessed with material things. We are not starving, our babies are not dying within a few weeks after birth, we don't sleep on the streets in human and animal filth, as millions of people in the world do.

In April 1997, Rosalynn and I visited a happy and relatively prosperous family who live near the top of a mountain about ten miles from Addis Ababa, Ethiopia. From the main road, we walked up and down a steep and twisting trail, and were welcomed in their home. It was just one room, about the size of a small bedroom in a working-class American house. The proud mother and her three children shared the space with their sheep and chickens, and they were laughing about a recent problem. The houses in the village had been wired with electricity, each having one light hanging from a cord. A well-meaning American friend had given this family a 100-watt bulb to replace the single dim bulb they had been issued. This had caused an overload, and the village lost power for two days. As punishment, the family was deprived of electricity for a month.

Their only income came from gathering fallen limbs from nearby eucalyptus trees and binding them into large bundles, which the mother would carry down the mountain to the city to sell for fuel. With the help of her children, she could make five round trips each week in good weather, producing a gross income of about three dollars. We walked over to her bundle prepared for the next day, which was about two feet in diameter and six feet long. Rosalynn could barely lift it off the ground, and I could never have put it on my back without help. We hated to imagine carrying it more than ten miles down the winding road to Addis Ababa. Yet this was a happy family, grateful to God for their blessings.

This was a vivid reminder to us of our tendency to be overly concerned about material things. We might also think of a few verses from the Sermon on the Mount: "Therefore take no thought, saying, 'What shall we eat?' Or, 'What shall we drink?' Or, 'Wherewithal shall we be clothed?'. . . for your heavenly Father knows that you have need of all these things. But seek first the kingdom of God, and his righteousness; and all these things shall be added unto you" (Matthew 6:31–33).

The point of these admonitions is summarized in the two words "seek first." All of us will have to face doubts, concerns, challenges, disappointments, sorrows, and apparent failures, as did the biblical heroes. Consider Peter, who denied Christ; Paul, who persecuted Christians; David, who committed murder to conceal his adultery; and Joseph, who was sold into slavery by his own brothers. For all of these, as there should be for us, there was an overriding priority of faith, a willingness to depend upon God for guidance through prayer, to sustain us in times of trial, and to forgive us when we repent.

Paul reminds us that this gives us not just an adequate existence but one of joy and all-encompassing peace. Regardless of our transient troubles, he says, "Rejoice in the Lord always; again I say, 'Rejoice!' "

Let's take a look at the man giving this advice. Paul was in prison, not knowing which day he would be executed because of his faith. He had been in jail several times and seldom received tangible support from members of the congregations he had helped to establish—he rarely even heard from them. Most churches were quite small, tiny enclaves of Christianity in large and mostly antagonistic communities. Paul was constrained to write a few letters that may or may not have been delivered, usually to a single member of one of the churches.

He had never preached to large and adoring crowds or been blessed with demonstrable success. Instead, as he told the Corinthians, five times he had been given thirty-nine lashes by the Jews, three times he had been beaten by the Romans, he had been stoned, shipwrecked on three occasions, often cold and hungry, and imprisoned several times. He could very well have looked upon his life as a failure.

Still, he gave the Philippians and us valuable advice about how to face our challenges. Don't be timid; instead, reach for greatness. If we're doubtful, get a partner, Jesus Christ. And remember, "I can do all things through Christ, who strengthens me." (Philippians 4:13)

Our Favorite Disciple

Peter said unto him, "Lord, . . . I will lay down my life for your sake." Jesus answered him, "Will you lay down your life for my sake? Truly, I say to you, the cock shall not crow till you have denied me three times."

JOHN 13:37–38

When I first taught a Sunday School lesson based on this text, at First Baptist Church in Washington while I was president, I began by asking the class, "Who is your favorite disciple?" Almost unanimously, the response was "Peter!" And then they called out multiple reasons for their preference: "I feel at ease with him." "He's human." "He was rough-hewn, a fisherman." "Peter was impetuous, he overdid things."

"When he failed, he really failed." "He admitted it when he had doubts."

Strangely enough, the Bible tells us much more about Peter than about any other apostle, including the names of his father and his brother, that he was married, his profession, where he lived, and that John the Baptist strongly influenced him.

Peter had an intricate relationship with Jesus and a roller-coaster career, with soaring successes and abysmal failures. Our class had a long discussion about failure—something we all have to face. One comment was "Peter bragged too much, and failed often, because he tried a lot." Maybe it's natural for us to identify with him.

Thomas Edison, one of the world's greatest inventors, had a visitor one day and took him down to his basement labora-tory to show him a new, experimental light bulb. Edison threw the switch and the bulb failed to light. The friend said, "Well, I'm sorry about your failure." Edison replied, "No, that was a success. Now I know one more thing that won't work."

One of our most admired politicians first ran for the state legislature in '32 with twelve other candidates. He came in eighth. Later he was elected, ran for Speaker, and was defeated badly. He left the legislature and tried to get an appointment as federal land commissioner, but someone else got the job. In '58, he ran for the U.S. Senate—and lost again. His life story was almost an unrelieved litany of failure. But two years later, Abraham Lincoln was elected president of the United States and became one of our nation's greatest political leaders.

So we relate to our leaders when they exhibit human weak-nesses and failures. Despite Peter's shortcomings, other dis-ciples seemed to recognize him as their leader, and Jesus seems to have been intrigued by him. Even today, we can see in this great apostle many of our own failings. Let's recall some of the events in his life and try to relate them to our own experiences.

Perhaps before other disciples, Peter knew who Jesus was and said, "You are the Christ, the Son of the Living God" (Matthew 16:16). But a few verses later, when Peter rebukes Jesus for predicting his own tragic fate, Jesus denounces him as "Satan." In our lesson text, John reports another swift change in the status of Peter, as he brags about himself only to be faced with the prediction of his betrayal of Christ. Shortly thereafter, Jesus went off to the Mount of Olives to pray. Knowing he was vulnerable to capture, he repeatedly asked his disciples to stay alert. More than once, Peter and the others went to sleep.

Peter was not afraid to express himself boldly, sometimes contradicting the statements of Jesus. He also had little reluctance to make public admissions of his doubts when they existed. One of the most poignant of these confrontations occurred at the Last Supper, when Jesus girded himself with a towel and began to wash the feet of his disciples. When it was Peter's turn, he said, "Lord, you will never wash my feet!" Jesus said, "If not, you will have no part with me." Taken aback, Peter responded, "Wash my feet, and also my hands and head" (John 13:3–9).

With all his good intentions, how could Peter make so many mistakes? His problem was similar to our own: He was filled with pride and considered himself self-sufficient—not needing God to help him withstand the inevitable human temptations. But he had faith, kept on trying, and eventually reached greatness in God's eyes.

CHAPTER FORTY-FOUR

The Span of Life

Now there were some present at that time who told Jesus about the Galileans whose blood Pilate had mixed with their sacrifices. Jesus answered, "Do you think that these Galileans were worse sinners than all the other Galileans because they suffered this way? I tell you, no! But unless you repent, you too will all perish. Or those eighteen who died when the tower in Siloam fell on them—do you think they were more guilty than all the others living in Jerusalem? I tell you, no! But unless you repent, you too will all perish."

LUKE 13:1–5

Why do bad things, even early deaths, happen to good people? And why do those who seem unrighteous sometimes enjoy long, financially prosperous lives? A few years ago in Alabama, a group was assembled in church preparing for their annual Easter pageant when a tornado struck. The building collapsed on them and twenty people were killed. Four were small children, excitedly anticipating the happy event; one was the four-year-old child of the church pastor. The timing and circumstances of this tragedy shocked Christians everywhere. How could innocent children be slaughtered in church, just a few days before celebrating the resurrection of Jesus Christ?

In one way or another, many of us have had to face the terrible question of premature, apparently unjust suffering or death of someone we know and love. When I first began teaching Sunday School at the Maranatha Baptist Church in Plains, there was a woman in my class whom I liked very much. She was a good athlete, and she and I would often go jogging early in the morning. Sometimes during class, I would glance at her and see tears running down her cheeks. I knew she had had a five-year-old son who had died, and something in the Bible lesson had reminded her of him. She had never overcome the torment of that personal tragedy.

Many people in biblical times had a pat way of dealing with this issue of incomprehensible suffering. They would claim that those who suffered (or perhaps their parents) were sinful in the eyes of God, even if no one could see what their sins were. The presumption was that God was punishing them for these sins. Disease was often attributed to evil spirits, or to moral and spiritual uncleanness. From this belief, it was a short, easy step to blaming victims for their suffering and ostracizing them so they wouldn't contaminate others.

Truth and falsehood are strangely intermixed in this doctrine of disease. It's true that some illnesses can be spread by human contact, which is why we have to take precautions when we encounter victims of contagious diseases. It's also true that many medical conditions are caused by human behavior. Unsafe sex, smoking, excessive drinking, poor nutrition, and the terrible living conditions of the poor and homeless all produce illness and suffering. People who fail to do what they can to free themselves from addictions and other self-destructive behavior help produce their own illnesses and death, and in that sense can be said to bring misfortune on themselves. But does this mean that they should forfeit our compassion and sympathy? I don't think so.

It's easy for us to become self-righteous in contemplating the suffering of others, especially when they have contributed to it in some way. It's comforting, too; it implies that, if we are well, we must be better, purer, stronger, or more moral than those others who are suffering. But common sense and reflection should show us that this belief, however tempting, is wrong. First of all, when measured against the only person who was without sin—Jesus Christ—all of us fall short of perfection. If illness or early death is a punishment for sin, then none of us should escape unscathed.

Second, it's plain that physical well-being and moral goodness don't go hand in hand. We all know people who have lived long, healthy lives without being moral paragons, while others have died young without doing anything to deserve such a fate. Jesus, of course, is the supreme example. His was the perfect life, a model of sinless love, but it was cut short at the age of about thirty-three by a death of unsurpassed cruelty and suffering. If Jesus' life is any indication, how can anyone claim that death and misery are generally imposed on those who deserve them?

We don't know the history behind Jesus' comments about the eighteen unfortunate people who were killed when the tower in Siloam fell on them. It sounds like a tragedy not unlike the tornado hitting the church in Alabama, or like many other calamities in the news almost every day. Jesus uses it as an example to warn his followers not to believe that those who suffer premature death have done something to deserve it. Were they, he asks, "more guilty than all the others living in Jerusalem? I tell you, no!" Yet Jesus goes on to say, "But unless you repent, you too will all perish." What can he mean?

Obviously, Jesus is not warning his followers that a tower will fall on them if they go on sinning. He has specifically disclaimed any such clear cause-and-effect relationship between suffering and sin. His message is subtly different from that. Don't concentrate, he says, on the number of years we have left on earth. At best, life is short, and its duration is unpredictable. Instead, concentrate on how we live—looking into our heart and soul and focusing on the most important questions: Who am I? Why was I created? And what am I doing to make my life on earth as meaningful as possible?

This is a difficult, challenging lesson. Death comes to all of us, and the time and manner of our death may not match what we think we deserve. We exaggerate the importance of longevity, with some people almost overwhelmed by fear of dying. But in the end, Jesus reminds us, the pain of earthly death is not the most important thing. What matters most is the eternal life that God has promised us. This is a gift that we

can enjoy not just at the end of our earthly existence but beginning now, in the way we live each day. If we repent, have
faith in Christ, and strive to embody his love and mercy in our
own lives, we can overcome the fear of a future death in the
joy and excitement of a present life that is ever more fully
united with God.

God's Call

CHAPTER FORTY-FIVE

Running the Race

Therefore, since such a great cloud of witnesses surrounds us, let us throw off everything that hinders and the sin that so easily entangles, and let us run with perseverance the race marked out for us. Let us fix our eyes on Jesus, the author and perfecter of our faith, who for the joy set before him endured the cross, scorning its shame, and sat down at the right hand of the throne of God.

HEBREWS 12:1–2

We all grow up with particular dreams and ambitions. When I was a child, my friends and I wanted to be firefighters, policemen, cowboys, or train engineers. Nowadays, some kids want to become astronauts and fly through space, or to become star basketball players.

I grew up during the Great Depression years, a difficult time for us as it was for almost everyone. But my daddy was determined to send me to college, even though money was hard to come by and he himself had only finished the tenth grade. The only two options for me to receive a free college education were the service academies, Annapolis and West Point. So from the time I was five years old, when anyone asked me, "What do you want to be when you grow up?" I responded, like a parrot, "I want to go to Annapolis to the Naval Academy." And ultimately I realized that goal.

In Paul's letter to the Hebrews, he uses the famous metaphor of a race to describe the goals we choose to pursue in life. I don't know for sure what kind of race St. Paul had in mind, but for me, the proper image for our lives is not a brief event like a 100-meter dash. It's more like a cross-country race—a long, difficult trek over unpredictable terrain with hills, valleys, holes, roots, and other unexpected obstacles. It's a race that tests not only speed but also willpower and endurance.

Cross-country was my major sport at the Naval Academy. Years after I left Annapolis, when I became president, my cross-country coach was interviewed by a reporter from *The Washington Post*, and I must say that when I read the article, I couldn't recognize his description of my running—he greatly boosted my performance! I never called a press conference to correct his error, however. I just basked in the glory.

In cross-country racing, we ran and earned points as a team. The first runner to cross the finish line scored one point; the second finisher scored two points, and so on; the team with the lowest point total won the race. I had modest talent, so my personal expectation was not to finish first or second, but I struggled mightily to cross the finish line in a respectable time and help the team as much as possible. Perhaps there's a parallel here to the race of life we all run.

In many areas of life, each of us pursues different goals. Think back to the beginning of the first real job you ever had. Maybe you made a promise to yourself: "Someday, I want to be the chief executive officer of this company," or "Someday, I want to be the senior lawyer in this firm," or "Someday, I want to be the superintendent of all the schools in this county." It may be that you are still pursuing that goal, or a different career goal based on what you've learned about life and your own abilities.

It's important and worthwhile for us to have career aspirations. But goals like these have one thing in common: all define success by the world's standards. When we dream of success in our careers, we are thinking of yardsticks that are primarily material: income, prestige, or authority over others.

Because work is so demanding, most of us spend the majority of our time in pursuit of these worldly goals. There's nothing wrong with them, but because the world in which we live is so intensely competitive, with far more people pursuing top ranks than can possibly achieve them, we're almost inevitably doomed to some degree of failure. Not everyone can become the chief executive officer. Not everyone can sit in the corner office. With failure come frustration and, perhaps, feelings of inadequacy; and with intense competition come, at times, anger, resentment, jealousy, and alienation from those against whom we are struggling. So if the goals we pursue in life are purely of a secular nature, we are almost bound to be frustrated and, to a greater or lesser extent, unhappy.

Yet it's possible to pursue a successful career and also to develop goals and ambitions of a different kind—high objectives that we can certainly achieve and that lead not to a life of failure and unhappiness but to one of excitement, adventure, and achievement. These are goals we can observe in the teachings and life of Jesus Christ. Rather than driving ourselves daily with questions about why we have failed, we can shift our focus toward other concerns, to questions like: How can I draw closer to God? How can I reach out to people who are different from me? How can I more fully demonstrate justice, compassion, or friendship in the way I live this very day?

I think that, deep down, the most important goal most people share, whatever their career ambitions, talents, or lifestyle may be, is a simple one: to live in a truly meaningful way. We all know—and we feel with special poignancy as we grow older—that we have been given just one opportunity to live, a precious gift from God that we're eager not to waste. Are worldly ambitions or material possessions enough to satisfy our hunger for a meaningful life? Most of us who pause from the stresses of our daily existence to reflect seriously on this question must answer no. Fortunately, in the life of Jesus, we have another model: a way of living that does not pit us against other people but helps us unite with them in fellowship and love.

Not everyone can finish first in a cross-country race. And not everyone can play basketball in the NBA, win a Nobel

Prize, or make millions in the stock market. But everyone can be successful according to the standards of God. Each of us can honor God through our lives' commitments, in our activities, and through giving and sharing our time and talents with others. And the joy and excitement of a life built around these values is greater than anything money can buy.

CHAPTER FORTY-SIX

Responding to God's Call

The word of the Lord came to me, saying, "Before I formed you in the womb I knew you, before you were born I set you apart; I appointed you as a prophet to the nations."

"Ah, Sovereign Lord," I said, "I do not know how to speak; I am only a child." But the Lord said to me, "Do not say, I am only a child. You must go to everyone I send you to and say whatever I command you. Do not be afraid of them, for I am with you and will rescue you," declares the Lord.

JEREMIAH 1:4–8

There are times in life when we all need special strength. Some of those times are obvious: when a loved one dies, when we lose a job, when an especially great temptation assails us.

Less obvious is the special strength we need to acknowledge when God has a calling for us, and to respond to that call.

How do we know when God is speaking to us? It's not always easy. One of my daddy's favorite stories to tell his Sunday School students was about a boy who worked from daybreak to dark on the family farm. This boy got it into his head that he was destined to receive a call from God. Sure enough, one morning, as he worked in the field, he looked up at the sky and seemed to see clouds forming the letters "GOP." "That's my call from God!" he said. "It's telling me that I need to Go Out and Preach." So he left the farm and began preaching. But no one wanted to listen to his sermons; he was just no good at it. Only then did he figure out what the message in the clouds had really meant: "Go On Plowing."

In the case of the prophet Jeremiah, God's message was unmistakable. God sent a special presence to Jeremiah and even touched his lips, saying, "Now, I have put my words in your mouth" (Jeremiah 1:9). So God made it very clear that there was a prophetic mission for Jeremiah. How did Jeremiah react to God's call? As we see in the verses quoted at the beginning of this lesson, it was a profoundly disturbing message for him to hear. Put yourself in his shoes. Jeremiah was a young, bashful kid, not a trained orator or a political leader, and he was being told to serve as a prophet to the nations. Notice that plural, "nations." That may have included Ethiopia and Greece, or Egypt and Babylon, as well as Israel and Judah: an enormous task. So this was a shocking statement.

No wonder Jeremiah responded as he did: "I am only a child." He felt inadequate for the job God was sending him to do.

This was a typical reaction of many people we read about

in the Bible who are called to some special task. When God called Moses to lead the Hebrews out of exile in Egypt, he repeatedly protested: "What if they do not believe me or listen to me and say, 'The Lord did not appear to you'? . . . O Lord, I have never been eloquent, neither in the past nor since you have spoken to your servant. I am slow of speech and tongue. . . . O Lord, please send someone else to do it" (Exodus 4:1, 10, 13).

Like Moses, Jeremiah felt inadequate to the task God was assigning him. What was God's response? It was much the same as to other leaders of Israel, or the reassurance later given to Mary, the mother of Jesus: "Do not be afraid, Mary, for you have found favor with God" (Luke 1:30). In effect, God said to all the chosen people, "Don't worry about a lack of talent, or about a challenging and unpredictable future. Just have faith, and I will give you the strength and ability you need."

How does this relate to us? Jesus has made the same promise to each of us. He knew that he would not be present in the flesh to comfort and sustain us forever, but he promised us the strength of the Holy Spirit: "The Counselor, the Holy Spirit, whom the Father will send in my name, will teach you all things and will remind you of everything I have said to you" (John 14:26). Like Jeremiah, Moses, and Mary, we will have adequate help from God in knowing what to do when God wants us to act.

We don't need any extraordinary gifts to be called by God to a special purpose in life. We don't need to be eloquent, handsome, powerful, or influential. We simply need to be willing to do something necessary for God's purposes. And we can't wait for a vision or a voice from heaven. Jesus has already set an example of humility, service, and compassion that is a permanent call to all his followers.

The talent it takes to carry out God's plan may be something very basic. Perhaps it's a compassionate feeling toward someone in our neighborhood who is lonely or unlovable—someone to whom we can reach out in acknowledgment or friendship. Perhaps it's the willingness to share someone else's burden or challenge, especially if it's that of a person hard to love. Or maybe we can take the initiative to forgive someone against whom we hold a grievance.

Living a life of purpose, then, doesn't require what the world considers special talent—just a readiness to respond when God calls, as Jeremiah did, or to follow the example of Jesus. If we examine our own hearts, minds, and consciences, perhaps we'll recognize some simple things God has in mind for us to do, ways of reaching out to express God's love for the world around us. These will always be compatible with our talents and opportunities. And if we answer God's call, even though we feel inadequate, we will have the help and strength we need.

CHAPTER FORTY-SEVEN

Riding Freely

Then Jesus said to them all: "If anyone would come after me, he must deny himself and take up his cross daily and follow me. For whoever wants to save his life will lose it, but whoever loses his life for me will save it."

LUKE 9:23-24

These words of Jesus are among the most famous in the Gospels. They are also among the most troubling. They certainly warn us that suffering in some form is part of the ministry of Christ. But in practical terms, what does this admonition imply? What does it mean for us to take up our cross in following Jesus?

First, there is one interpretation many people make that I

think is wrong. Some people apply this verse to any kind of trouble. According to this reading, taking up our cross could mean suffering from cancer or arthritis, having an unhappy marriage, being expelled from school, or going bankrupt in business. Those who follow this interpretation would say that Jesus is urging us here to accept such tribulations with strength and courage. There's wisdom in that idea. All of us suffer pain, disappointment, even tragedy, and to turn a time of suffering into an opportunity to grow spiritually by disciplining ourselves to accept it bravely is a good thing and a powerful consolation. But it's a mistake, I think, to feel at such times, "Well, I'm suffering; therefore, I'm fulfilling Jesus' admonition to take up my cross."

Jesus is talking here not about the troubles that all creatures must face but rather about suffering for *his* sake, or, as he puts it in verse 24, "losing one's life for me." We don't suffer cancer or have an unhappy marriage for Jesus' sake. Jesus has a different kind of suffering in mind. On the other hand, we don't need to take Jesus' words literally. True, in too many parts of the world there is still persecution of Christians on account of their beliefs, and to this day there are martyrs who actually give up their lives in defense of the word of God. We honor them and their courage, as we should. But those of us who are fortunate enough to live in lands where we are free to teach and practice our faith are still called upon to take up our cross each day. How so?

The best way, I think, is by emulating Jesus' life so fully that we set ourselves apart from the world, even while we live in the world, loving and serving it. The Gospels show us that Jesus addressed the same kinds of daily problems we face today—disease, poverty, prejudice, loneliness, hatred—with generosity and love in a way that would be considered strange and wonderful, in his time and in ours. And we know how the world responded to him—first with praise and admiration, but then with rejection, contempt, and violence.

Living as Christ commands is not easy; sometimes it's not even safe. But we can try. If we work every day for the Lord, speaking out against injustice and hatred, freely sharing what we have, and constantly seeking opportunities to help those who cannot help themselves, we will probably not run the risk of losing our lives, as Jesus did, but we may suffer in other ways. Maybe people will think we're a little odd; maybe some will look down on us. If we're in business, maybe we'll lose a few customers, because some people may find that being around us makes them uncomfortable; maybe we'll lose some income when we pass up business deals our consciences can't approve. Maybe we'll even find ourselves isolated from some of our closest friends and family, who don't share our beliefs and values. To accept, with God's help, any of these forms of deprivation is one way to take up our cross. In each case, others must benefit.

Clarence Jordan, a man who has had a great influence on my life, is one of many modern examples of this lesson. Back in the 1940s, Jordan founded Koinonia Partners on a farm not far from my hometown of Plains, Georgia. Koinonia was a biracial community, one of the few places in the Deep South where white and black people could live, work, and worship together at that time. It was not easy for them. The local merchants boycotted their farm produce, and members of the Ku Klux Klan attacked the farm more than once. They were falsely accused of being communists. But the residents persisted, demonstrating to the world that whites and blacks could live together in peace and friendship. This was the birthplace of the self-help movement known today as Habitat for Humanity.

Someone once asked Clarence Jordan whether he'd ever participated in the famous freedom rides during the civil rights movement of the 1960s. "No," he replied, "but I've always ridden freely." Jordan had an ethical, moral, and spiritual standard for his life, and he lived by it boldly. Sometimes it brought him acclaim, and at other times it brought him brickbats—or worse. But no matter what, he followed faithfully what he believed God was calling him to do. If we live out this philosophy of riding freely, declaring, "I'm going to follow the path God has laid out, no matter what the outcome," there are times we'll get into trouble and maybe even suffer deeply in mind or body as a result. But, of course, we can all expect to suffer in life anyway—isn't it better to suffer for good rather than for evil? (Peter makes this very point in one of his epistles—see 1 Peter 4:12–16.)

And Christ promises us that when we do take up his cross, we're following him on the only path that leads, in the end, to life.

CHAPTER FORTY-EIGHT

The Unfaithful

She is not my wife, and I am not her husband—that she put away her whoring from her face, and her adultery from between her breasts, or I will strip her naked and expose her as in the day she was born. . . . Upon her children also I will have no pity, because they are children of whoredom. . . .

Therefore, I will now allure her, and bring her into the wilderness, and speak tenderly to her. From there I will give her her vineyards, and make the Valley of Achor a door of hope. There she shall respond as in the days of her youth.

HOSEA 2:2–4, 14–15

The contrast between these two statements is startling when we realize that in both it is the prophet Hosea speaking to his children and about the same woman, his wife, Gomer. God had instructed Hosea to marry her, in spite of the fact that she was known to be a whore—and she continued her prostitution after their marriage. As a cuckolded husband, Hosea had full legal authority to strip her naked and cast her out of the family's home.

The Book of Hosea contains an almost inseparable interweaving of his anguished cry to his children and the voice of God, who calls out to a remnant of faithful Israelites. This unhappy marriage relationship parallels that between God and the unfaithful people of Israel.

The text reveals that Gomer received nice rewards from her lovers, including food, clothing, and drink. And we learn that the Israelites also had a good life at this time (about 700 B.C.). They were prosperous, free, and at peace. However, they thought that their blessings came from the pagan god Baal, whom many of them were worshiping. In effect, they were saying to Jehovah, "We don't really need to retain our somewhat restrictive relationship with you, because we have much more freedom with other gods and still have good crops."

The troubling aspect of the lesson on unfaithfulness is that we're not supposed to equate ourselves with God or Hosea but with Gomer. In order for us to be faithful, there must be a commitment for us to honor—otherwise, there's nothing to betray. Marital vows are not the only kind; many types of commitments shape our lives. What is the origin of these restraints, goals, obligations, and promises? Beginning as infants, we absorb them from our parents, siblings, friends, teachers, from religious experiences and training for our professions, and from government laws, rules for athletic contests, and other accepted norms. If we have never read a Bible, listened to a sermon, or heard the name of Jesus, Moses, or Isaiah, we should still know God through our awareness of what has been created and of apparently unexplainable miracles. At each stage in our development, we are constrained by potential punishment and encouraged by rewards. We must choose whether to obey the rules or face the consequences for flouting them.

But we also have higher standards available to us that are purely voluntary —elements of idealism that transcend simple duties or obligations. These can come to us through various forms of affection, as we experience when we become infatuated with a sweetheart and feel this evolve into sacrificial love. An equivalent feeling can exist for our children or our grandchildren. These relationships are usually reciprocal, and the pleasure they create for us is a reward for our faithfulness.

We might be guided by a still more exalted standard, when we are willing or even eager to exceed normal expectations, perhaps with some sacrifice of our own well-being and without our admirable acts even being known. This is the highest form of moral aspiration.

Where do we derive these most transcendent ideals? For Christians, they come primarily from our knowledge of the life of Jesus Christ, who set a standard of perfection, generosity, gentleness, humility, service, compassion, and love. In what ways, then, are we unfaithful? As Christians, we are unfaithful when we betray or ignore the teachings of our Savior, all of which are designed both for our own good and for the benefit of others. Even the miracles of Jesus were not earthshaking or designed to exalt his own stature or to prove that he was the Messiah, but they set a moral example for us, emphasizing our commitment to alleviate suffering and to rescue the lonely and the despised.

Like Gomer, then, we are all unfaithful and deserving of separation from God. Yet just as Hosea reached out to his unfaithful wife, God reached out to the unfaithful Hebrews. In the same way, we know that Christ is reaching out to us, even though we do not persistently honor our commitments as Christians. Our forgiveness through Christ is total, as was Gomer's when Hosea said she would be "as in the days of her youth," when she was still a virgin.

In all cases, forgiveness has not been earned, but redemption has been made possible through grace, mercy, and love. This is a difficult story, but it's still beautiful.

CHAPTER FORTY-NINE

The Lord Looks at the Heart

Samuel consecrated Jesse and his sons and invited them to the sacrifice. When they arrived, Samuel saw Elias and thought, "Surely the Lord's anointed stands here before the Lord." But the Lord said to Samuel, "Do not consider his appearance or his height, for I have rejected him. The Lord does not look at the things man sees. Man looks at the outward appearance, but the Lord looks at the heart."

1 SAMUEL 16:5–7

The story of Saul, Samuel, and David, and how the kingship of Israel came to be transferred from Saul to David, is a fascinating study of power, legitimacy, authority, and obedience—issues that cause us to ponder and speculate to this day. Of course, for the author of the biblical books of Samuel—and for believing Jews and Christians today—God's will is supreme and is the measuring rod against which the fallibilities of humans must be judged.

In the fifteenth chapter of 1 Samuel, just before the passage quoted here, King Saul, with the help of God, has won victory over the Amalekites. But the king is rejected because he disobeys God by sparing Agag, king of the Amalekites, and the best of their sheep and cattle. God tells the prophet Samuel, "I am grieved that I have made Saul king, because he has turned away from me and has not carried out his instructions" (verse 10).

It's somewhat troubling to us to see God demanding ruthlessness in battle. Looking ahead through the centuries, it's impossible to imagine Jesus, with his message of mercy and forgiveness, making a similar demand. But whatever we might think of God's order to Saul, the fact that he failed to obey it meant that Saul no longer merited the kingship.

God then sent Samuel to Bethlehem, saying, "I have chosen one of Jesse's sons to be king." Samuel was supposed to anoint, on God's behalf, the one whom God would reveal. We now know who the chosen one will be, but Samuel does not know. When he sees Elias and the other sons of Jesse, he assumes that it will be one of them. But God has in mind the youngest, David, who is off tending the sheep when Samuel arrives.

I think we can identify with each character in this story: Saul, because we have all been disobedient and failed to live up to a responsibility we have been given; Samuel, whose difficult task is to speak of God's wishes despite condemnation and danger; and the sons of Jesse, each a promising young man hoping to be exalted by God's favor. But in a different way, all of us are called to fill the role of David, who becomes God's anointed.

The Bible refers to every Christian as a saint. That doesn't mean we are perfect; we all know we're not. It means that we are set aside for the service of God; anointed, spiritually if not physically, as God's servants on earth.

What qualified the youthful David to be chosen by God? At the time, he was not a fine warrior, charismatic leader, or wise thinker, nor did he have a track record of notable achievements that would justify his selection as king. He did not exhibit the personal qualities that we think of as marking a leader. He didn't take the initiative or ask to be chosen but was just minding his own business, taking care of the sheep. But through Samuel, God sent for him. It was God's choice, not David's, that David should be anointed.

With God's presence, through the power of the Holy Spirit, each of us is given the potential of exaltation, of greatness—not greatness in the sense of fame or glory, with headlines in the newspaper or stories on the TV news about our deeds but, rather, the greatness that God measures. The Lord looks at the heart, we are told. There are simple things about us that might never be known by most people: what we think, what we pray, how we feel, the small, meaningful things we do—or fail to do—for another person. In God's eyes, these are the deeds for which we are anointed, and they may make us worthy of exaltation.

Saul fell from God's grace because of his arrogance in disobeying God's command. To replace him, God chose one of the humblest of his servants, the youngest son, the shepherd boy—who was destined for greatness. Centuries later, Paul wrote about God's choices in his first letter to the Corinthians: "God chose the foolish things of the world to shame the wise; God chose the weak things of the world to shame the strong. He chose the lowly things of this world and the despised things—and the things that are not—to nullify the things that are, so that no one may boast before Him. . . . Therefore, as it is written, 'Let him who boasts do so in the Lord' " (1 Corinthians 1:27–29, 31).

If we strive, whether persistently or only intermittently, to serve Christ, there are many things that need not worry us. We don't have to worry about how wise or clever we are—God chose the foolish. We don't have to worry about how powerful we are—God chose the weak. We don't have to worry about how popular we are, or even whether we'll amount to anything much—God chose the despised and the ones who are nothing. None of those human measurements counts when it comes to performing great acts in life—great acts as defined by God, acts of humility, obedience, and love.

CHAPTER FIFTY

Real Wealth

Jesus said to his disciples, "I tell you the truth, it is hard for a rich man to enter the kingdom of heaven. Again I tell you, it is easier for a camel to go through the eye of a needle than for a rich man to enter the kingdom of God."

MATTHEW 19:23–24

God creates us with a variety of needs, desires, interests, talents, and opportunities. But these things don't define what we'll be. They're like the bricks, lumber, wallboard, shingles, and tiles we might see piled on the road near a construction site. It's what we make from the raw elements of our personalities that defines who we are; and this is where priorities and choices are crucial.

In these well-known words of Jesus, our Lord is warning us about the importance of setting the right priorities in our lives. I don't think Jesus is opposed to money or material possessions as such; what concerns him is the tendency we have to equate our material possessions with what is valuable. The problem in both cases is making some material thing more important in our lives than God—an idol, in effect.

We don't have to be wealthy to fall into that trap; a person can be just as covetous by being focused on small things as by hoarding millions of dollars. What material things receive an inordinate amount of attention in our lives? For some of us, they may be the latest car, the finest kitchen equipment, or the property that adjoins ours. Some of us feel undressed unless we're decked out in the latest fashions; others feel our lives are empty unless we travel to some new, exotic place twice a year. One of my weaknesses is for computers. I enjoy working on a word processor (I write my poems and books on one in my office at home), I find E-mail a fast and easy way to communicate with our family, and I use the Internet to locate information that would otherwise require research in a library. I guess I'm on my fifth computer now. No sooner do I get acquainted with one than I want a newer machine that is faster, has more vivid images, and can do things my current one can't do.

None of these desires is bad in itself. But material wealth can be a particularly treacherous priority for us, especially in our society, where advertising and the media remind us constantly of the pleasures and prestige of consumption. The more we are interested in amassing things, the more we are thrown into competition with others—our neighbors, our colleagues at work, our adversaries in business. There will always be something I covet that I can't have, and when this happens I'm immediately tempted to engage in disputes, conflicts, and jealousy. And the more I focus on increasing my own store of possessions, the less I'm inclined to think about sharing my time, talent, or treasure with others. After all, being generous won't help my bottom line!

So the pursuit of wealth, while natural and harmless in it-self, can carry serious spiritual dangers.

One way of testing whether our priorities are correct is to get into the habit of speaking to God, in prayer, about the things we want. If we take prayer seriously and really open ourselves to the presence of Christ whenever we pray, we'll find that our desires and wishes will be directed into channels that are truly nurturing and healthy. Imagine kneel-ing in your bedroom and praying, "In the name of Christ, my Savior, let me obtain a new computer or automobile, or the farm next door." Prayers like this sound wrong, almost shockingly so. We all have self-centered desires like these, but if we try to share them with God, their shallowness becomes apparent.

We need to accept Jesus as our partner in setting priorities. Prayer can help us do that. When making our needs and de-sires known to God, we are most often praying in the trans-mitting mode—speaking and not listening to God. Yet if we're sincere, we can't help but sense God's response and reaction to the desires we express; we shift, almost automatically, into the receiving mode. It's one of the benefits of habitual, daily prayer.

There's nothing bad about a shiny car, a nice house—or a powerful new computer! But before we focus all our time and energy on seeking these goals, we should try bringing them before God in prayer. As we shape and mold our desires, we may find ourselves pursuing the simple spiritual riches more avidly than costly material things.

CHAPTER FIFTY-ONE

If We Have Faith, Let's Show It!

What good is it, my brothers, if a man claims to have faith but has no deeds? Can such faith save him? Suppose a brother or sister is without clothes and daily food. If one of us says to him, "Go, I wish you well; keep warm and well fed," but does nothing about his physical needs, what good is it? In the same way, faith by itself, if it is not accompanied by action, is dead.

JAMES 2:14–17

The letter of James is one of my favorite books in the Bible. But through the ages, it has been a controversial part of Scripture. Martin Luther, the great churchman who helped start the Protestant Reformation, was so dubious about James's message that he called it "an epistle of straw." James continues to have his detractors, especially regarding the issue of faith versus works, about which he writes more than any other New Testament author. Some people say that James puts works— that is, deeds of charity, courage, and compassion for others— ahead of faith, or even substitutes works for faith. After I wrote *Living Faith*, there were letter writers who made the same accusation about me. I've thought about these letters, and believe that the criticisms are unjustified, certainly about James. As we'll see, he wanted us to understand that both works and faith are important in the life of a Christian, and that we can't have true faith without good works, and vice versa.

It's clear that an imbalance between faith and works is a constant danger. Some of us get so proud of our works that we think that's all there is, and neglect our spiritual lives—prayer, worship, fellowship, and study. We sometimes seem to place our works above Christ's supreme sacrifice as our path to salvation—as though we can earn a place in heaven by being so good that God is actually in our debt. This attitude is obviously wrong; it devalues the grace of Jesus, which is given to us without being earned and which we can never deserve, because we all fall so far short of moral and spiritual perfection.

Yet as James tries to show, the opposite attitude is equally wrong, when we place our faith so far above works as to imply that good deeds are unnecessary and unimportant. All we need to do, we believe, is walk down the aisle of the church during a revival meeting when we're ten or eleven years old and accept Christ as our Savior, and from then on just being regular church members meets our obligations as Christians. Some of

us even go a step further and think all this is preordained—
that we have been selected for eternal life while others never
even have this opportunity.

On an institutional scale, we see this kind of attitude in-
fecting some of our most famous and outwardly most successful churches. I think of a particular church in one of the big
cities of the South. The new building cost $35 million, com-
plete with all the pleasures of a huge health resort to serve
the congregation, which is large and growing by leaps and
bounds. Unfortunately, at the same time the new facility was
being built, members canceled plans for an outreach ministry
in an inner-city neighborhood, saying they couldn't afford it. I
guess the expense would have interfered with the building of
their sports complex.

Don't misunderstand; I don't see anything wrong with
physical fitness or with ministering to the needs of our own
congregations. But there is something wrong with becoming
so committed to caring for our needs and pleasures that we
forget about the practical ministry of Jesus Christ. It's also
nice when membership rolls increase, but some churches grow
because joining them is like gaining membership in a huge
fraternal order or a country club.

That's the danger James is warning us against. James isn't
saying that faith is unimportant. He's saying: If we have faith,
let's show it! Prove it as Jesus did, by ministering not only to
those like us, our friends and neighbors, but to the poor, the
hungry, the lonely, and the despised. Become active, inquisitive, questioning, adventurous Christians. Take some of the
blessings God has given us—our time and talents, our education, our financial status, our security—and say, "I want to in-

vest this, in the name of Christ, in the same way that Jesus invested all that he had for us."

How do we do this? What's a practical way to reach out to someone in need or trouble? It depends on us—our background, our neighborhood, the amount of time and the specific talents we have to offer. Each of us has something unique and valuable to give. A habit of very small things is much more important than a few dramatic ones. We can make a gesture of forgiveness to someone against whom we've had a grudge; offer friendship to someone who is lonely or neglected; volunteer to be a big brother or sister to a local kid in need of guidance, or give time at the nearest hospital.

Or join one of my favorite organizations, Habitat for Humanity and work side by side with some of the poorest people in the world, helping to provide them with decent homes. There are Habitat projects in over 1,300 U.S. communities and more than 45 foreign countries. Habitat has branches on 450 college campuses and at over 100 high schools. Almost anywhere, we can help Habitat build a better world.

There are many ways to put our faith into action, limited only by our imagination. In the end, James's message is a simple one. To be saved, we need faith, surely; but self-satisfaction and self-glorification are not the end of faith. Rather, service to others, compassion, and justice exemplify the Christian life. When we emulate Christ by working to make these things real in our lives, we strengthen our faith as well.

CHAPTER FIFTY-TWO

Take a Chance

Whoever watches the wind will not plant;
whoever looks at the cloud will not reap. . . .

Sow your seed in the morning, and at evening let not your hands be idle, for you do not know which will succeed, whether this or that, or whether both will do equally well.

ECCLESIASTES 11:4, 6

As a person who grew up and still lives in a farming community, and has done his share of planting, cultivation, and harvesting, I find these images from Ecclesiastes particularly intriguing. And because of the provocative, even paradoxical nature of their message, more than one interpretation is possible. Let me share some of my thoughts about these curious, fascinating verses.

In a way, it would be easier to understand the author if he had written, in verse 4, "Whoever does *not* look at the clouds will not reap." That would just be a basic piece of farming wisdom. Any farmer in South Georgia knows that our crops will suffer if we don't pay attention to the weather. If we plant our peanuts when the ground is too cold or wet, the seed will rot; if we get a long dry spell, they won't sprout. So the smart farmer does pay attention to clouds, winds, rain, sun, and all the other weather signs. What, then, does the writer mean by seeming to say just the opposite?

I think he is warning us about the danger of seeking perfection in our lives. The farmer has to watch the weather signs, sure. But if we watch and ponder the weather and the other conditions too closely—if we measure and remeasure the humidity, the temperature, and the soil conditions—if we seek out and pay attention to all kinds of advice from every farmer, seed salesman, or extension service expert in the county—we may end up in a quandary, wondering, "Is this the right day to plant? Will tomorrow be better, or the day after that, or the day after that?" Before we know it, the time for sowing will be gone.

So if we wait for perfection in our lives, for exactly the right moment, then we may never act! This message applies to all of us.

If we've made a commitment to faith in Christ, we've promised to serve God according to the pattern Jesus set. Yet how many of us are really living that way? Instead, we wait for a better time. It's not deliberate; it just happens, year after year. And then there's retirement—we've got to be sure we have enough set aside for that, too, don't we? Before we know it, our lives have slipped away, with the commitment to serve God in Christ permanently on hold while the worldly things take precedence.

Ecclesiastes is warning us not to let that happen. Don't wait until everything is perfect before we act; in an imperfect, uncertain world, be bold! Go ahead!

Verse 6 gives another perspective on the same theme. It's often difficult to take risks in life. How do we know which seeds will grow best if we plant them? Will we succeed or fail at what we try? Maybe it's better not to take a chance rather than accept the possibility of failure.

Of course, that attitude leads to a timid, diminished life. Failure is a reality; we all fail at times, and it's painful when we do. But it's better to fail while striving for something wonderful, challenging, adventurous, and uncertain than to say, "I don't want to try, because I may not succeed completely."

In September 1994, when Sen. Sam Nunn, Gen. Colin Powell, and I returned from Haiti, having helped to resolve the crisis caused by a military coup and avoided the need for a planned U.S. invasion, President Clinton admitted that he'd never believed our mission could succeed. And frankly, there were times we'd felt the same way. During the thirty hours we spent in Haiti desperately trying to negotiate a settlement, there were at least four occasions when it seemed that the discussions had broken down and war was inevitable. But people in Port-au-Prince and Washington refused to give in to despair, and a settlement was reached that gave victory—and peace—to everyone concerned. It was not a miracle, just the result of human beings persisting in the face of uncertainty and risk, being willing to take a chance.

Every life offers similar opportunities. "Should I reach out to that man who hurt me deeply with an ugly comment or a cruel deed several years ago? Perhaps I could call him on the phone or knock on his front door, offering reconciliation and a chance at renewed friendship. But that would be a risky thing to do. What if he slams the door in my face, or shouts 'Go to hell!' and hangs up the phone? Maybe it would be better not to try!"

The Book of Ecclesiastes offers an antidote to that attitude. We'll never know whether something new and wonderful is possible unless we try. Let's stretch our hearts, stretch our minds, be adventurous! Serve God with boldness, and who knows what wonders the Lord may work?

Index of Scriptural References

Index

ABOUT THE AUTHOR

JIMMY CARTER, thirty-ninth president of the United States, was born in 1924 in the small farming town of Plains, Georgia, and grew up in the nearby community of Archery. His father, James Earl Carter, Sr., was a farmer and businessman; his mother, Lillian Gordy, a registered nurse.

After receiving a B.S. degree from the United States Naval Academy in 1946, he served as a submariner in both the Atlantic and Pacific fleets and rose to the rank of lieutenant, working under Admiral Hyman Rickover in the development of the nuclear submarine program.

When his father died in 1953, he resigned his naval commission and returned to Plains. He worked his own farm, and he and his wife Rosalynn operated Carter's Warehouse, a farm supply company. He was elected to the Georgia Senate in 1962 and was elected governor of Georgia in 1970.

In 1976, Carter was elected president of the United States, serving from 1977 to 1981. Noteworthy accomplishments of his administration included the Camp David Accords, the treaty of peace between Egypt and Israel, the SALT II treaty with the Soviet Union, and major domestic programs in education, energy, and environmental protection.

In 1982, he founded The Carter Center, a nonpartisan and nonprofit organization that addresses national and international issues of public policy. Carter Center fellows, associates, and staff join with President Carter in efforts to resolve conflict, promote democracy, protect human rights, and prevent disease and other afflictions throughout the world. President Carter was awarded the Nobel Peace Prize in 2002.

Mr. Carter is the author of fourteen books, including the spiritual autobiography *Living Faith* (1996). Jimmy and Rosalynn Carter are the parents of three sons, Jack, Chip, and Jeff, and a daughter, Amy. They live in Plains, Georgia.